Living Faith

Living Faith

convictions that bring faith to life

Glenn Parkinson

CreateSpace Independent Publishing Platform

To my daughter, Renee

Acknowledgments

For me, both preaching and writing are team efforts. My wife, Micki, not only edits my written work, but she is also a tremendous partner in developing the original messages. She even designed the cover. Her creativity and wisdom are amazing. Flo Wolfe once again contributed her very helpful expertise to critique and proofread the original project. Many thanks to Mindy Haines for getting my preaching notes into useable form. And I am grateful to God for all my friends and coworkers at Severna Park Evangelical Presbyterian (PCA), who encouraged me to enjoy the truths these pages explore.

Contents

The Power of Convictions

As the body apart from the spirit is dead, so also
faith apart from works is dead. (James 2:26)

Only faith that is practiced is alive. The words of James are
often seen as a threat, inciting guilt to "do more" in order to be a
good Christian. But to me, they are a promise that there is meant
to be more to the Christian faith than bare religion. Leading up to
the above quote, James remembered how Abraham was called
God's friend. I want to be God's friend.

I've tried to capture what I think James is getting at in the
word-play, *living faith*. As an adjective, living faith describes faith
that is alive, or real. As a verb, living faith (as in living out one's
faith) expresses the dynamic of friendship with God, how he
guides and inspires how one actually lives.

A memorable instructor at seminary over four decades ago
told me that the role of a pastor would inevitably require a good
deal of compromise. In order to serve with integrity, he told me to
decide up front "what I would go to the wall for." When he spoke
those words, I had no idea what I believed that deeply. But over
time, I found that along my faith journey there have been a
number of crossroads, places where life choices called me to
decide what I actually believe. At that point, something about my
faith which had previously been vague, general or untried, rose to
the forefront. I then discovered what I really believe by the

decision I made. And from that point on, integrity led me to make similar decisions up to the next defining crossroad.

I think of such defining decisions as convictions. I believe that the key to living faith is making a series of conscious decisions to live according to clear biblical truths. Such convictions are not merely ideas to confess. What makes them convictions is the decision to incorporate each one into who I am. Like jumping off the high dive, there is no going back. Like conceiving a child, giving birth to a conviction profoundly shapes what life has now become.

I don't know that this book contains every truth I would go to the wall for. But I do know that I have decided to build my life on each one. The process has not been elegant, but it has defined my journey so far. Along with my creeds and vows, these convictions concretely define what I mean by "faith."

The book itself is not an autobiography, however, It took initial form as sermons, now adapted for this purpose.

> The Preacher sought to find words of delight, and uprightly he wrote words of truth. The words of the wise are like goads, and like nails firmly fixed are the collected sayings; they are given by one Shepherd. (Ecclesiastes 12:10-11)

I believe faith receives truth from our Shepherd with sheer delight. For that to happen, it must goad, or prod, me to action. To have faith that is alive, I must live my faith. And for that to happen, I need nails firmly fixed, upon which I can rest my soul. I think of my convictions as these nails. They are not goals to accomplish; they are truths I can count on, no matter what. They are truths I have decided to count on, no matter what.

I recommend my convictions to you. But beyond considering this particular list, I encourage you to develop your own collection of convictions, truths which you have decided to believe regardless of any circumstance you may encounter. As you make them, write them out. Let them chronicle your journey with Christ. Few things are more precious to the Christian or more potent in dealing with adversity than knowing what you are willing to believe.

God Is Who He Says He Is

> Then Moses said to God, "If I come to the people of Israel and say to them, 'The God of your fathers has sent me to you,' and they ask me, 'What is his name?' what shall I say to them?" God said to Moses, "I AM WHO I AM." And he said, "Say this to the people of Israel: 'I AM has sent me to you.'" (Exodus 3:13-14)

When we think of the beginning of the Bible, we think of the grand first chapter of Genesis, "In the beginning God created the heavens and the earth …" Not only is Genesis the first book in our printed Bible, but it deals with the first things, like the creation of the universe, our first ancestors and the origin of sin and salvation.

And yet, in a way, Exodus 3 is the real beginning of the Bible because it describes the calling of Moses, who wrote the first five books of the Old Testament, including Genesis. And the first subject in this encounter was the true identity of God. The Hebrews believed that names should represent their owners, so Moses asked who God is by asking his name.

After all, the world calls upon many gods. Every nation has their own version, and their own name. A primitive culture might use the name of an animal or a natural phenomenon to associate divinity with some admired trait. Modern societies do the same thing in more sophisticated ways, still worshiping our own values and desires, still naming our "gods" to suit the lives we wish to live.

But when the Living God revealed his name to Moses, the name he gave was fundamentally different. God said to Moses, "I AM WHO I AM." And he said, "Say this to the people of Israel: 'I AM has sent me to you.'" God's name is the Hebrew sentence

Yahweh (sometimes pronounced Jehovah), meaning "I am who I am," a name-sentence almost universally translated into English as the LORD (all capitals). In the Bible, whenever you see "LORD" in all capitals, it represents a personal name, not a title. It is the name Yahweh.

What the name means is: "Moses, tell the Israelites that I am not whatever they want to define me to be. I am not whatever they think I am. I am not whatever you think I am, Moses. I am not the product of anyone's art or imagination. I am not defined by your limited logic or your untethered desires. I am … who I am. I am objectively real. Your religious sensibilities do not define me and your cultural fads do not change me. I do not exist in your mind; in fact, my existence is a good deal more fundamental than yours. I am who I am."

The only way we can know the God who is who he is, is for him to explain himself to us. As the Apostle Paul observed, "For who knows a person's thoughts except the spirit of that person, which is in him? So also no one comprehends the thoughts of God except the Spirit of God. (1 Corinthians 2:11)

I can know some things about another person from observation: height, weight, so on. But I cannot know anyone as a person unless he reveals to me his thoughts using words I can understand. Similarly, we can know some things about God from observation: his power, creativity. But we cannot know God himself as a person unless he reveals his own mind to us in words we can understand. This is what we call special revelation, or just revelation.

Revelation is God telling us who he is, "in words not taught by human wisdom but taught by the Spirit, interpreting spiritual truths to those who are spiritual." (1 Corinthians 2:13)

Moses did not make up the Bible using his own wisdom. He expressed the truths of who God is, using words that expressed the Holy Spirit's revelation. Moses was joined over the centuries by other prophets, until God became flesh in Jesus Christ. Christ commissioned a group of special prophets called apostles to tie it all together—explain Jesus as the embodiment of all God's revelation. The Scripture they wrote, the Bible, is God's revelation to us concerning who he is. Christianity is based on the revelation of God given to the prophets and apostles, starting with Moses. If you believe in Jesus, then your faith rests on revelation, not intuition or social convention but revelation, what God has taken the initiative to reveal about who he truly is.

Whenever we substitute our own thinking or society's values for apostolic teaching, we drift into idolatry. Idolatry is not just about little stone statues. The Apostle John linked Christian idolatry to misunderstanding who Christ revealed God to be.

> The Son of God has come and has given us understanding, so that we may know shim who is true; and we are in him who is true, in his Son Jesus Christ. He is the true God and eternal life. Little children, keep yourselves from idols. (1 John 5:20-21)

Biblically understood, Jesus is the completely accurate revelation of God. But the pressure to redefine God is very powerful—social pressure from outside and pressure of personal preference from inside.

God is not a generic Person, however. He is a real, objective Person. He is who he is. Since he has revealed himself in Scripture, we may say: he is who he says he is. Confidence in biblical revelation is the most fundamental element of a living faith.

Such faith is challenging for two reasons. First, the Bible is bound to reveal things about God that we won't like. Does that sound like heresy? Blasphemy? No, because the only way we would like everything we discover about God is if either: 1) we were as perfect as he is, or 2) we made him up according to our personal specifications. Otherwise, there are bound to be points of revelation with which each of us will disagree, things about God that don't feel right to our fractured feelings.

Be prepared to discover that in some ways God runs this world differently than you would. The Living God may occasionally make you uncomfortable. He may frustrate your opinions and your desires. The question is, are you the judge of who God is, or do you accept the revelation of himself that he has given? Are you willing to trust that as you grow, you will learn to think differently? God may not always be what you think he ought to be. No doubt, you would be God differently. But will you affirm that is your problem, not his? Will you refrain from the idolatrous urge to change him, and instead ask him to change you?

The second reason that revelation is difficult to accept sounds similar, but what I mean is very different. Again, the Bible is going to reveal things about God that you will have a very hard time accepting. I am not, however, speaking now of things that frustrate you. I am speaking instead of wonderful things that hurt because they seem too good to believe.

Sometimes, beautiful things can hurt. Like when you are alone not by choice, and you see a couple holding hands, smiling together, embracing. It's beautiful, but it hurts. Or when you see children sleeping in parent's laps, and feel an emptiness in your own lap for the child you wish you had. It's beautiful to see such things, but it hurts. Or when you watch young people hiking, sporting and just enjoying being young, and you realize that those days are behind you in this world. Or when you see others rising up to tremendous success, attaining large goals, and you compare that to your own modest accomplishments. It hurts when you see something wonderful, that you can't quite believe you can ever have yourself.

If you read the Bible with a mind opened by the Spirit of God, he will show you such things. For the God who is, is so much better than you could dream. He's so much better than any puny and petty idol. As grace penetrates the fog of your own sin, your view of the Living God becomes breathtaking. God is pure, with nothing to hide. He is simple in his goodness; no hidden faults or unwholesome agendas. The Lord is so good that he cannot be scratched or dented by evil. His hatred of evil is completely uncompromising, yet his grace is boundless and stunningly beautiful. God's grace is stainless steel next to our rusted nicety. It towers with Sequoia magnificence above our scrub pine, a sparkling stream free of our refuse.

The God revealed in Scripture is so wonderful that it hurts at first to look at him. His glory is painful to people like us, with compromised consciences aware of so many moral failures. His love is too much for us to hope for. It truly is beyond our reach. We will never deserve to know the love of such a One. Never … and we know it.

But if God has revealed who he is in Christ, then we can, indeed, have what we do not deserve. God is not something less, just because we find it hard to hope in such goodness. God does not limit his greatness to our imagination. Rather, our hope must stretch to embrace the God is who he says he is.

What does living such a faith look like? … or, in the case of Jonah (our only negative example in this book), what does it *not* look like? …

Jonah

> When God saw what they did and how they turned from their evil ways, he had compassion and did not bring upon them the destruction he had threatened.
>
> But Jonah was greatly displeased and became angry. He prayed to the LORD, "O LORD, is this not what I said when I was still at home? That is why I was so quick to flee to Tarshish. I knew that you are a gracious and compassionate God, slow to anger and abounding in love, a God who relents from sending calamity. Now, O LORD, take away my life, for it is better for me to die than to live." (Jonah 3:10-4:3)

One generation after Solomon, a civil war fractured the nation of Israel. Ten of the twelve tribes rebelled, retaining the ancestral name of "Israel." Their capital was Samaria. Their monarchy was marked by assassination, political coups, and idolatry that corrupted worship of the LORD. The two southern tribes took the name "Judah." Their capital was Jerusalem. Their slide into idolatry was not as fast as their brothers to the north. God raised up prophets to call both sides to repentance. They reminded both royalty and commoners of God's covenant with Abraham and Moses. They called people to faithfulness. They warned that unless the kings and nations repented, God would raise up foreign powers to defeat them and take them captive.

In the sixth century, the Babylonians to the east would defeat southern Judah and take them away into a seventy year exile, from which some would one day return to rebuild the land. But long before that, in the eighth century BC, the great nation of Assyria would defeat the northern ten tribes. The Assyrian conquest would be worse than the later victory of the Babylonians, for the Assyrians would destroy Israel completely. Its people would be scattered, never to return.

Several decades before the terrible Assyrian conquest, one northern prophet received an unusual commission from God. "The word of the LORD came to Jonah son of Amittai: 'Go to the great city of Nineveh and preach against it, because its wickedness has come up before me.'" (Jonah 1:1-2)

Nineveh was the capital of Assyria, one of the truly great ancient cities. Through God's repeated warnings to Israel, Jonah knew that Nineveh would, in time, crush everything he loved. So, you might think that Jonah would jump at this assignment. Surely the prophet would enjoy declaring God's judgment against the nation he despised? Perhaps a weakened Assyria would postpone Israel's judgment at their hand.

Well, Jonah did jump at the chance. He jumped the other way.

> But Jonah ran away from the LORD and headed for Tarshish. He went down to Joppa, where he found a ship bound for that port.
> After paying the fare, he went aboard and sailed for Tarshish to flee from the LORD. (Jonah 1:3)

Tarshish was a port in southwest Spain, clear across the Mediterranean. In other words, Jonah tried to get as far away from Nineveh as he possibly could. The text says that he was trying to flee from God. We see why he did that when Jonah eventually ends up in Nineveh and warns them of God's judgment. They repent, and God decides to spare them. That's when Jonah explained that he originally ran away because he knew God would spare anyone who repents.

Jonah fled the Lord because he knew that God was gracious, so gracious that he would even spare the Ninevites if they repented. Jonah did not want the Ninevites to be spared. Assyria was going to smash Israel. He wanted them smashed first. He certainly didn't want to be an instrument of God's grace to them. So he ran. He wanted the Lord to judge his enemies. He didn't want to warn them of judgment. And sure enough, look what happened. They repented and God forgave them!

It's important that we understand Jonah's problem. In general, Jonah did not despise God's sovereign mercy. As a prophet, Jonah often preached God's mercy. Jonah actually composed a beautiful song of grace while in the whale.

> Then Jonah prayed to the LORD his God from the belly of the fish, saying,
> "I called out to the LORD, out of my distress, and he answered me; out of the belly of Sheol I cried, and you heard my voice ....
> When my life was fainting away, I remembered the LORD, and my prayer came to you, into your holy temple. Those who pay regard to vain idols forsake their hope of steadfast love. But I with the voice of thanksgiving will sacrifice to you; what I have vowed I will pay. Salvation belongs to the LORD!" (Jonah 2:1-9)

In general, Jonah had no problem with God's grace. Also, Jonah had no problem with grace being offered to the Gentiles. When God sent a storm against the Gentile ship he used to run away, he offered to sacrifice himself to save the Gentile crewman. (Jonah 1:8-12) Jonah had no prejudice against Gentiles in general. He wished them well. He would welcome the salvation of anyone who would honor Israel's God.

Anyone, that is, except Assyrians! For Jonah, Assyria was the devil. In all God's warnings to Israel to repent, Assyria was the demonic force God would one day use to chasten a disobedient people. Assyria was evil. Israel lived in terror of their shadow and Jonah knew that one day soon, Israel would become their prey. What God said about his grace was great in general, but what he said about his grace to Assyria in particular seemed absurd and unacceptable.

The Book of Jonah is not really about the whale (only three verses mention the big fish). It's about the breadth of sovereign grace. It is broader than the boundaries we are comfortable with. It is so broad, it reaches to all God's enemies, even if they happen to be our enemies.

The Lord tried to expand Jonah's perspective regarding mercy. In a later scene, Jonah wanted Nineveh destroyed, but mourned the loss of a shade plant. In contrast, God destroyed the shade plant, but mourned the potential loss of a city with so many people.

Jonah's problem goes down to the fundamental conviction of our faith: that God is who he says he is. Living faith is not something we make up; it is based upon divine revelation. Living faith does not carve out what we want God to be, and then worship the idol we create. Rather, we believe that God revealed himself in Jesus Christ, whom we know through the New Testament apostles and Old Testament prophets who gave us the Bible.

But Jonah reminds us how difficult it is to consistently embrace the God of revelation, because there are times when we learn things about him that we do not like. And when we discover something about God that we do not like, we are tempted to rebel. Not that we reject the idea of divine revelation wholesale. Jonah remained a prophet, after all. We simply rebel against a particular detail of divine revelation. "O LORD, is this not what I said when I was still at home? ... I knew that you are a gracious and compassionate God, slow to anger and abounding in love, a God who relents from sending calamity." In general, Jonah praised God for being gracious, but when this quality of God resulted in something Jonah found offensive, he rebelled. He ran away from it.

Even a prophet can rebel against divine revelation. "Lord, what you are doing is simply unacceptable. Don't you understand who these Assyrians are? How am I going to face my fellow prophets, neighbors, children and tell them that I was involved in bringing your grace to these people? I refuse to be a party to this ... I'm going to Tarshish."

Whoa! ... the storm, thrown overboard, the whale, vomiting him up on the beach ... "Ok, I guess I'm not going to Tarshish. I'll do what you command. But Lord, I still don't like it. I'm ashamed to do this. I'm angry about it. Now, O LORD, take away my life, for it is better for me to die than to live."

This is how we instinctively react when Scripture touches something sensitive. Like when a doctor pokes around an acute pain and says "Does this hurt?" God said to Jonah, "Do you have a right to be angry about the vine?" "I do," he said. "I am angry enough to die." (Jonah 4:3) Ooooh, something hurts! The idea of mercy to Nineveh turned his stomach. Maybe Jonah learned that hatred from his father, Amittai. Maybe he absorbed it from his culture. Whatever the reason, God's mercy to these people rankled Jonah. God's mercy is fine for me, fine for people I can tolerate, but not for *them*. Jonah didn't want to face God's feelings in this matter. He only wanted to run away.

Before you think it unusual for real believers to be embarrassed or disappointed with God, please remember Christ's own disciples, who later became the apostles of the church. They were initially embarrassed about Jesus spending up-close time with notorious sinners. They believed that since a holy God hates sin, holy people ought to keep socially removed from sinners. Yet, Jesus had dinner with them, and even went to their parties. It was a scandal. They could not embrace that part of who he was. And when they could not approve of him, they felt justified in being embarrassed.

Similarly, when Jesus first told them about the cross, those same disciples were scandalized. Jesus was Israel's king. God was bringing his kingdom to pass through him. How could that happen if he was condemned and executed as a criminal? Peter actually rebuked Jesus.

In both cases, the disciples later learned that their thinking on those subjects was flawed. Before God's Spirit was through with them, they would delight in imitating Christ by reaching out to the most notorious sinners. They even counted it a privilege beyond words to die like him in the service of God. But there was a time when they were embarrassed by who Jesus really is.

Have you ever felt embarrassed by God? Embarrassed by something in the Bible? I don't mean embarrassed because other people make fun of your faith, I mean embarrassed because the Bible teaches something which you don't want to believe, such as:

- God commands us to be caretakers of the planet, not simply consumers.
- God commands us to actively help the poor.
- God does not allow something we want to allow, like homosexual relations.
- God does not forbid something we want to forbid, like Moses' marriage to an Ethiopian.

Sometimes, God's character and plans are hard for me (the author) to stomach. And it doesn't even have to involve a challenging doctrine like God's wrath, or mysterious teaching like predestination. It can be something as wonderful and delightful as God's grace, something I normally rejoice in, as Jonah did. But, when it butts up against my most deeply held prejudices it doesn't seem so wonderful.

Are you ever angry with God? When I ask that question of myself, I am forced to consider attitudes, feelings or behaviors that are at odds with God's Word, but which I prefer to cherish. Somehow, I actually feel justified protecting them. They are right; I am right. I don't want to talk about it or examine it. I have relied on my own prejudices, pride and self-centered habits to hold me together. Part of becoming who I am today is the result of carefully defending an island of self will in the midst of my sea of faith. These hold-outs against God's righteousness or purity—yes, and even his grace—are the twine I have used to hold myself together all these years. The Bible would have me cut those cords so God can rebuild a powerful superstructure of righteousness, compassion and purity. But I'm not so sure I want such a makeover. I think I'll just keep the old twine, thank you. I've already decided how I want God to be - how I am determined God has to be.

Christian, do you want to know how you are behaving like Jonah? It's where God asks of you, "Do you really have a right to be angry about this?" And you scrunch up in anguish and misery, crying, "I do. I'm angry enough to die." Do you want to know how you are hurting like Jonah? It's where you are running away, fleeing from God. In that one particular, that one area of life, you refuse to acknowledge his will with joy and devotion. And you want to get as far from him as possible. Do you want to know how you are trapped like Jonah? It's where you are hiding from the storm that accuses you, hoping that your lack of faith will not be discovered by the unbelievers up on deck.

God is not what we define him to be. God is who he says he is. This is the living faith that not only falls in love with Christ, but is determined to grow in that love as I discover all that Christ

16

reveals. Even when it means abandoning some of my deepest prejudices. Even when God's character illuminates warped beliefs about life that I learned from my childhood or developed on my own. Faith that God is who he says he is affirms that the Christ of the Bible is perfect, and dares to hope that he will mold my heart into his image.

Augustine of Hippo famously urged us to "believe so that you may understand." Augustine did not promote irrationality. He simply pointed out how minds crippled by an innate inability to trust God can be made well. God is who he says he is, so we must base our understanding of God on what he says. This is the foundation of living faith.

The ironic thing is that Jonah knew this. God reminded Jonah of his boundless blessings by saving him from the ocean depths through a great fish. Inside that fish, Jonah hung on to the truth that limitless blessing flows from the Living God of infinite grace. He realized that "Those who pay regard to vain idols forsake their hope of steadfast love." (Jonah 2:8) Yet, he was willing to forsake God's steadfast love because he would not give up his idol of hatred. With respect to the Assyrians, Jonah insisted that God be different that he said he was.

Can you imagine how the final chapter of this book would read if Jonah had learned from his experience in the sea? He could have gone to Nineveh, preached, and watched a miracle of repentance. True, this city might still launch a terrible strike against Israel some time down the line. But in his own day, Jonah could have seen the Lord fabulously honored. God's grace is glorious! Even Israel's enemies respond, bowing to God and embracing his mercy. God is glorified and his prophet has the privilege of being part of it all!

The Lord longed to rejoice with Jonah, to share his happiness with his prophet. Instead, the book ends with Jonah sulking by himself, holding tight to his bigotry against Assyria, defending his rebellion against God, and miserably curled up under a dead tree while a whole city repents below.

What do I do if I find in the Scripture something about God I don't like? What do I do if I believe that in some particular way, the Lord is wrong. He embarrasses me. I just can't follow the Bible in this one area. What do I do?

First, find out if what you think the Bible teaches really is what it teaches. This may take some time and effort, and some study on your part. Enlist the help of pastors and books written by people who know the Bible better than you do. They may not have all the answers, but you would be foolish not to benefit from their study. Perhaps you have misunderstood what God has said. Maybe the conflict doesn't really exist.

But what if it does exist? Then recognize the problem as your problem, and confess it to God. Don't hide it; don't hide from it. Never hide from your Lord. Jonah demonstrated our tendency to run away from God when we have a problem with him, but running away only leads to disaster for us.

We don't need to run away. God will help us understand. God wants us to understand. Face the conflict squarely and humbly; put your feelings into words and pray them to God. "Lord, I'm embarrassed about what the Bible says concerning this thing. I confess that what you say here makes me very upset." Please, don't yell at God as if your feelings were justified. Just openly confess your feelings and ask him to help you understand. Ask God to open your eyes to more clearly see his mercy or justice or purity or whatever it may be. Approach this as a golden opportunity to better grasp his true character. Ask him to train your mind to better understand how he is worthy of your love. Ask him to train your emotions to feel his worthiness more deeply. Ask him to teach you new behaviors that pursue his will.

Jonah is the only negative example in this book. From him we learn what living faith doesn't look like. It doesn't look like running away when you see something about God you don't like.

But along the way, Jonah has also taught something about how hard God works with faith to make it alive. He does not want you running away from him. And if you persist, he will come after you as he did Jonah, because he loves you. He doesn't want you embarrassed or angry at him, curled up in yourself, missing the great things he is doing all around you. He will come after you, and find a way to remind you of his grace, even if he needs to use a big fish.

When he does, be sure to take away what Jonah left in the belly of the whale … "Those who pay regard to vain idols forsake their hope of steadfast love. But I [sing] with the voice of thanksgiving." Don't give up on God's steadfast love. Trust the God who is who he says he is.

Living Faith

God Is In Control

I know how to be brought low, and I know how to abound. In any and every circumstance, I have learned the secret of facing plenty and hunger, abundance and need. I can do all things through him who strengthens me.

And my God will supply every need of yours according to his riches in glory in Christ Jesus. To our God and Father be glory forever and ever. Amen. (Philippians 4:12-13,19-20)

If God is who he says he is in the Bible, then he controls all things. Living faith will have confidence in God's sovereignty across the board—from matters of life and death to the most mundane details.

The Bible text above illustrates faith on both levels. Under house arrest in Rome, the Apostle Paul daily faced the prospect of a negative ruling from Nero Caesar, followed by execution. But on a more mundane level, he also needed money to pay for his rented house-prison. Compared to a martyr's death, paying the rent may be small potatoes ... but the rent still had to be paid. The Book of Philippians is a thank you letter for financial support, which Paul understands as an example of God's sovereign care.

Living faith in God's sovereignty enabled Paul to live in confidence. "I have learned the secret of facing plenty and hunger, abundance and need." And God's control was not just an internal feeling Paul had. The unexpected financial gift from the Philippian church met his needs in a way that demonstrated that God's sovereignty is an objective reality. The Lord owns the cattle on a thousand hills. (Psalm 50:10) Providing for his people as they seek to serve him is not hard for God to do.

Biblically speaking, sovereignty is about God's power and his authority to accomplish anything he wants to accomplish. That is to say, the sovereignty of God is not about power in an abstract sort of way. It's about the Lord's ability to exercise his rights, which are unlimited. God's control is about his power to accomplish his own goals. Therefore, when Paul said that he could do everything through Christ who strengthened him, he didn't mean everything in a literal sense, everything he could imagine or think of: become rich, jump over the moon, or lose thirty pounds overnight. What he meant, of course, was that he could do everything God called him to do. If that meant to die for Christ, he could do it well. If it meant to live for Christ, he was not only ready to accomplish that another day, but God would see that the rent was paid.

Understanding that God's sovereignty has to do with God's goals, not mine, is the secret of being content whether in plenty or in want. This is not a Zen-like state of mind that doesn't care about stuff, but it is, rather, an overriding passion to see God's will accomplished more than anything else. God's financial provision through the Philippian church wasn't some perk of faith just so Paul could avoid working for a living. The unexpected gift was an example of God controlling the details in order to accomplish his will in Rome, which was to advance the gospel through his apostle.

The sovereignty of God is about God's power to accomplish anything he wants to accomplish. It involves tremendous power that he manifests both inside us and outside of us in the world at large. "Ah, Lord GOD! It is you who have made the heavens and the earth by your great power and by your outstretched arm! Nothing is too hard for you." (Jeremiah 32:17) "I have spoken, and I will bring it to pass; I have purposed, and I will do it." (Isaiah 46:11)

God can do absolutely anything he pleases, but his sovereignty is directed only at what he pleases. It doesn't exist in the abstract or to advance our own whims. Paul speaks of "the purpose of him who works all things according to the counsel of his will" (Ephesians 1:11)

So when we say that God is in control, what we mean is that no matter what is happening, we can be sure that God's purposes are not being frustrated. Our purposes may be frustrated, but God's never are. So, the conviction that "God is in control" is really very little comfort to someone who is not particularly interested in God's agenda. If I think God's power is a neutral force I can tap into for my own purposes, I will not find it; I'll be strictly on my own. But if I stay in the center of God's purposes, then God's power is going to be all around me.

Israel was a nation of slaves in Egypt. They had no control over their own destiny. They had to make bricks seven days a week. The Egyptian government killed their infants to keep the population down. God said that when he looked for the scrawniest, weakest, most pitiful group of people in the world, he chose them. (Deuteronomy 7:7) God called them out of slavery to worship him. By doing this, God demonstrated his purpose to bring fallen humanity back into a right relationship with him. This is a relationship in which we worship him for who he is, and he blesses us beyond our dreams.

In calling Israel out of slavery, the Lord fulfilled a centuries-old promise to Abraham to reach all nations through one chosen nation. But from the perspective of the Israelite slaves, they had, overnight, been unexpectedly drawn right into the vanguard of God's activity in the world. God called and they followed, not with perfect faith or perfect obedience, but they did follow. And suddenly, they were caught up in the most miraculous journey ever taken by any people. The exodus crackled and sparked with the energy of God's power. God worked in things outside of Israel's control, doing things beyond their reach so they could survive and prosper. Like pushing back a sea to allow Israel to escape the only superpower in the region. Or dropping food from the sky, or releasing water from the ground. Like winning battles over experienced desert armies, or collapsing the defensive walls of a stronghold with nothing more than the sound of God's praise.

You see living faith in this sovereign God in leaders like Moses and Joshua, giving them endurance and loyalty and love and confidence and effectiveness way beyond what is normal. "Have I not commanded you? Be strong and courageous. Do not be frightened, and do not be dismayed, for the LORD your God is with you wherever you go." (Joshua 1:9)

And when it was over, God had done something considered impossible in the ancient world.

> For ask now of the days that are past, which were before you, since the day that God created man on the earth, and ask from one end of heaven to the other, whether such a great thing as this has ever happened or was ever heard of. Did any people ever hear the voice of a god speaking out of the midst of the fire, as you have heard, and still live? Or has any god ever attempted to go and take a nation for himself from the midst of another nation, by trials, by signs, by wonders, and by war, by a mighty hand and ban outstretched arm, and by great deeds of terror, all of which the LORD your God did for you in Egypt before your eyes? (Deuteronomy 4:32-34)

Before Jesus, the great symbol of rebirth was the exodus. A nation in bondage and fear and hopelessness, a nation that was dead, came to life by the sovereign power of God. But this was not their plan. Rather, they became immersed in what God was doing. In fact, they found themselves dead center in God's principle project on this planet: redemption. Therefore, his power was all around them, a pillar of cloud by day and a pillar of fire by night. They saw every promise fulfilled, and accomplished things far beyond their natural abilities.

Living faith exults in God's sovereignty because it travels in the middle of God's purposes. Bravely muttering "God is in control" while seeking our own agenda is fruitless. But "the eyes of the LORD range throughout the earth to strengthen those whose hearts are fully committed to him." (2 Chronicles 16:9) The key is to embrace God's agenda as our own. Then we can have justified confidence and contentment in any situation, knowing that God Almighty rules and overrules the path I walk with him.

Where did you and I get our agenda for what we want to accomplish in life? From TV commercials? From movies? From our clique in school? To say that God isn't going to exercise his sovereign power to help us attain our goals, is not to say that he cares nothing about us. On the contrary, God cares more about us than we imagine. But if I have nothing particularly worth while to do with my life, I shouldn't expect God to empower me with supernatural opportunities or abilities. He has something much, much better in mind for me.

Christian, God calls you with a holy calling to be his servant and to be his child, to reflect his character, his healing and his gospel. You don't have to be an apostle but you do need to know how God has called you to serve him in your church, in your family, in your job and in your community. And if that means more to you, if glorifying God and pursuing his agenda means more to you than anything else, if your desire is to glorify him, whether by death or by life, then you will enter into the territory where God's power crackles and sparks, where a pillar of cloud goes before you during the day and a pillar of fire by night. Not that you are "controlling" God's power, but you are traveling where the Almighty is moving.

Living faith finds God's sovereignty in the stuff of life. But mere discussions about the sovereignty of God can become ponderously academic. "Can God make a rock so big he cannot move it?" "How can God be sovereign and man still have free will?" Such questions are not useless, and it's important to sharpen our understanding, But questions like these are not where faith lives. Faith lives where I live, where I face death as a slave to sin and God calls me out with a mighty hand and an outstretched arm to worship him.

Living faith affirms that God is in control and he is accomplishing his purpose in this world right now. Living faith wants to answer God's call to worship him, to dedicate our lives afresh to his glory, whatever that may mean for us personally. Then watch out as God brings provision, encouragement and opportunity from unexpected sources, and God's Spirit brings uncanny contentment and confidence to your soul.

What does such living faith look like? ...

Esther

> Then Esther spoke to Hathach and commanded him to go to Mordecai and say, "All the king's servants and the people of the king's provinces know that if any man or woman goes to the king inside the inner court without being called, there is but one law—to be put to death, except the one to whom the king holds out the golden scepter so that he may live. But as for me, I have not been called to come in to the

king these thirty days."

And they told Mordecai what Esther had said. Then Mordecai told them to reply to Esther, "Do not think to yourself that in the king's palace you will escape any more than all the other Jews. For if you keep silent at this time, relief and deliverance will rise for the Jews from another place, but you and your father's house will perish. And who knows whether you have not come to the kingdom for such a time as this?"

Then Esther told them to reply to Mordecai, "Go, gather all the Jews to be found in Susa, and hold a fast on my behalf, and do not eat or drink for three days, night or day. I and my young women will also fast as you do. Then I will go to the king, though it is against the law, and if I perish, I perish."

Mordecai then went away and did everything as Esther had ordered him. (Esther 4:1-17)

Looking at Jonah in the first chapter, we considered the conquest of the northern kingdom of Israel by the Assyrians in 8th century BC. Later, in 587, the Lord chastened southern Judah by allowing Nebuchadnezzar of Babylon to conquer Jerusalem and deport most of its citizens to Babylon. Babylon itself was taken over by the Medes and Persians, becoming the Persian Empire. At that point, Jews were allowed to return to Jerusalem to rebuild the city, but a great many stayed in their Persian home. Sixty years later, during the reign of King Ahasuerus of Persia (also known by his Greek name, Xerxes), large numbers of Jews remained in the eastern half of the Persian Empire; many in the great imperial cities.

The Book of Esther is the remarkable story of one such expatriated Jewish girl who becomes the Persian Queen. She could adopt that role only by downplaying her racial identity and her relationship to the Jewish cousin who raised her, a man named Mordecai. To repay her cousin, Esther quietly has him promoted as a local city judge. This puts him in contact with a very high ranking official named Haman. Haman is a vain man who requires all minor officials to grovel before his greatness, something which Mordecai refuses to do. In an egotistical rage, Haman resolves to destroy not only Mordecai, but also all of Mordecai's people, the Jews. Without mentioning the group by name, he convinces Xerxes that he has uncovered a subversive minority in the empire. The busy king gives him full authority to exterminate everyone involved. Unwittingly, the King had just ordered the execution of all Jews in his empire.

Mordecai learns of this catastrophe and gets word to Queen Esther. Mordecai humbles himself before God in sackcloth and communicates with Esther through the network of servants. He informs her of this impending disaster and begs her to go and intercede for the Jews before the King. This brings us to the text quoted above.

Esther responds that to appear before the king without an invitation automatically invokes the death penalty, which the king would have to specifically cancel or she would die. Mordecai's response is our focus, "Do not think to yourself that in the king's palace you will escape any more than all the other Jews. For if you keep silent at this time, relief and deliverance will rise for the Jews from another place, but you and your father's house will perish. And who knows whether you have not come to the kingdom for such a time as this?" Esther decides to intercede and what follows is a remarkable example of how God takes care of those who chose to trust in his sovereign power. (If you aren't familiar with the story, find the Book of Esther in the Bible and finish it. It's amazing.)

I've lost count of all the conversations I've had with people who want to discuss the philosophical and theological subtleties of God's sovereignty and human free will. The topic is mysterious because our minds are not clever enough to draw a picture of how eternity intersects with time. But we make the question much more difficult than we need to by assuming that God's sovereignty and our free will are in opposition to each other. The truth is exactly the opposite: they only make sense when taken together.

The human spirit responsible for intelligent choice could not exist apart from a sovereign God. Contemporary science takes a schizophrenic view of the universe: a huge, predictable machine resting on a quantum sea of unpredictable chaos. There is no room for free will in this vision, either in the machine or in the chaos. The only way a human spirit could possibly have free choice is if the universe is ultimately the creation of a God who transcends the universe, and we are made in his image. And a God who transcends the universe—who exists outside of matter and energy, space and time—a God who created the universe and sustains it—must, of necessity, be completely and utterly sovereign. He must be totally in control. Such absolute control expresses itself, in part, through the free human choice he enables. The freedom of mankind and the sovereignty of God are not mutually exclusive. The one depends on the other. The Westminster Confession of Faith brilliantly understands this relationship. It states that true human choice exists, not in spite of God's sovereignty, but because of it. (WCF III 1)

Although it is impossible for our finite minds to draw a picture of it, it is certain that God's total, complete sovereignty is the only way that human beings—beings with true freedom and real significance—can exist. So, perhaps we should not be too surprised that in the Bible, observations of God's sovereign power often arise as we are called upon to freely obey him. In fact, within our text, we see one of the great affirmations of divine sovereignty matched with an equally profound appeal to responsible choice, all in the same verse. On the one hand, "if you keep silent at this time, relief and deliverance will rise for the Jews from another place," while on the other hand, "who knows whether you have not come to the kingdom for such a time as this?" This is a plea for Esther to freely invest her life in God's purposes. Apparently, living faith in God's sovereignty leads us to freely trust and obey him.

"If you keep silent at this time, relief and deliverance will rise for the Jews from another place." Centuries before, God revealed to Moses that he had a purpose for Israel. He decreed that they would be the channel of salvation for every nation in the world. In Mordecai's day, that purpose had not yet been fulfilled. Therefore, Mordecai knew enough of God's purpose to realize that Haman could not completely destroy the Jews. Mordecai knew that because God is in control. God is sovereign.

The Lord is the one who says, "[I declare] the end from the beginning and from ancient times things not yet done, saying, 'My counsel shall stand, and I will accomplish all my purpose.'" (Isaiah 46:10)

The sovereignty of God has to do with the purposes of God, and not one purpose of his shall fail, not one. Whatever God has purposed to accomplish shall come to pass. God knows the end from the beginning, because he controls it all. He sees the past, present and future all at once because he is outside of time and space. When God speaks of the future, he speaks of that which he sees as truly as he sees what is our present. The New Testament will later speak of, "the purpose of him who works all things according to the counsel of his will." (Ephesians 1:11)

God's sovereignty is all about the completion and fulfillment of his purpose. That means, to the extent that we know God's will, we know the future; we know something of what shall and must be. Since God has revealed his eternal purposes, we know for a fact how things are going to play out.

We don't know most of the details, of course. We only know what he has revealed. Mordecai does not know what God has planned for him personally; he is in sackcloth, praying for mercy. Mordecai does not know what God has planned for Esther; he pleads with Esther to invest herself in God's kingdom. He does not know what she will decide. What Mordecai does know is that whatever Esther decides, God's purposes for Israel are not going to be thwarted by Haman, or anybody else for that matter.

Living faith understands God's sovereignty in terms of his revealed purposes. "The secret things belong to the LORD our God, but the things that are revealed belong to us and to our children forever, that we may do all the words of this law." (Deuteronomy 29:29)

God has his own purposes for everything; for every star, for every snowflake, for every human being. But the vast ocean of details concerning his purposes are secret, in that he has not chosen to reveal them. We aren't supposed to guess at the details; we're supposed to live them out through the choices we make, for good or ill, as we affirm or deny what he has revealed.

Sometimes, we wish God revealed more about his secrets for our lives. How long will I live? Will I beat this cancer? Is it his will that I stay in the job I have now, or should I move to Cincinnati in search of greener pastures? Personally, I wish I could look ahead about four days each week and copy down the sermon I'm going to write. That would save me a lot of work! But, you know, if I just copied down my sermons from the future instead of having to study and pray through them, I'd never grow. If you knew every detail of your future, you might become frightened or complacent, but no wiser.

What God has chosen to reveal, to a large extent, is his Law. His Law describes his purposes in a way that's helpful and practical. The Law of God is a general description of his purpose for the human race. God's will for his redeemed people is that they become transformed and renewed into the ethical, emotional and intellectual image of his Son. That is God's sovereign purpose for his people. "Those whom he foreknew he also predestined to be conformed to the image of his Son, in order that he might be the firstborn among many brothers." (Romans 8:29)

That, Christian, is your predestined future. You will grow to be like Jesus, and nothing can stop that from happening. The opportunities that allow that to happen in this life … we must wait to see. How fast we are transformed in this life depends largely on our choices. But the fact that in eternity, every believer will each reach God's purpose of reflecting his Spirit just as Jesus does—of that, there is no doubt. God has said it, and it shall be. He has spoken, and it shall come to pass.

Mordecai can look at whatever God has revealed about his ultimate plans and know that those plans shall be accomplished. "If you keep silent at this time, relief and deliverance will rise for the Jews from another place." "Esther, my dear, I'm not worried about God's plans. Anything that we do, or refuse to do, has already been taken into account by the Lord. We can't mess up his plans and neither can we accomplish them all by ourselves. God is in control. But my dear Esther, because God is in control, you have a decision to make. We don't know how this catastrophe will play out. We don't know how God will preserve our people and what will become of us. But you might possibly become God's means for saving the entire Jewish nation from extinction."

"Who knows whether you have not come to the kingdom for such a time as this?" Biblically speaking, confidence in God's sovereignty never makes our choices insignificant. Instead, God's sovereignty gives our choices real meaning. This is because the God who ordains the ends, also ordains the means. That is, God not only ordains outcomes, but he also plans for the prayers, work and faith of people whom he empowers to make those plans happen. He doesn't tell us those details ahead of time. We get to freely involve ourselves in his sovereign purposes, but God has not chosen to accomplish his redemptive purposes without us. He intends to build his kingdom alongside his children, alongside us. Mordecai did not say that God would wave his hands and deliver his people. He said that deliverance would rise from another place. God would raise up somebody else to do what needed to be done to provide deliverance—not because God needs us, but because that is how God's sovereignty works. It works through our responsible choices.

Living faith in God's sovereignty never puts us on the sidelines. Having established that God's purposes for Israel are not threatened by Haman, Mordecai then presents a challenge to Esther: "Will you go to Xerxes and use your influence to avoid this catastrophe? Will you willingly invest your life in the sovereign purposes of God? His purposes will come to pass, whatever you choose. You don't have to be involved if you don't want to, but you get to choose whether God will work through you to accomplish his design. Look at the opportunity you have, because of your position, because you are the Queen. The opportunity to accomplish God's will defaults to you. What do you say?"

God is just as much at work accomplishing his purposes today, as ever. As always, the secret things belong to him, but we can choose to use the things he has revealed to direct our choices.

That is why we can all find ourselves in this passage. God's sovereignty is the focus for our choices, just as much as they were for Esther. God is accomplishing his will today. You don't know the details of its formation, but you do the know general outlines of God's kingdom. The question before you and me is the same one that Mordecai put before Esther. Since she knows where God is taking things, won't she choose to be the one who moves his kingdom forward? God will move it forward regardless of what we decide. But it's our choice as to what part we have in it all.

The question for you and me, the every-day question that determines how we plan and make decisions, is how can I use the opportunities given me by God to further his purposes in this world? I live in the twenty-first century, in the midst of very specific challenges and opportunities. In God's providence, I am a father or mother; I'm a pastor or a mechanic or a school teacher or a government contractor. I work in a specific place with specific people. I am in one particular church out of hundreds. I have specific children. Haven't I been put where I am to accomplish God's purposes, where I am? Mordecai phrased it diplomatically as a question, "who knows but that you have come to royal position for such a time as this?" But surely, he was making a statement. Surely, it was no coincidence that Esther, a secret Jew, had become a beloved queen at a time when this king was about to destroy all the Jews. She had the opportunity to be used by God to bring his purposes to pass—in this case, save the Jews from extinction. Sure, she could let God save the Jews some other way, but why? Why, when she was right there and this privilege was in her lap? What else is life for, but to be used of God to bring his purposes to pass? What else matters? What else will last?

Only God's purposes will last. Psalm 90 declares, "Before the mountains were brought forth, or ever you had formed the earth and the world, from everlasting to everlasting you are God." Apart from his purposes, all our efforts amount to nothing.

> You sweep them away as with a flood; they are like a dream, like grass that is renewed in the morning: in the morning it flourishes and is renewed; in the evening it fades and withers …
>
> The years of our life are seventy, or even by reason of strength eighty; yet their span is but toil and trouble; they are soon gone, and we fly away. (Psalm 90:5-6,10)

That's why Psalm 90 ends with, "Let the favor of the Lord our God be upon us, and establish the work of our hands upon us; yes, establish the work of our hands!" As we give ourselves to accomplishing God's eternal purposes, his favor rests upon us and the work of our hands is established in this life. Our choices are made meaningful, turned into something that will last.

Esther is a great story because she stood at a crossroads in Old Testament history. She was given a crucial opportunity to make a difference for the Lord, and she took it. She is such a vibrant example for us because we each face the same choice every day of our lives. It doesn't matter whether the issues are great or small because the greatness of any action is not how great the world thinks it is, but whether it accomplishes something of God's eternal purposes. If our lives do not pursue God's purposes, then they won't count much in the ultimate scheme of things. We would be wildflowers that look pretty for a few days and then are gone and forgotten. But if our service and our prayers go toward advancing God's eternal and inevitable plan, then what we do will matter for all time; no matter how large or small our actions may be.

When you and I use the opportunities at hand to pursue the Lord's revealed purposes, then God manifests his power in us to bring his design into being. We become his hands and his lips to accomplish the things prophesied in Scripture; tasting in this age the redemption which will be perfected in eternity.

The Lord is so excited whenever he sees people like Esther investing their lives in his desire. They are the ones who have a vision of God's divine sovereignty, and therefore hear, "the voice of the Lord saying, 'Whom shall I send, and who will go for us?' Then I said, 'Here I am! Send me.'" (Isaiah 6:8)

Sure, God could choose somebody else, but why would we want him to?

Living faith chooses to be the instrument of God's power to bring love and righteousness into being on this planet, rather than let someone else do it.

> In a great house there are not only vessels of gold and silver but also of wood and clay, some for honorable use, some for dishonorable.
>
> Therefore, if anyone cleanses himself from what is dishonorable, he will be a vessel for honorable use, set apart as holy, useful to the master of the house, ready for every good work. (2 Timothy 2:20-21)

Living faith does not want a life that will be mostly thrown out at the end of the day, useless shards of self-centered effort thrown in the dust bin. Living faith wants to be an instrument for noble purposes, made holy and useful to the Master, prepared for any good work he has for us to do.

In God's providence, you have a particular job, accomplishing a particular benefit for society, working with particular people. And where you work, there are challenges. Maybe not as bad as the challenges facing Esther and Mordecai, but significant for those involved. Maybe management is poor, maybe people are uninspired, bored or angry at how they are treated. Maybe some of those around you are excruciatingly lonely, or overburdened with family crisis, or terrified out of their mind about dying before they ever discover why they are alive. And you are there. Who knows but that you have come to your position for such a time as this? Jesus could be made visible where you work through your courage to stand up to injustice, or through your compassion and mercy to those who are hurting. What could it mean if Jesus were made visible where you work? Yes, God's kingdom will be built regardless of what you do, but what you choose at work will, in part, determine where and how his kingdom is built.

This week, or next, you'll run up against the next family crisis. In God's providence, you are either single with particular friends or you have a particular spouse and particular children and other family members. And in your family, there are challenges. Maybe someone is buried under depression or is wandering off into self-destruction for lack of any direction. Maybe a loved one can no longer live independently or another is crossing a milestone in becoming a responsible adult. And you are there. Who knows but that you have come to your position for such a time as this? Jesus could be made manifest in your family through you, through your willingness to get involved and help, through your forgiveness or the time you invest to earn the right to impart wisdom. What could it mean if Jesus were made visible in your family? Yes, God's kingdom will be built regardless of what you do, but in his providence, what you choose at home will, in part, determine where and how his kingdom is built.

Living faith looks like Esther walking into the King's presence unannounced. It believes God is in control. It approaches every opportunity with the confidence that God has placed me here for just such a time as this.

The World Is Not What It Should Be

> The creation waits with eager longing for the revealing of the sons of God. For the creation was subjected to futility, not willingly, but because of him who subjected it, in hope that the creation itself will be set free from its bondage to corruption and obtain the freedom of the glory of the children of God. For we know that the whole creation has been groaning together in the pains of childbirth until now. (Romans 8:19-22)

A tight Gone with the Wind camera shot on Scarlet O'Hara, in all her shock and misery. Then the camera angle widens … and widens … panning across the overwhelming devastation of Civil War Atlanta. The Apostle Paul would take that view to maximum, capturing all of history, all the world as we know it. Sin is not just a personal calamity we must face; it is a universal catastrophe gripping the entire planet, with innumerable casualties. The creation is frustrated, in bondage to decay, and groaning.

I must confess that my first reaction to this text, as a physics graduate, was to think in terms of matter and energy and physical forces. Somehow, sin had impacted gravity and brought decay into the world. I still wonder if something like that might be true, but I no longer think that Paul had that in mind. The context is all about the human consequences of sin. By the end of this chapter, he illustrates this bondage as trouble, hardship, persecution, famine, nakedness, danger, sword, and death. Paul is talking about the universal human tragedy of sin. When he speaks of decay, he's not thinking about alpha particles and radioactivity; he's thinking about the way the human spirit has decayed from its original design. We see this decay not only in our personal struggle with sin but also all around us, in all of society and in the ways we use our institutions to abuse each other and the planet. The whole world is groaning in frustration and bondage.

A fundamental aspect of the biblical world view is that God designed everything to be good, and human sin, instigated by Satan, has ruined it all. We call this "the Fall." The Fall of humanity has knocked every aspect of human civilization out of alignment with God's intent. Humanity still works, but we no longer work the way God intended. Atomic energy can provide cheap power for millions, but we also use it to make bombs. Rockets can be used to explore space, but also to drop those bombs on civilian targets. Things meant for good, we use for evil.

God gave us the capacity to live in his image, exercising benevolent dominion over all life in this wonderful planet, living together as one big, happy family. But we have "improved" on God's design. Our first parents chose a predisposition to exalt self and distrust our Creator. What is more, they have passed that predisposition on to us. It has worked itself out into every form of sin imaginable.

God doesn't like what we have done. And God is determined to put a stop to our sin. God is determined to execute justice and retribution and see that every person, every family, every nation face the sins they have committed.

However, this judgment, this curse upon what we have turned this place into, has been suspended. God's sword is stayed in mid-thrust, so that he may first reclaim a multitude of sinners before judgment falls, saving them by pure grace—simply because he is merciful. After bringing a multitude safely into a great ark named "Jesus Christ," God's judgment will flood the world, but not harm his people. Their judgment will have been borne by Jesus on the cross, who shields them from the downpour with his own sacrifice.

And so, from a biblical perspective, the world as we now know it is in a temporary, transitional phase. It doesn't feel transitional, because it is the only world humanity has known throughout our brief recorded history. But human history is not really that long; it's just a short slice of time. And all of it has transpired within this temporary suspension of God's judgment. Ours is a world that is no longer innocent, a world systemically infected with sin but not yet judged and remade by God—a broken world in a transitional period of grace. A time in which people seem to get away with sin and injustice, when oppression is imperfectly opposed and disease, accident, pain and death are the norm. A temporary phase in which God is saving a people for himself before his judgment closes it all down and locks individual destinies forever.

We live in an age when the wounds of sin are treated only superficially. We have government to restrict evil, but it has limited effect. We have families to promote righteousness, but their impact is spotty. We have medicine, but the relief it brings is partial, and oh, so temporary. The creation is subjected to "futility" and "bondage to corruption."

The world as it is today is not what it should be. God originally made it to be better, and one day it shall be better. We live in a transitional period of grace before judgment, with access to God's mercy, while still unavoidably saddled with sin and misery.

This profound insight is critically important in making sense out of life. It announces a uniquely positive message and role for believers in this world, and offers sanity when the world throws nasty things our way.

A living faith that this world is not what is should be can give us a uniquely positive message and role. When you have no way to see life in a larger context, you assume that whatever is, is all there is. There are fringe populations in South America and in the Philippines who live in rubble outside of major cities. They eat out of the city dump; they live in cardboard houses. That is normal for them. That is what life has always been for them. If you were a child growing up in such a family, that would be all you would expect to know.

But in Florida, people have sat in rubble after devastating hurricanes and tornados. For a day or so they were shell-shocked, but they did not assume that the chaos around them was all there was, and the way it always had to be. They had a larger context. They knew it was better before. They knew it would be better again. So they rolled up their sleeves and worked together to rebuild. You watch people in catastrophe who have a larger perspective, and it's quite inspiring. From an economic perspective, many Americans have a positive attitude that puts disaster, even something as big as 9/11, in a larger context. We know we can rebuild.

But what is true for us economically is not the case morally. As a culture, we are losing any notion of a larger moral context. Some of the powers that be are actually trying to erase the knowledge of God's design out of our social memory. And the idea that God would judge anyone, let alone the world, is laughed at. As a result, we have entire generations who know nothing but life in a moral dump. We can't recognize the dignity of an unborn baby. We can't figure out what sex is for and how relationships work. We don't know when they've had enough of anything; appetites of all kinds are out of control. In terms of moral choices, we're eating in the dump, in the gutter, and we think. "That's just the way life is," because we have no larger context.

Biblical Christians have a larger context in which to view life, because we know that this world is not what it should be. We know there is an "oughtness" to life. We know that an objectively real God created this world with a wonderful design, one that reflects his own nature. But our chosen outlook, our sin, ruined it all. And sin has not only ruined individual lives, it has crashed the creation. The creation was subjected to frustration and bondage to decay, not in the sense that my personal faults directly cause a tornado in Florida, but in the sense that human sin (which I share) has alienated this world from its Creator and earned his judgment. Because that judgment is suspended, we still enjoy many of the blessings we were designed to have. But since we are under judgment and alienated, those blessings are compromised and do not work well anymore.

Now, we have thorns to contend with. Now, bearing and raising kids is no picnic. Now, couples blame each other instead of cleave together. Now, brother murders brother. It's all there in Genesis. It's as though our father gave us the keys to the car and we immediately wrecked it. Oh, it still runs, but the grinding gears won't go more than five miles per hour.

Christians have the advantage of seeing this life in a larger perspective. We understand that this world is not what it is supposed to be. It is supposed to be better, and God's Word tells us how it can be better. We fully expect God to intervene, to deal with sin once and for all and reinstitute his design. We don't even need a constitutional amendment; it's going to happen. Jesus will return and see that it happens.

Living faith sees this world and this life as something in transition, a broken period of grace between what used to be good and what shall be better. Our society desperately needs people who believe that, people who know what's wrong with this place and who have some idea how to at least partially fix what's wrong.

It's tragic that some Christians take this divine perspective and use it to spew self-righteous condemnation all over our morally lost society, like a fifth-grade bully terrorizing first graders who don't have a clue. That's a far cry from the One who said, "Father, forgive them, for they know not what they do." (Luke 23:34) The Lord emphatically told us that this is not the time for condemnation. Of course, we need to humbly warn people that condemnation is coming, but this is not the time for us to condemn anyone. "For God did not send his Son into the world to condemn the world, but in order that the world might be saved through him." (John 3:17)

No, believing that this world is not what it should be rightly generates a uniquely positive message and role. We have the context of Eden to remind us of what God wants. We weren't meant to eat in the dump, so we can get busy restoring some order. We have the prospect of Paradise to assure us of what God will bring about, so we needn't feel discouraged that our efforts now are imperfect. We know that ultimate restoration is inevitable. Christ will return and God will have his way. We are therefore free to link hands with those who wish to join us and build something that looks a little more like Paradise, right here and now. And we can share our hope of Paradise with all who are interested. That's a great message and a great role to have.

A living faith that this world is not what it should be sustains us when the world throws nasty things our way. The world in which we live is not only infected with evil, but it is also laced with danger. There is no one reading this who has not been hurt over the last year. Eden did not have lay-offs or divorce or old age; Paradise will not have war or racism or drugs. We have these things now, in this transitional period under God's suspended curse, when Heaven and Hell are held back and the Lord roots through the rubble to save us.

Just as many lack the context in which to understand right and wrong; they also lack the context in which to understand pain and suffering. It always strikes them by surprise. Whether it's an earthquake or a flood or a heart attack or a child custody suit, the response is almost always the same: "Why me?" "Why is this happening to me?" and they really don't know the answer. The unspoken assumption goes something like this: This world is normal. If God exists, then he is in heaven and all should be well with the world. God's judgment is not part of the picture. Then something nasty happens: a root canal, diabetes or unplanned job move—or maybe something really nasty: a child runs away, a kidney fails, fire takes your house. And … "Hey, what's wrong? I thought everything was OK! God is all powerful, right? God is all loving, right? So how come I'm hurting? What's wrong?" Faith doesn't work—nothing works—if this world is the way its supposed to be.

Christians ought to know what's wrong. The Christian should not be tormented by "Why? Why?" We should know why. Christians should know that this used to be a Garden of Eden and shall be a Paradise. But right now, we live in a war zone under God's suspended curse. And life is not normal in a war zone. Knowing that doesn't take away any of the pain, but it does take away confusion and bitterness.

The trouble is, very few Christians these days see this life as a temporary phase of brokenness between something that was better and will be so again. Modern Christianity is afraid to be heavenly minded, on the assumption that it does no earthly good. God's judgment and future glory are doctrines we confess to be orthodox, but our working horizon often extends no further than anyone else's. We lack the clear, positive vision of God's lost design and future purposes which would sustain us in the trials we must endure along with everyone else.

45

Many believers today are fixated on this world in its present form. Scripture says, "Do not love the world or the things in the world." (1 John 2:15) Yet we look lovingly to this life to answer all our needs and fulfill all our desires. Scripture says, "The world is passing away along with its desires." (1 John 2:17) Yet we persist in giving most of our attention to what is temporary and ignore God's design, which shall be permanent. No wonder we join others asking, "Why me?"

Christian, you and I need a living faith that accepts the broken and transitory nature of this world. We can still taste many original blessings, but this world is under God's suspended judgment, and until Christ returns nothing will work right. When I live in that faith, then I stop asking "Why me?" I don't have to question God, or question my salvation, or question my faith. I realize that I'm not hurting because something is wrong with my faith; I'm hurting because something is wrong with this world. I'm living in the chaos of a spiritual war zone in which Christ's Spirit is fighting for souls. I can endure the present crisis, because I know that it is neither normal nor permanent.

If this world were either Eden or Paradise, we'd be in real trouble, wouldn't we? Or if there were no Eden or Paradise, we'd be in equal trouble. In either case, there would be nothing for us but despair. Like children growing up in a perpetually war-torn city, that would be all there would ever be to life, all we would ever know. We would think nothing of living in holes and picking through the dump for food, always with a constant, confused, pathetic "Why?" every day.

But faith that this world is not what it should be changes all that. Seeing this world in terms of its past and its future, we want to get busy cleaning it up—simply because now we know what it's supposed to look like. No need to shout condemnation at other folks still scrounging in the rubble. We want to clean up our own corner of this mess and reclaim some dignity and hope, dignity and hope we can share with other lost souls as God finds them, too.

What does such living faith look like? ...

Nehemiah

> We all returned to the wall, each to his work. From that day on, half of my servants worked on construction, and half held the spears, shields, bows, and coats of mail. And the leaders stood behind the whole house of Judah, who were building on the wall. Those who carried burdens were loaded in such a way that each labored on the work with one hand and held his weapon with the other. And each of the builders had his sword strapped at his side while he built. (Nehemiah 4:15-18)

Nehemiah was one of those Jews, like Daniel and Esther, who did very well in Persia after the Babylonian exile ended. They remained faithful to their religion, but managed to be so helpful that those in power wanted them around anyway. Nehemiah was cupbearer to Artaxerxes, a Persian monarch reigning about thirty years after the Xerxes we read about in Esther.

A cupbearer was the official wine taster for the king, whose job was to check for poison with his own body. The position was obviously one of considerable trust. So, we're not surprised to read in ancient documents that the cupbearer was sometimes known as a "chief advisor." We should not think of Nehemiah as holding an official cabinet position, but rather as part of a "kitchen cabinet," or what has been known since Franklin Roosevelt's day as the Executive Office.

The reign of Artaxerxes was marked with rebellion in the far-flung provinces of the huge Persian empire. The Persians responded by allowing their subjugated people groups to reestablish their local religions, in hopes of building a good will that would earn the blessing of many gods and their worshipers. To that end, Ezra was sent to Jerusalem to restore the teaching of Moses and rebuild the Temple of the LORD.

However, when Ezra attempted to rebuild the walls of the city, competing regional neighbors told the king that the Jews were planning a revolt. As a result, Artaxerxes halted work on the walls. When Nehemiah heard of this turn of events, he was deeply moved. He had never been to Jerusalem, but he was convinced that God's people needed freedom to live out the divine covenant made with them. He was convinced that the Empire—indeed, the whole world—needed to see God's people living out the covenant of grace. He was convinced that God could only be glorified as he should be, if his rule were properly modeled in the Holy Land.

After much prayer, Nehemiah suggested to the king that he be given the task of rebuilding the city walls and re-forging the Jewish identity. These were goals Artaxerxes already desired. He did not personally know and trust Ezra, but he did trust Nehemiah, so he appointed him as temporary governor of Judah and sent him with all the authority he needed to rebuild the wall and thus reestablish the city. Before he was finished, Nehemiah would actually make two extended trips to Jerusalem as governor over a period of twelve years. The book of Nehemiah is about a man with a vision to see God glorified in this world through his people.

But it is also about the hard work and perseverance necessary to bring God's will to fruition in our chaotic world. Nehemiah lived at a time when Old Testament faith was in as much disrepair as Jerusalem's walls. When Nehemiah arrived in Jerusalem, he found that God's people had almost forgotten their holy calling. There was no sense of brotherhood; the rich lent to the poor at interest, making themselves rich by keeping their brothers poor. There was no appreciation of worship; the Sabbath was treated like any other business day. There was no godly leadership; leaders used positions of influence for personal privilege instead of service. There was no passion to reach and teach the next generation of Jews. They were taking foreigners as spouses. and abandoning the use of Hebrew, thus cutting off their children from the language of the Scriptures.

And all of these problems were fed by a hostile external environment. Sanballat, the governor of Samaria to the north, opposed any reestablishment of Jewish identity in Jerusalem. He wanted Samaria to be the only viable political and religious center in the region. Gesham led a powerful confederation of Arab communities to the west and south. He, too, did not want to see any reestablishment of Jewish power. There were also Jewish leaders like Tobiah, who feared losing their share of established influence. These people had economic, political and military power and they were not afraid to use it. Jerusalem would never have independence as long as it was at the mercy of men like these.

That is why Nehemiah focused on the city wall. After the introduction of gunpowder in Europe in the twelfth century, the invention of the canon would made city walls obsolete. But before then, walls were the most effective form of defense. A city with walls could independently develop on its own. A city with walls had integrity. That's what the Jews in Israel needed: integrity. Rebuilding the wall would rebuild the people's integrity as the people of God. It would turn Jerusalem from a laughing stock into God's city on a hill, able to model the covenant of salvation that God offers the world.

Nehemiah recorded the threats and opposition of those who didn't want the wall completed.

> Now when Sanballat heard that we were building the wall, he was angry and greatly enraged, and he jeered at the Jews. And he said in the presence of his brothers and of the army of Samaria, "What are these feeble Jews doing? Will they restore it for themselves? Will they sacrifice? Will they finish up in a day? Will they revive the stones out of the heaps of rubbish, and burned ones at that?" Tobiah the Ammonite was beside him, and he said, "Yes, what they are building—if a fox goes up on it he will break down their stone wall!" (Nehemiah 4:1-3)

Nehemiah's initial response was to pray, and then later,

> When [their enemies] heard that the repairing of the walls of Jerusalem was going forward and that the breaches were beginning to be closed, they were very angry. And they all plotted together to come and fight against Jerusalem and to cause confusion in it. (Nehemiah 4:7-8)

Nehemiah continued to pray, but he also posted guards. He identified weak places in the wall and had people stationed by families to defend those places. Nehemiah made sure they were ready for any attack. Some of the people focused on guarding the others. People who carried materials held them in one hand while hefting a weapon in the other. People who were building had a sword strapped on at the ready. The builders stayed in the city overnight to double as a night watch. Nehemiah himself continually made a circuit around the city, with a trumpeter next to him who could call the people to rally at any point to repel an attack. The governor didn't even pause to change clothes, but remained on duty every day.

Nehemiah devised plans to keep the building project on target. And all the while, Nehemiah prayed. The results?

> So the wall was finished on the twenty-fifth day of the month Elul, in fifty-two days. And when all our enemies heard of it, all the nations around us were afraid and fell greatly in their own esteem, for they perceived that this work had been accomplished with the help of our God. (Nehemiah 6:15-16)

Just about everybody feels that this world is not what they wish it to be. We see so much pain and horrible evil and we wish the world were different. We think of our own pain and the challenges we face just to live, and wish our lot were more pleasant. So, we make up our minds to change the world, at least the little section we live in. We use whatever tactics match our personalities and resources: wit, force, intimidation, seduction— anything to make the world over into our own idea of what we want.

But, of course, we compete with a whole civilization trying to do the same thing. We are all outfoxing each other, all trying to make the world what we wish it were. And at some point, usually around middle-age, we realize we aren't going to succeed. We aren't going to be able to remake the world in our image. It is a bitter and disappointing discovery, to realize your life will not be all you wish it were, because you have neither the power nor authority to fundamentally change it.

How different it is for the person living in the faith that this world is not what it should be—*should be*, not in the sense of what

I wish, but in the transcendent sense of what God wishes, or what ought to be. Such faith perceives a great *should* lying over the world, a moral rightness that is simply God's character: the inner moral attributes of the one who created all that is for the purpose of displaying his character. People with a living biblical faith know what the world should be because God has revealed his character in his covenant of redemption, also known as the gospel. We see its outlines in the model of Old Testament Israel, and then gloriously fleshed out for all the world in the person of Jesus Christ.

To think that the world is not as I wish it to be, pits me and my puny strength against the world, but to live in the faith that the world is not what God says it should be, links me to God's plan, God's purposes and God's strength. The one who has grasped that the world is not what it should be understands that his or her life is part of a much longer process of redemption. God is remaking the world from the inside out, redeeming individuals by planting faith in the heart so faith can grow and transform the soul. Then bringing those tender, growing souls together to form oases of fellowship in a morally barren wilderness—oases that remind the desert of the garden it once was and will be again. At final judgment, the entire earth will be remade into an oasis.

In the Old Testament, there was only one tiny oasis: Israel, represented by its capital, Jerusalem. God temporarily disciplined Jerusalem with the Babylonian exile because its people would not honor his covenant. They bore his name, but blasphemed it through their lukewarm and adulterated religion. But he said that he would bring them back, stronger and more faithful after this discipline. That is why Nehemiah was willing to invest twelve years of his life to rebuild that city. Nehemiah wasn't doing it for himself. He was nicely positioned in Susa with a great job. Nehemiah had it made. But Nehemiah jumped at the opportunity to get involved in God's plan. God was crafting a covenant to reconcile the world to himself! The world desperately needed Jerusalem to shine as a witness to the Lord's character and plans.

Those who realize that this world is not what it should be, become idealists. They see beyond what is; not to what they might accomplish in their own strength, but to what God is accomplishing in his strength. They exchange their smaller hopes for God's published dream. They see beyond what is, to what assuredly shall be, knowing that God's sovereign dream will come to pass in time. While others sweep sand in the desert to build their own kingdom, these folks work with God to create the only true oasis in a barren world. They become idealists.

Ah, but those who realize that the world is not what it should be become realists, too. Things are not as they should be for a reason—three reasons, actually. First, there is the devil, a fallen angel. Things are not as they should be because of a being of immense power and malevolence. For centuries, the devil used superstition to magnify and exaggerate his power. In today's secular societies, the devil uses our sophistication as a perfect camouflage in which to hide. But make no mistake; he is still a roaring lion seeking those he can devour. Second, there is the flesh; that is, our sinful nature. Things are not as they should be because we are born spiritually and morally broken. That doesn't make us any less human or valuable, but it does predispose us to exaggerated self-reliance, self-centeredness and self-destruction. Third, there is the world. Things are not as they should be because the devil and human sin together have baked fear and lies into all our institutions and structures so that they perpetuate sin all by themselves.

In God's sovereignty, he has made room in his plans for freedom of choice. He has made room in his plans for both the devil and human sin. God will reconcile a vast multitude to himself, but getting there is going to take a lot of work; a lot of work from God and from anyone who wants to work alongside him. Living by the conviction that this world is not as it should be creates idealists willing to hope, and realists willing to work.

Nehemiah was an idealist, willing to interrupt his nice life to become governor of God's people during one of their most challenging periods, because a Holy City without integrity was not the way it should be. God would have it differently, for God is bringing redemption to this world.

Nehemiah had a vision of God's future order, but what a realist he was. He didn't expect it to be easy just because it was God's will. God allows for sin in this world, so accomplishing his will is going to cost something. It certainly cost God something— the cross—and it's going to cost us something too. Nehemiah was ready for personal sacrifice and a lot of practical improvising. He was ready to work hard, persevere and adapt to fresh attacks by the world, the flesh and the devil.

And please note that the hard work that needs to be done must begin with unifying and directing God's people. Of course, there is tremendous good we can do in society at large, but the church must always begin by putting its own house in order. Nehemiah went back to his job in the Persian empire, but not until he spent twelve years restoring to God's people a vision of who they were.

A young college student named Glenn was having a great time as a new believer. A whole new side of him was growing that before, he didn't even know existed. An early high point was a two-week leadership training camp in Michigan where he gained a vision of the Lordship of Christ. On one of those weekends, he and his small group attended the closest local church. It was the first time in his young Christian life that he had ever been in a church that did not meaningfully trust the Bible as

God's Word. The message had no substance and contained no biblical truth. For the first time, he saw the walls of the church in ruins. It was not the way it should be, the way God wanted it. God's Word should be central in his church; it is the light for our path. Glenn said, in his youthful idealism: "I could preach better than that, if I just read the Bible and sat down. Why have church if you're just going to ignore what the Bible says?"

Well, I came to learn that preaching and pastoring is much harder than I thought. But nearly 50 years later I remain willing to invest in that work because I know I'm working with God on something God wants to accomplish.

A young woman named Micki was a brand new Christian when she took an accounting job at a fine evangelical seminary. She thought she was just one step away from heaven, until a beloved professor ran off with a secretary. Then she discovered that seminary students could neglect their bills like anyone else. She saw that Christ's future leaders need a tremendous amount of encouragement and pointing to Christ if the walls of his church are to remain strong. My wife remains willing to invest in that work because she knows she is working with God on something he wants to accomplish.

Surely, Christian, you see places where the walls of the church are cracked or collapsed. What do you do? Do you keep your distance, stay in Susa where life is good and just shake your head at the crumbling city on the hill?

What we can do instead is accept that this world is not what it should be, and the first thing that needs to be repaired is God's church. Let the world do its worst. Realize that temptations are on their way. Let Satan roar. It doesn't matter. These walls are going up. If we have to endure insults and threats from outside the church, we will. If we have to confess our own sin, work on our own fellowship, raise up better leaders, learn to worship properly, retool how we are raising our kids, we will. If we have to build with one hand while carrying the sword of the Spirit in the other to protect ourselves, we will.

Living faith looks like Nehemiah building a city wall. It grasps God's dream and therefore understands that this world is not what it should be.

God Will Make All Things Right

> Then I saw a great white throne and him who was seated on it …. and they were judged, each one of them, according to what they had done. (Revelation 20:11,13)

> Then I saw a new heaven and a new earth … And he who was seated on the throne said, "Behold, I lam making all things new." (Revelation 21:1,5)

In this section of Revelation, we are looking at a symbolic vision of the end of history; that is to say, the end of this phase of human history. It began when human sin set in motion the way things are now, the order of things examined in the previous chapter, a phase of history in which the world is under God's suspended curse and sin often seems to win.

This vision in Revelation tells us that a day is coming when God will make all things right. At Christ's return, God's curse will finally come crashing down on this sinful world, sin will finally lose and God will reinstate his blessing and bring his design to completion on this planet. This vision is not a newsreel of those events, of course. Visions reveal the meaning of events through pictures. What we see here is a vivid, unforgettable picture of what it will mean for God to make all things right.

First, God will make all things right by judging unrepentant sin, all sin not covered by his grace. "Then I saw a great white throne and him who was seated on it. From his presence earth and sky fled away, and no place was found for them." (Revelation 20:11)

What an image, a kingly throne descending from heaven, as the sky and the earth retreat in awe! The point, of course, is that when God manifests himself there is no competition for attention.

God dominates everything. He has been hidden, but one day he will be hidden no longer. The image is of a great Monarch on his throne to judge his subjects, to weigh complaints against them, to weigh their loyalty, to weigh their deeds and hearts, then reward or punish them appropriately.

> And I saw the dead, great and small, standing before the throne, and books were opened … And the dead were judged by what was written in the books, according to what they had done. And the sea gave up the dead who were in it, Death and Hades gave up the dead who were in them, and they were judged, each one of them, according to what they had done. (Revelation 20:12-13)

Here is the bodily resurrection of all people. These are not the disembodied souls temporarily kept in Heaven or Hades after death. No, every body is raised. It doesn't matter whether they were buried on land or at sea, each person stands before God as a whole person, body and soul together, ready to account for all thoughts of the soul and all the deeds of the body.

We see a stack of books—a contemporary vision might portray computer logs—since God's judgment involves a thorough review of one's life, with special attention given to our choices.

> Then Death and Hades were thrown into the lake of fire. This is the second death, the lake of fire. And if anyone's name was not found written in the book of life, he was thrown into the lake of fire. (Revelation 20:14-15)

Death is God's punishment for sin, anyone judged to be a sinner must die. Biblically speaking, however, death is not a cessation of existence. (Notice that these people have already died once, and they still exist.) Rather, death is a banishment from the Lord's presence, an exile from all blessing. Adam and Eve died on the day they first sinned (Genesis 2:16-17). Death began when they were cast out of the Garden. Those who die outside of grace during the present age of the world are separated from God temporarily. This vision makes it clear that at Christ's return, they are cast away from God's presence forever. The image for this banishment is a lake of fire which we usually call Hell.

Jesus said more about Hell than anyone else in the Bible. He liked to use an object lesson one could actually see from the southern steps of the Temple. From there, he and his disciples looked across the valley at the hill called Hinom, *Gar Hinom* in Hebrew. We pronounce it "Gehenna," and it is often translated to English as "Hell." When Jesus spoke of Hell, he pointed to an actual location as an illustration. Gehenna was the place where children were once offered in fire as sacrifices to the pagan God Moloch. Jesus taught that Hell is like that, a place for idolaters whom God excludes from worship, people who burned their future to ashes in the worship of false gods. Jesus also spoke of Hell more abstractly as an outer darkness, a place of weeping and gnashing of teeth, a place where people live forever without any experience of God's blessing.

What does Hell literally look like? Since the images of fire and darkness are mutually exclusive, we don't know. But being lost in darkness, or having the fruit of one's life burned to ashes must describe Hell pretty well. The just punishment for all who prefer to live on their own by rejecting the authority of the Living God, is to be condemned to receive exactly what they long for: life without him forever. Such punishment is both terrifying and eminently fair.

The first thing God will do, therefore, to make all things right is judge unrepentant sinners, all those not covered by his grace. He will exile them forever.

The second thing God will do to make all things right is remake the world, re-order it so that his blessings will be experienced to the full by those reconciled to him.

> Then I saw a new heaven and a new earth, for the first heaven and the first earth had passed away …
> And I saw the holy city, new Jerusalem, coming down out of heaven from God, prepared as a bride adorned for her husband. (Revelation 21:1-2)

A new heaven for the angels, a new earth for humanity. Believers will be resurrected along with everyone else. In renewed bodies we will stand before God on a renewed earth. The earth will be "new" in the sense that Paul taught us earlier: liberated from its bondage to decay and brought into the freedom of God's children. The new order of things, pictured as a Holy City, will come down from heaven. God will institute an order where sin does not exist and blessing abounds.

> And I heard a loud voice from the throne saying, "Behold, the dwelling place of God is with man. He will dwell with them, and they will be his people, and God himself will be with them as their God." (Revelation 21:3)

Who are these whom God claims as "his people"? How did they escape his judgment? Remember that Revelation 20:12 mentioned another book, a unique book not of deeds but of names, names of the redeemed. The redeemed are those who have already been judged through a surrogate or a substitute. This God-provided Savior was willing to receive divine judgment in their place. When these people rise on the Day of Judgment, their sins are already old news. Their sin was punished when Jesus took their place in judgment on the cross. With their sin dealt with, they are counted as righteous.

Just as the essence of Hell is the absence of God's presence, the essence of this new earth is God's presence with us. The vision sees the whole earth as his temple, a staggering idea developed later in the chapter. This is not to say, of course, that the entire new earth will literally look like a temple, with columns and incense. The point is that every forest, shore, sea, mountain, village and city will function as a temple where God is worshiped, honored, obeyed, and glorified through every human activity. Gone is all the misery we experienced before while his judgment was suspended. The glorious point of the vision is expressed in verse 5, "I am making everything new!"

Living faith counts on the fact that God will make all things right. He will do this by personally intervening through the Person of Jesus Christ, who will return to this planet literally, visibly, personally, bodily and tangibly. This was part of the apostolic gospel.

> [God] commands all people everywhere to repent, because he has fixed a day on which he will judge the world in righteousness by a man whom he has appointed; and of this he has given assurance to all by raising him from the dead. (Acts 17:30-31)

Jesus was sent to this world not to judge, but to save, and he has been saving for over 2,000 years. But when he returns, it will be to execute God's now-suspended judgment. Jesus will completely end the way this world presently works. He will reverse creation's bondage to decay. He will complete what the

Garden should have become, a Holy City. He will make all things right.

A living faith understands that we cannot find the answer to this world's problems in this world. This is a profound thought. The way this world works will only change at the return of Christ —not before.

This is not to say that we're unable to make the world better than it is; we can and we must. We can because God has given us wisdom to know his design. We must because he is healing our hearts to long for his design and care about the misery of others.

But making this world a better place, whether the scope is a nation or a single home, will not change what this world essentially is. Think of Jesus' concern for the poor, his own compassion and how he taught us to care for the poor. Yet, he told us plainly, "The poor you always have with you." (John 12:8) We care for the poor because we can. We care for the poor because we must. But we will never eliminate poverty in this world; there will always be poor people. Selfishness and injustice is how this world works. We cannot change that, not with all the education, religion, or programs we can muster. A living faith understands that the answer to this world's problems does not lie in this world.

Living faith believes the answer is coming in the next phase of human history. Indeed, it has already broken into our history! God, in the Person of Jesus Christ, is the answer. His Spirit is making things better now, as a kind of down payment, relieving poverty of both body and soul, establishing outposts of the new order in every faithful church.

And yet, all these good things of the Spirit are but a foretaste. Jesus himself is returning and he will make all things right. At his return, evil will be properly exposed and dealt with. Those whom he has previously cleansed of sin will be perfected and given the inheritance God originally intended. Thus, God's terrible judgment will have a marvelously cleansing and renewing effect.

> ... waiting for and hastening the coming of the day of God, because of which the heavens will be set on fire and dissolved, and the heavenly bodies will melt as they burn! But according to his promise we are waiting for new heavens and a new earth in which righteousness dwells. (2 Peter 3:12-13)

Living faith does not look for a utopia in this age of history. There are always plenty of opportunities to make this world a better place, but there is nothing we can do to change the way this world works. Christians should not fall for the promise that some program or leader or political party or educational reform or philosophy or artistic movement will make the world operate differently. We do not expect any such knight to come charging in to save us.

We do not look for such saviors because we are already expecting the genuine article.

> Then I saw heaven opened, and behold, a white horse! The one sitting on it is called Faithful and True, and in righteousness he judges and makes war. His eyes are like a flame of fire, and on his head are many diadems ... And the armies of heaven, arrayed in fine linen, white and pure, were following him on white horses. From his mouth comes a sharp sword with which to strike down the nations ...On his robe and on his thigh he has a name written, King of kings and Lord of lords. (Revelation 19:11-16)

This vision portrays the impact of Christ's return—leading the cavalry over the hill to rescue God's people and liberate this world from bondage.

Typically, we tend to frame our lives with the same temporal goals as everyone else: going to college, raising a family, retiring to the shore. We mold our lives around these goals and endure hardships because those goals lie on our horizon and encourage us on.

But what if we looked further out to see God's goals on a wider horizon, so that what he is inevitably bringing to pass could frame our lives, guide our plans, direct our choices and lift our spirits?

Living faith sees every current challenge, hardship and opportunity framed by a powerful view of history. The values of this world are irrelevant, because this world is not what it should be. Living faith eagerly invests in whatever will be of value at Christ's return, regardless of its perceived worth today. This is because God will make all things right.

What does such living faith look like? ...

Jeremiah

> And I bought the field at Anathoth from Hanamel my cousin, and weighed out the money to him, seventeen shekels of silver ....
>
> "Thus says the LORD of hosts, the God of Israel: Take these deeds, both this sealed deed of purchase and this open deed, and put them in an earthenware vessel, that they may last for a long time. For thus says the LORD of hosts, the God of Israel: Houses and fields and vineyards shall again be bought in this land .... I will bring them back to this place, and

I will make them dwell in safety. And they shall be my people, and I will be their God. I will give them one heart and one way, that they may fear me forever, for their own good and the good of their children after them. I will make with them an everlasting covenant, that I will not turn away from doing good to them." (Jeremiah 32:9-15,37-40)

This is another text from the exile period. It involves the second invasion of Nebuchadnezzar of Babylon, this time to overthrow Jerusalem itself. In terms of military might, we're looking at a David and Goliath style match up. Unfortunately, King Zedekiah was no David. The repeated idolatries of Judah's kings had brought God's wrath upon them. The Babylonians were about to smash Jerusalem and destroy Solomon's Temple, not in spite of the Lord's power, but because of it. The Lord's prophets, like Isaiah, had prophesied this moment in history for some time; God was causing it to happen as judgment.

As the invasion nears, the prophetic mantle falls upon Jeremiah. The doom he prophesies is not a vision of the distant future, as it was when Isaiah had preached. Rather, that siege army right out there is going to destroy this city! As you can imagine, this was not a popular message to a nation at war. At the time of our text, Jeremiah was in the courtyard of the guard (jail), imprisoned by the King for preaching what the King deemed traitorous. But our text is not really about Jeremiah's prophecies of doom. Instead, it is about a seemingly insignificant personal matter which God used to underscore his larger message of hope.

When you think of the word prophecy, you normally think of oral preaching or a written text like the one before us. However, while God always communicates in words, in the Old Testament he sometimes used actions to illustrate those words. Such an action might be an historical event, or a Temple ritual, or it might be what scholars sometimes call an "enacted parable." The most famous New Testament example is when Jesus washed the disciple's feet to make a point.

An enacted parable is something God tells a prophet to do in order to symbolize a message. For example, Ezekiel was told to lie on his left side in front of an etching of Jerusalem to symbolize the siege of the city. Hosea was told to marry a faithless woman to illustrate how God felt about Israel's betrayal. These actions were always explained in words, but they dramatically underscored the truth at issue and served as a memory device.

As Jeremiah sits under arrest for predicting God's imminent judgment, the Lord tells him to expect a visitor with a business proposition, one which he is instructed to take. Sure enough, along comes Hanamel, Jeremiah's cousin, to tell him of a piece of property that just came on the market, a field in Anathoth in the territory of Benjamin. Jeremiah grew up in Anathoth, a little town about two and a quarter miles northeast of Jerusalem.

For Israel, the whole concept of a divine inheritance was bound up with the land. When, for whatever reason, a piece of family property came on the market, the closest relative was morally obligated to buy it if he could, just to keep it in the family.

But we must remember that, like the rest of the countryside, Anathoth has been overrun by Babylonians, who have annexed the nation and are on their way to smash the capital. It's not hard to see why Hanamel has fled to Jerusalem or why he is no longer interested in his property! The amazing thing is that he has the gall to offer it to Jeremiah as his cousin languishes in prison. Imagine Jim Bowie turning to Davey Crockett at the Alamo, and offering him a great deal on a little ranch a mile or so out of town, right about where Santa Anna is camping right now.

I think it is safe to say that, if God himself had not spoken to Jeremiah just before Hanamel's visit, Jeremiah would have laughed out loud. Not that Jeremiah laughed very much. He was known as "the weeping prophet" because God called him to serve in Jerusalem right through its downfall. It's just that the situation would have been so funny, in a darkly humorous sort of way. The Babylonians are about to plunder the Temple of Jehovah, many will die, the King will be blinded and carried off as a captive, there will be another, devastating depopulation as thousands of Jews are forcibly resettled in Babylon. Jeremiah doesn't even know if he will live to get out of jail. The whole Jewish civilization is about to fall apart and here comes cousin Hanamel, "Jeremiah, would you buy my field? I'm giving you first chance because you're my closest relative."

If that seems strange, here is something even stranger: at the command of God, Jeremiah bought it! He made it legal there in the courtyard where everyone could see.

Why? Because God wanted one of the last memories of that generation to be of someone keeping the inheritance in the family, making an investment in the kingdom—just before Jerusalem falls. In the days to come, there would be so much sadness, so much death and destruction and humiliation. It would burn nightmares into their souls. The Lord wanted to give them something to help them hope. Jeremiah had already given words of hope. Several prophets promised that God would resettle them one day back in Israel. But the Lord wanted them to remember something that would make them smile when they feared they would never see home again.

"Zeb, I don't think we will ever return to the promised land."

"O, I don't know, Zeke. Remember how Jeremiah bought his cousin's field just weeks before the end? It seemed like the stupidest land deal in history."

"True, but he used to say that after seventy years of exile, God will bring us all home. He said he wanted to keep the inheritance in the family."

"That's right. He quoted the Lord as saying, "I will gather them from all the countries to which I drove them in my anger and my wrath and in great indignation. I will bring them back to this place, and I will make them dwell in safety. And they shall be my people, and I will be their God. Fields shall be bought for money, and deeds shall be signed and sealed and witnessed in the places about Jerusalem, for I will restore their fortunes, declares the LORD."

"Yea. I guess if a prophet felt that way, there must be something to it. We'll get home, all right."

Throughout the whole exile period, thousands and thousands of people would remember Jeremiah's prophecies of doom and how they had not listened. They would remember their sin and their guilt. Their misery would not allow them to forget it. But God wanted them to remember more than their sin and more than their misery. He wanted them to remember his covenant of grace. Sin does have its consequences, yes, but God is sovereign to preserve his people and bring them to ultimate blessing. So God told Jeremiah to do something unusual. Just before the city falls, invest in some local real estate. Let them know that investing in my future kingdom is a great deal, a sure thing.

In Jeremiah's mind, this little field in Anathoth stood for the same thing that the whole land of Israel had stood for in Abraham's mind. The land of Israel was an historical symbol—what the Bible calls a type—of God's ultimate kingdom. Until Christ came, it was the concrete representation of the eternal inheritance of faith. Long before, God had assured Abraham that he personally would have a wonderful inheritance from God, but he would not receive it in his lifetime. Abraham gathered that, while the land was an inheritance in an immediate sense, God was ultimately talking about something else. The New Testament explains it this way,

> By faith [Abraham] went to live in the land of promise, as in a foreign land, living in tents with Isaac and Jacob, heirs with him of the same promise. For he was looking forward to the city that has foundations, whose designer and builder is God ...
>
> These all died in faith, not having received the things promised, but having seen them and greeted them from afar, and having acknowledged that they were strangers and exiles on the earth. For people who speak thus make it clear that they are seeking ... a better country, that is, a heavenly one. Therefore God is not ashamed to be called their God, for he has prepared for them a city. (Hebrews 11:9-16)

Biblical faith is grounded in the past, and we exercise our faith today. But living faith also enjoys a great hope of the future. It's true that this world is not what it should be, but Jeremiah illustrates hope that God will make all things right. This age will dissolve into another in which everything is exactly as it should be. In that age, evil will be perpetually rejected and will never be able to get the upper hand again. In that age, those redeemed by grace will willingly exercise their freedom to obey God and glorify him by becoming all they were meant to be.

Jeremiah preached about an amazing grace, expressed in terms of a future return from exile. That return would be the final way that Israel would model the covenant. Their return from exile would model Christ's work in the hearts of believers all over the world. "I will give them one heart and one way, that they may fear me forever, for their own good and the good of their children after them. I will make with them an everlasting covenant, that I will not turn away from doing good to them." Israel modeled that promise for a few centuries, until the time was right for Christ. That promise is being fulfilled right now as Christ assembles his church, and in the age to come, the fulfillment will mature into a perfect new heaven and earth.

God told Jeremiah to make what the world would consider a really stupid business decision, a decision that only made sense because God would keep his Word and bring them back. In essence. Jeremiah made an investment that only made sense if the gospel is for real. What a statement, what an enacted parable of hope. In the years to come, when many a Jewish family longed to go home, they could remember Jeremiah buying his cousin's field on the eve of disaster. A real field that to this day lies somewhere northeast of Jerusalem. Jeremiah expected his grandchildren to literally work that field. And like Abraham, Jeremiah expected an even better land for himself someday, an eternal kingdom.

That's living faith. Living faith is being sustained during a season of difficulty by the promise of a better season to come—not a simple wish for a better time, but the sure and certain promise of such a thing. Just as God swore to discipline Israel with a taste of his much-deserved wrath, he also swore to bless them down the road with a long drink of undeserved mercy and grace.

> Now these things happened to them as an example,
> but they were written down for our instruction, on
> whom the end of the ages has come.
> (1 Corinthians 10:11)

God did those things historically with Israel, so we could have pictures of what judgment and grace look like. We need such insight because millions of us are called to live our brief lives in this world in spiritual exile. Saved people, redeemed people, must live in this fallen world as strangers and pilgrims. We need to be sustained through this period by a living faith that this age will one day run its course, and we will see the world fully renewed, never to fall again.

Living faith produces outrageous lives. It does things that only make sense if the gospel is true, only make sense if I end up living forever in a world that God makes right.

What would be some contemporary equivalents of Jeremiah's land deal? How about training our children to make service their career goal? That is, to consciously choose a career based upon how their skills and passions can be sacrificially offered in the service of God and humanity? Whether their job be non-religious or religious, we could teach them to use their careers as a stewardship, rather than just an opportunity to live well. That might not make a lot of sense to some members of our families, it might sound like a waste. But we could assure them that it makes all the sense in the world because we will get to offer the fruit of our lives to Christ at his return and look forward to an eternal reward.

How about generous financial investments in things that do not benefit us? Gifts to traditional charities, a full tithe to the church, anonymous gifts to Christian brothers and sisters in need, taking leadership in fund raising efforts for all manner of good causes, planning our estates to contribute something substantial to the work of Christ? What kind of financial sense does such serious giving make in this day and age? It only makes sense if you plan on taking part one day in a profoundly different economy—an economy where what you gave here is the only thing you were able to take with you into eternity.

How about postponing some personal gratification, not just for a few weeks or years, but for a whole lifetime, in order to focus on the needs of this age? Right now, I am called by God to be a pastor, but I don't really think there will be a need for pastors in glory. That's why, when I left physics for the pastorate after college, I didn't think of it as giving up science. I only laid it aside for a little while, for this brief lifespan. From a worldly perspective, that was a truly stupid thing to do. I will die without realizing many of my childhood dreams. Postponing my desires for an entire lifetime only makes sense if there will be a new heavens and a new earth someday where I will be able to study and invent forever.

As missionary Jim Elliot used to say, "He is no fool who gives what he cannot keep to gain what he cannot lose."

Christian brothers and sisters close to you need to see that sort of living faith in your life, just as you need to see it in theirs. When the days are weary and the nights are long and they wonder if this is all God has for them, this not-so-wonderful life that is cracked and peeling. They need to see you doing something outrageous; something that doesn't make any sense at all unless Christ really is coming back to build Paradise.

And folks who do not have a saving relationship with the Savior, they need to see living faith most of all, because they do not know what real hope is. Their hope involves the weekend or a brief retirement. Such tattered frills are all they think they can hope for. By sacrificing some of those tatters because you expect to live forever in blessedness, you become a living parable of a hope that could be theirs, by faith.

Living faith looks like Jeremiah buying a field he will never use in this life. It knows that the world as it is now, is not all that will ever be. It radiates hope by living in a way that makes no sense at all … unless Jesus is coming back and God will make all things right.

Jesus Makes All The Difference

In the beginning was the Word, and the Word was with God, and the Word was God.

No one has ever seen God; the only God, who is at the Father's side, he has made him known. (John 1:1,18)

In many ways, Christianity is similar to all the other great religions of the world. It has rituals and forms of worship, as do the others. It promotes a philosophy of life, as do the others. It promotes a particular way of living, which is something all religions do. Of course, the details of worship, philosophy and lifestyle vary, sometimes significantly, but all religions are similar in that they all deal with these kinds of things. But there is one thing that makes Christianity absolutely unique—not in detail, but in substance. Christianity depends completely on one particular individual: Jesus Christ.

Now I know that every other religion has its founder or founders, too. But what is important about them is what they said and what they did. If someone else, at the same time and place, said and did essentially the same things, these religions would have taken off just as well and been essentially the same movement. From the Islamic perspective, if another prophet had the position Mohammed had and said exactly the same things he did, and did exactly the things Mohammed did, that religion would be pretty much the same. If someone perfectly paralleled Siddhartha Gautama, Buddhism would be just as valid in the eyes of its followers as it is now.

But if anyone else lived in Israel in the first century, and said everything Jesus said and behaved the way Jesus behaved, Christianity would not be valid. If I were to go back in time, learn Aramaic, and appear in Jerusalem a few years before Christ ... if I called myself "Glenn, the Christ," and preached all the things Jesus preached, and by the power of God, performed all the miracles Jesus performed … even if I ran afoul of the authorities and ended up dying on a Roman cross, presumably suffering, at least in the physical sense, in exactly the same way … I would still not be the Christ and any religion founded on me would be an exercise in futility.

Of course, what Jesus said and did is crucial to the Christian faith. But in terms of biblical religion, our salvation not only depends on what Jesus did; it depends upon the specific identity of the one who did it. Nobody could be the Savior of the world other than Jesus because the validity of his words and deeds hangs on who he uniquely is. Jesus himself makes all the difference.

"In the beginning was the Word, and the Word was with God, and the Word was God." This verse highlights a surprising quality about God. A quality which, at first, seems counter-intuitive, but which upon reflection makes perfect sense. It is that God is not only a personal being, but also an interpersonal being. He is able to relate personally within himself. Or, to put it another way, the one God consists of more than one Person.

Scripture teaches that God is complete within himself. He needs nothing. Since he is the Creator of everything else, he must have been perfect before the universe was. But one person alone is incomplete, lacking a relationship. When God created Adam, he said, "It is not good that the man should be alone" (Genesis 2:18) Why? Was there something wrong with Adam? No, he was a complete person, but there are aspects of personhood that cannot be fully expressed alone. You cannot express all there is about love by yourself. If you are going to express love, or trust, or compassion, or fairness, or any other personal quality, you need another person to do it with. "So God created man in his own image … male and female he created them." (Genesis 1:27) God's image is best expressed by two persons in union, together creating a third.

There was nothing incomplete about Adam as a person. A human being doesn't need to be married to be complete as a person. But God is interpersonal. In his own being love is given and received. No created human being can give and receive love alone. For finite, physical creatures to reflect God's interpersonal nature, there has to be at least two of us—and the way God designed sex, there are soon three of us—each giving and receiving life from the other two in a harmonious order. A family pictures God more perfectly than an individual can. The Scriptures reveal God as three persons inextricably bound together as one God. Not three Gods. Not one God looked at from three different angles. But one God in three persons. When considered together, Christians call these three Persons, "the Godhead," or the "Trinity."

What our famous text declares is that these three Persons are not clones. They relate in a distinct way. "In the beginning was the Word, and the Word was with God, and the Word was God." Since God is a spirit, the particular divine Person John speaks of doesn't have a human name or a human face, but is called simply, "the Word." Apparently, when the first Person of the Godhead desires a thing, the second Person of the Godhead is the creative voice who gives expression to that thing. "He was in the beginning with God. All things were made through him, and without him was not any thing made that was made." (John 1:2-3)

This second Person of the Trinity, the Word, is especially dear to us because "The Word became flesh and dwelt among us." (John 1:14) Personal divinity was never claimed by Siddhartha or Mohammed or Confucius. Only one man has ever claimed this with any credibility. The Word did not stop being

God and turn into a man. He didn't manipulate a human body as a puppet. Rather, without ever ceasing to be God, he added to himself a human nature.

The baby born in Bethlehem was as typically human as you or I. He wasn't in any way a super-baby. He had all the needs a normal baby has. The only human difference between him and any other baby was that his soul was not predisposed to sin. This is because he was fathered by the third Person of the Trinity, called the Spirit of God, through a humble and willing virgin girl.

After the birth of his human nature, the the Word of God could have a human name, and was given the name "Jesus." Once he wrote that the Word became flesh, John stopped referring to "the Word" and from then on used the name "Jesus" to refer to this absolutely unique Person who is both divine and human.

At the core of Christianity lies the conviction that Jesus has a uniquely dual nature. On the one hand, Jesus Christ is God, and is to be worshiped. On the other hand, Jesus Christ is a man who relates to God exactly as a human being should, and is, therefore, our perfect example of what it means to be human.

There has never been a Christian who can fully comprehend what I just wrote. I certainly can't. I have no model or diagram that can remove the mystery. How can one Person have two distinct natures at the same time? Natures that never overlap—no part of Jesus' humanity ever becomes divine and no part of Jesus' divinity ever becomes human. Jesus is not a hybrid. He isn't a demigod or a super-man. He is one Person who is both divine and human at the same time—with all the infinite attributes of divinity and all the temporal limitations of humanity. The Person who is Jesus, in his deity, knows the end of history from the beginning, while that same Person, in his humanity, does not know the day of his return.

Christianity is absolutely unique because Jesus is absolutely unique. It's as if we are all two dimensional people (imagine flat people in a flat, two dimensional world), and Jesus is a flat person too. But he alone also has an infinite third dimension in addition to his flatness that we don't have, a dimension that we can't even see in our flat world. Jesus is as human as you or I, but behind that humanity—part of the same Person—is something infinite and wonderful.

It is because of who Jesus is that he was able to accomplish a real and true salvation like nobody else could. "No one has ever seen God, but God the One and Only, who is at the Father's side, has made him known." Except for Jesus, all the world's religions are guided by prophets and philosophers. No philosopher or prophet has ever seen God. God is a spirit; he has no body and he has no equal. God's essence is not the sort of thing physical eyes can see. No human being lives in eternity, outside of the universe God made. Who among us could possibly speak for him authoritatively? In answer to that question, only one figure has ever risen in all of human history and asserted to have come into the world from God's intimate fellowship, sharing complete union with him.

Because of Jesus' unique identity, he can make God known to us. What he says is not speculation, surmise or deduction, or the passing on of a vision. The Jesus who walked and talked on this earth to teach us about God ... is God. John the Baptist explained it this way,

> He who comes from above is above all. He who is of the earth belongs to the earth and speaks in an earthly way. He who comes from heaven is above all. He bears witness to what he has seen and heard, yet no one receives his testimony. Whoever receives

his testimony sets his seal to this, that God is true. (John 3:31-33)

Jesus came as the culmination of a long process of God's self-revelation. "The law was given through Moses; grace and truth came through Jesus Christ." (John 1:17) Into the structure of one chosen society, the Law shaped themes, principles, promises, and models concerning forgiveness and judgment—all the categories we needed in order to understand God's plan of salvation. That salvation itself, both grace and truth, came in a Person who fulfilled those themes, principles, promises and models. Grace and truth are not just ideas on a piece of paper. Grace and truth were embodied in a specific Person. God himself brought us his grace and truth by coming to us in Jesus Christ. It is because of who Jesus is, that he can reveal God to us.

And he does more than just reveal God. "To all who did receive him, who believed in his name, he gave the right to become children of God." (John 1:12) The name Jesus means "the Lord who saves." Jesus can find us in our isolation, as we slide toward the grave alienated from our Creator, and he can save us. And he can bring us home.

I don't have the authority to do that. I can't give you the right to be God's child. I could sell you a $10 button displaying "Child of God," but that button would not put you in a right relationship to the Lord. I could bless you, pour water on you, and preach to you for hours. I could give you a certificate declaring that you are a child of God, and sign it myself. But nothing I could do, could actually reconcile you to the Lord. Why? Because I'm not God! Only God can reconcile you to God. We are all by nature wayward children, alienated from the Heavenly Father, disowned by him. Who has the authority to welcome us home? What religious leader has the authority to reconcile us with our

Creator? Does any pastor or bishop or prophet or imam or rabbi or guru have that authority?

"To all who ... believed in his name, he gave the right to become children of God." So who gave Jesus the right to give us that right? (Remember the scene in the first Christopher Reeve Superman movie ... Lois falls from the top of a skyscraper. Superman goes public for the first time and flies up to save her, "Don't worry Miss, I've got you." Lois responds, "You've got me? Who's got you?") Jesus claims that he can save us from falling into sin and Hell, but what gives him the authority to bring us into God's family? What could give anyone such authority?

What gives Jesus the authority is the unique fact that he is God! That's why he is the only one with the right to welcome us into God's home. Jesus, alone throughout history, stands up and says, "I and the Father are one." (John 10:30) "I am the way, the truth and the life." (John 14:6) "I am the light of the world. Whoever follows me will not walk in darkness, but will have the light of life." (John 8:12) "I am the resurrection and the life. Whoever believes in me, though he die, yet shall he live, and everyone who lives and believes in me shall never die." (John 11:25-26)

Salvation is not some philosophy or substance that we need. What we need is for God to be our Savior. Jesus can bring mankind and God together again because, in Jesus, mankind and God is together. He is the perfect interface. "For there is one God, and there is one mediator between God and men, the man Christ Jesus." (1 Timothy 2:5)

Jesus can make God known to us and he has the right to bring us back to God, all because of who he is. To living faith, Jesus makes all the difference.

What does such living faith look like? ...

Nicodemus

> Jesus answered him, "Truly, truly, I say to you, unless one is born again he cannot see the kingdom of God." Nicodemus said to him, "How can a man be born when he is old? Can he enter a second time into his mother's womb and be born?" Jesus answered, "Truly, truly, I say to you, unless one is born of water and the Spirit, he cannot enter the kingdom of God." (John 3:3-4)

When Jesus first visited Jerusalem with his disciples, he immediately confronted the priests and religious leaders at the Temple. Most were hostile, but there were those who watched and listened and understood that Jesus was something special. Jesus demonstrated an understanding of the covenant, the way of salvation, that cut to the heart of the matter. He had an understanding far superior to that of the Temple priests. This caused great uneasiness in the religious establishment, but there were a few independent thinkers who were captivated by this remarkable man. So, one evening, when it was dark and no one could see him, Nicodemus came to talk with this preacher from Galilee. A member of the ruling council, Nicodemus came in the evening because it would not be safe for his reputation to come in the daytime. Learned and responsible church leaders were not supposed to believe in this man. Even so, Nicodemus came. "Rabbi, we know that you are a teacher come from God, for no one can do these signs that you do unless God is with him." (John 3:2) Nicodemus came confessing his faith as best he could, and desiring to learn more.

Jesus' response is not what he expected. He corrects Nicodemus, explaining that he is not, in fact, a believer, at least not yet. Note how Christ closes the interview,

> Are you the teacher of Israel and yet you do not understand these things? Truly, truly, I say to you, we speak of what we know, and bear witness to what we have seen, but you do not receive our testimony. (John 3:10-11)

Jesus clearly identifies Nicodemus as among those who do not yet accept his testimony. Why is this so? Was there something wrong with Nicodemus' confession? Not really. Nicodemus probably confessed Christ as well as the disciples could have, at that point. He acknowledged the validity of Jesus' miracles, validating him as a divine messenger. Nicodemus certainly thought he was confessing his faith to Jesus. And yet, Jesus finds it necessary to warn him about his spiritual condition. Why?

Because Nicodemus came at night. Nicodemus came when no one would see him. He did not want word to get back to his colleagues that he was taking this Jesus seriously. They believed Jesus had attacked the Temple. Supporting him could bring serious repercussions. If a showdown developed, Nicodemus didn't want to be caught in the crossfire.

Nicodemus' fears were certainly justified. On Jesus' last visit to Jerusalem, he would stir up a hornet's nest and it would be over exactly what Nicodemus found so convincing—his miracles. After the resurrection of Lazarus in nearby Bethany,

> The chief priests and the Pharisees gathered the council and said, "What are we to do? For this man performs many signs. If we let him go on like this, everyone will believe in him, and the Romans will come and take away both our place and our nation." ... So from that day on they made plans to put him to death. (John 11:47-53)

That would be two years later. For now, the miracles were just causing a whirlwind of notoriety and debate . Even so, to acknowledge that Jesus' miracles were genuine would put you on the side of a prophet who threatened the authority of the ruling council. Leaders like Nicodemus were not willing to take that risk. Much later, the Apostle John wrote of men like Nicodemus:

> Many even of the authorities believed in him, but for fear of the Pharisees they did not confess it, so that they would not be put out of the synagogue; for they loved the glory that comes from man more than the glory that comes from God. (John 12:42-43)

In the Book of John, you learn that the verb "believe" can have several meanings. It's possible to believe in Jesus on one's own terms, but not on his terms. Nicodemus appreciated and affirmed what Jesus stood for, but Jesus did not see that as saving faith. Nicodemus did not yet believe in him because Nicodemus came at night to hide his interest. For Jesus, faith that will not follow him into the light is no faith at all.

> This is the judgment: the light has come into the world, and people loved the darkness rather than the light because their works were evil. For everyone who does wicked things hates the light and does not come to the light, lest his works should be exposed. But whoever does what is true comes to the light, so that it may be clearly seen that his works have been carried out in God. (John 3:19-21)

Anyone can develop a kind of faith in Jesus, but the kind of faith we can generate on our own cannot save us. We can intellectually affirm the things Jesus says. We can emotionally appreciate the things Jesus does. We don't need God's help to do either of those things. Saving faith, however, trusts Jesus himself and therefore walks through life alongside him in the open. Saving faith does not remain in the shadows. "Whoever does what is true comes to the light." Such a naturally transforming faith is so radical a thing that only God can generate it in the human spirit. That's why Jesus' immediate reply to Nicodemus is "Truly, truly, I say to you, unless one is born again he cannot see the kingdom of God."

Nicodemus is quite taken aback at this. He thought his faith was pretty special to come see Jesus at all! But Jesus responded by painting a much bigger picture of what saving faith is all about, and Nicodemus obviously had a hard time understanding what Jesus was trying to say. Jesus said that to see the kingdom of God, a man had to be born *anothen*, Greek for "from above", or "from the top." Jesus probably intended to speak of a birth from heaven, or a spiritual birth. But *anothen* could also be understood as "again," just as it does today when a musician says, "let's take it from the top"—he means: let's start at the beginning or let's start over again. Nicodemus misunderstood the remark as referring to being physically born all over again. "How can a man be born when he is old? Can he enter a second time into his mother's womb and be born?"

Jesus goes on to clarify that he was speaking of a rebirth from above, a spiritual rebirth, explaining, "That which is born of the flesh is flesh, and that which is born of the Spirit is spirit." (John 3:6) In other words, "I'm not talking about physical rebirth. I'm talking about a new spiritual life."

Jesus' reference to spiritual birth through water should have tipped off Nicodemus, an Old Testament scholar, about the image Jesus is thinking about.

> I will sprinkle clean water on you, and you shall be clean from all your uncleannesses, and from all your idols I will cleanse you. And I will give you a new heart, and a new spirit I will put within you … and you shall be my people, and I will be your God. (Ezekiel 36:25-28)

God once promised the Old Testament nation of Israel that he would bring them out of exile, wash them clean from sin and give them a new spirit of faith, a spirit that would desire him and desire his Law. Jesus is essentially saying that he is the fulfillment of that promise. He can provide that new washing from sin and new heart to love God. He can give a new spirit that is determined to embrace God's will without reservation.

Finally, to further underscore that he is thinking about Ezekiel, Jesus refers to a life-giving wind blowing in every direction. Just after the Ezekiel quote above, the Old Testament records Ezekiel's vision of the valley of dry bones. Note that we translate the same Hebrew word as "wind," "breath," and "spirit," suggesting some rich wordplay. In Ezekiel's vision of the valley of dry bones, the wind/spirit comes from all directions, representing God's Spirit as God breathes/inspires life into dead Israel. Jesus says that through him, God is breathing new spiritual life. Like the wind, you can't see how it happens and you don't know who will come alive next, but before he is finished Jesus will breath spiritual life into people from the four corners of the earth. With renewed hearts, they will all openly follow him.

Nicodemus left perplexed, wondering about the nature of his own faith. He thought he believed in Jesus. But he didn't want anyone to know about it. So, did he really believe, or did he just wish he believed? Surely faith is something internal, but how can you know it's for real unless it is also external? How could Nicodemus know that his faith was real unless he were willing to stand up, risk the disapproval of his peers and confess his faith publicly … in the light?

Nicodemus was not the only one Jesus allowed to go home wondering about his faith. You may remember the "rich young ruler" who came asking for salvation. Or the Jewish crowd in John 8 whom John specifically says "believed" in Jesus—believed in some sense, yet by the end of the chapter, they wanted to stone him to death. Or the religious leaders we have already read about who wanted to believe, yet remained quiet for fear of losing their religious and political position.

Jesus once taught a parable about four kinds of soil, paralleling four responses to him. Some reject him out of hand. Others confess him instantly, willing to walk down any aisle, but when obedience is required, their faith quickly withers away to nothing. There are even those who stick with the church long term, but who are so entangled with the cares and worries of this life that they never get around to actually acting on their faith. All of these people believe something, but those varieties of faith are not saving faith.

James reminds us in the New Testament that even the demons believe in Jesus, in their own way. They know exactly who he is. But simple head knowledge, however accurate, is not saving faith. Saving faith involves a change of heart that embraces the love of God in Jesus Christ, himself. This kind of faith not only trusts him for forgiveness, but also trusts him to be our Lord. Saving faith creates a relationship with Christ so deep it is willing to actually follow him. "Whoever is ashamed of me and of my words, of him will the Son of Man be ashamed when he comes in his glory and the glory of the Father and of the holy angels." (Luke 9:26) "Everyone who acknowledges me before men, I also will acknowledge before my Father who is in heaven." (Matthew 10:32)

This is the transforming faith brought to life by the Holy Spirit of God when a person is born from above, or as many prefer to phrase it, born again.

The good news is that, with Jesus, all our religious theory can become real. It's like marriage. You can talk about marriage in great detail. You can describe God's will for marriage perfectly. You can expound all the right arguments and give all the best illustrations. You can wax eloquent on what marriage means. But you can also actually get married! At that point, marriage stops being abstract and becomes a flesh and blood relationship.

You can make the same point about any relationship, can't you? What do you believe about your country? What do you believe about your community? What do you believe about your church? Debate it all you want; hang whatever professions of faith you will upon the walls of your home. Fly whatever flag you wish. It's when the abstraction turns into real human relationships that it gets real: in actual church ministry, community service, or alongside comrades on the battlefield. It's what you do with relationships that shows what you actually believe.

Israel had no lack of faithful worshipers, if worship were defined merely by talk. The Pharisees were men of great faith, if all God had to do was listen to them. But how can God be satisfied with mere speech when, at the same time he can see our hearts? After a few years, Jesus exploded against the Pharisees, "You hypocrites! Well did Isaiah prophesy of you, when he said: "This people honors me with their lips, but their heart is far from me." (Matthew 15:7-8) They preached eloquently about faithfulness to God … yet continually found ways to ignore his will, and actually tried to kill him when they met him face to face.

The Christian faith has a wonderful theology, and many churches have fine confessions, but an individual's faith is revealed by whether or not he or she actually follows Jesus Christ. The point is not that we could merit salvation by how well we follow Jesus. He endured a bloody cross because we cannot follow him all that well. The point is that not a drop of Jesus' blood will cover the sin of anyone who is ashamed to follow God's Son.

In Jesus, God Almighty condescended to come into our world, so that we could see him. So that we could see God for who he really is. So that our relationship could become personal, mediated, experienced through the Person of Jesus. Jesus cried out, "Whoever believes in me, believes not in me but in him who sent me. And whoever sees me sees him who sent me." (John 12:44-45) The Holy Spirit opens our eyes to look at Jesus Christ—his perfect life, atoning death and glorious resurrection—and see in this living Person, the relationship God wants with us. He came to put flesh and blood on our relationship with God. To be born again is to discover by the Holy Spirit's power that Jesus makes all the difference.

If you find God in Jesus Christ, you can't keep your relationship with him in darkness. You can't hide it when you go to school or work. You can't hide it from your children, as you talk about problems they have with their friends, or teach them how the family budget is allocated, or explain what marriage and sexuality and career goals and child raising are all about. You can't hide the Lordship of Christ from your politics. You can't ignore what he means to you when you encounter crushing need in the world. You can't open your heart in a one-hour worship service and then lock it up when you go out into society at large, too afraid and ashamed to be seen with him.

I am painfully aware of how easy it is for me to assert all this, in a country where we are still free to worship as we choose. There are many places today where Christians face real persecution for their faith. Many have to weigh the virtue of going public and perhaps being killed, against remaining secret believers and continuing to serve Christ underground. Such Christians are willing to die for him, but choose to live for him under the radar. I'm not trying to address their fragile situation. I don't know that I have the wisdom to do so.

What Nicodemus began to discover that night, however, is that when the Spirit of God awakens your spirit to find him in Jesus, you will put Christ above everyone and everything else. That's just what you do with God; he becomes first in your life. It's not an artificial requirement. It's what a soul naturally does with God when he embraces you. Our relationship to God comes alive with Jesus.

This is not the kind of transformation we can accomplish on our own. That's why the Bible is so clear about God's having to create a new spirit within us. "Therefore, if anyone is in Christ, he is a new creation. The old has passed away; behold, the new has come." (2 Corinthians 5:17) "because of the great love with which he loved us, even when we were dead in our trespasses, made us alive together with Christ." (Ephesians 2:4-5) "And you, who were dead in your trespasses and the uncircumcision of your flesh, God made alive together with him." (Colossians 2:13) "since you have been born again, not of perishable seed but of imperishable, through the living and abiding word of God." (1 Peter 1:23)

> When the goodness and loving kindness of God our Savior appeared, he saved us, not because of works done by us in righteousness, but according to his own mercy, by the washing of regeneration and renewal of the Holy Spirit, whom he poured out on us richly through Jesus Christ our Savior, so that

being justified by his grace we might become heirs
according to the hope of eternal life. (Titus 3:4-7)

The Holy Spirit takes all the truth about God and about you
that is revealed in his Word, and brings it all together in Christ.
Jesus makes all the difference. That's how you can tell real faith
from the plastic religious imitation. That doesn't mean you are
perfect in following Christ. Far from it. It just means that your
link to God—your link to reality, to all that is good, to all your
peace, hope and joy, your link to everything that makes life
meaningful and worthwhile—that link is Jesus. Living faith may
well talk to Jesus at night, but it is also seen walking with him in
the morning. When Jesus makes all the difference, you know that
your heart has been touched by the Spirit of God. Such faith is not
an imitation manufactured by us. It's the real thing. Turn it over
and look at the base; it says "Made in Heaven."

John intentionally traced Nicodemus' journey of faith through
his Gospel. Nicodemus lived in Jerusalem and we see something
of him each time Jesus visited the city. This was the first visit. By
the second visit, the Pharisees were actively opposed to Christ
and discussed seizing him and putting him on trial for
blasphemy. One voice, however, was raised in Jesus' defense:
Nicodemus. "Does our law judge a man without first giving him
a hearing and learning what he does?" (John 7:51) As you read
John 7, you can cut the tension with a knife as the Pharisees
wonder whether any of their own number secretly believes in this
prophet from Galilee. Nicodemus took a risk. He still did not
confess his faith, but he did temporarily prevent a train wreck.

On Jesus' last visit to Jerusalem, the ruling council met in
special session to seek his death. It's probable that the gathering
in the middle of the night was somewhat select. Men like
Nicodemus and Joseph of Arimathea (a self-professed disciple of
Jesus) were probably not notified. In the early morning hours, the

council declared Jesus' teaching blasphemy and pressured a death sentence from the Roman governor on the grounds of treason. When did Nicodemus hear of the trial? Did he see Jesus led through the streets carrying a cross? Did he see this man he knew was from God nailed to the cross and killed? Did he hear Jesus use the cross as a pulpit from which to offer forgiveness?

We don't know. But we do know that on that horrible day, when every disciple but one deserted the Lord in fear, when only his family and a few women friends stayed by his side, when no one dared ask for his body for fear of being labeled a traitor along with Jesus and possibly share his fate … On that horrible day, one man, Joseph of Arimathea, went to ask Pilate for the body. No matter what the consequences to his career or his safety, Joseph would not let Jesus rot on the cross. He would give his Master a decent burial, whatever his own associates thought of him. That's because Joseph was a believer.

But John says that as Joseph went out alone, past the ostracizing stares of all his peers, Nicodemus came alongside him with spices for burial. The two of them went to the top of Golgotha, for all to see, and took down Christ's body. They lovingly wrapped it and buried him in Joseph's tomb.

Nicodemus finally took a stand in broad daylight. Apparently, the miracle promised in Ezekiel happened to him. His heart of stone had come alive. The Spirit of God had breathed into his soul, causing him to be born from above. Christian tradition has it that Nicodemus went on to became a notable disciple, indeed.

Living faith does not look like Nicodemus coming to Jesus by night. But it does look like him walking up to the cross in broad daylight to stand beside the one who makes all the difference.

I Am A Disciple of Jesus

I will not leave you as orphans; I will come to you. Yet a little while and the world will see me no more, but you will see me. Because I live, you also will live.

These things I have spoken to you while I am still with you. But the Helper, the Holy Spirit, whom the Father will send in my name, he will teach you all things and bring to your remembrance all that I have said to you. (John 14:18-19,25-26)

When Jesus invited someone to follow him as a disciple, he meant it quite literally. "Follow me" meant "say goodbye, get a good pair of sandals and let's get going." While Rabbis often taught during scheduled hours in small areas around their home, Jesus taught at all hours while traveling from place to place. The disciples followed as he traveled all over, teaching individuals, small groups and large crowds. He taught at weddings and funerals, in the synagogues and in the streets where prostitutes worked. He taught beggars along the road and the wealthy around the dinner table, in the fields with farmers and in towns with merchants. He taught in the Temple with priests and on the sea with fishermen. Jesus taught with babies in his arms or with his hands upon the sick and infirm. He taught in the midst of life, all kinds of life.

The disciples learned to imitate Jesus because unlike many other rabbis, his purpose was not only to teach his disciples to understand the commandments, but also to live them as they were intended. He wanted not only to teach truth, but also win hearts to those truths resulting in genuine trust and obedience. Jesus discipled his disciples, reconciling them in a practical way with God and with each other as they learned how to live, worship, serve and share God's good news.

At the Last Supper, it seemed as if this discipleship were coming to an end, because Jesus spoke of leaving them. In what is called the Upper Room Discourse, we read, "Little children, yet a little while I am with you ... Where I am going you cannot come." (John 13:3,33) "A little while, and you will see me no longer." (John 16:16)

Jesus knew that Judas would betray him that night and that he would be executed. He confidently anticipated his resurrection and ascension back to heaven. Therefore, this was the final meal they would eat together.

If Jesus were anyone else, this would, indeed, have been the end of his discipling ministry. He would have left the church in the hands of the new apostles. His part would be over, finished. They would have to develop and mold the church on their own. Many people and some churches seem to think that is exactly what Christianity is, something a carpenter from Nazareth started and then handed over to others to develop and perfect, an ancient philosophy passed down from one generation to another, evolving, repeatedly recreated by each generation as one layer of disciples trains another in their own image.

Have you ever played that game where you stand in a line and someone whispers a sentence to his neighbor, who whispers it to his neighbor until you go through the whole group? It's funny to see how the message has changed by the end of the line. Many Christians see Christianity like that, a second or third-hand experience—or more like a fiftieth-hand experience—far removed from Jesus Christ. That would make the church whatever its current leaders wish to make it. But that understanding of the church is not at all what we read in our text.

Jesus doesn't say his own involvement is coming to an end. Instead, he tells them how it will continue. "I will ask the Father, and he will give you another Helper, to be with you forever, even the Spirit of truth." (John 14:16)

"Helper" is an attempt to translate a Greek compound word, *paraclaytos*, which means someone who is called to come alongside. Notice that Jesus says that he's going to ask the Father to give another helper. Well, who has been walking alongside them so far? Jesus, that's who. Therefore, Jesus is promising that God will send them someone who will continue to give the help he had been giving.

Jesus identifies this helper as the Holy Spirit, who is another member of the Godhead. The Holy Spirit is a person of the Trinity who is not incarnate, who has not become flesh or taken a human name (that's why he is simply called "the Holy Spirit").

Jesus says, "You know him, for he dwells with you and will be in you." (John 14:17) The Holy Spirit lived with the original disciples because he is united with Jesus, and Jesus had been living with them for three years. After Jesus left, the Holy Spirit would be united with Christ's disciples directly. He would walk alongside each of them.

This is the amazing truth that makes Christian faith a living faith: the Holy Spirit continues the personal discipleship of Jesus Christ! The Holy Spirit enables the incarnate Jesus to personally disciple his people from heaven. This is what Jesus meant when he said, "I will not leave you as orphans; I will come to you. Yet a little while and the world will see me no more, but you will see me." When Jesus says, "you will see me," he isn't thinking of his final return, because he refers to a time when the world cannot see him. (When he physically comes back, every eye will see him.)

Jesus promises that even after he leaves them (after his ascension), his disciples will continue to see him, even though the world cannot. He promises to personally come to his disciples to continue their discipleship. How? By sending the Holy Spirit to make him visible —not to our eyes but to our faith. "I will ... manifest myself to him." (John 14:21) "[My Father and I] will come to him and make our home with him." (John 14:23)

The Holy Spirit accomplishes this as the Spirit of truth (vs. 26) who keeps the words of Jesus alive and brings them to each disciple, as if Jesus were speaking to them personally (giving them "ears to hear"). The Old Testament prophets and New Testament apostles were inspired by the Holy Spirit to give us the full content of Jesus' words. But the Holy Spirit not only inspired the Scriptures, he also enables each believer to respond to them as if Jesus himself were speaking directly to them with his authority.

This is what living faith is all about: the continuing personal discipleship of Jesus Christ in the life of his church and the lives of his people! When Jesus spoke about the true shepherd of God's sheep, he said,

> The sheep hear his voice, and he calls his own sheep by name and leads them out. When he has brought out all his own, he goes before them, and the sheep follow him, for they know his voice. A stranger they will not follow, but they will flee from him, for they do not know the voice of strangers ...
>
> I am the good shepherd. I know my own and my own know me, just as the Father knows me and I know the Father; and I lay down my life for the sheep. And I have other sheep that are not of this fold. I must bring them also, and they will listen to my voice. So there will be one flock, one shepherd. (John 10:3-5,14-16)

In the church of Jesus Christ, we don't make disciples of ourselves. We are Christ's agents, his partners, to make disciples of him. From another perspective, Jesus is with us, making his own disciples through us. How? Through the Holy Spirit. While still in the upper room, Christ said,

> I still have many things to say to you, but you cannot bear them now. When the Spirit of truth comes, he will guide you into all the truth, for he will not speak on his own authority, but whatever he hears he will speak … He will glorify me, for he will take what is mine and declare it to you. (John 16:12-14)

The Holy Spirit does not conduct his own independent discipleship program. He does not speak on his own, or about himself. Jesus continues to disciple us from heaven as the Holy Spirit takes the words of inspired Scripture and enables each believer to spiritually hear Jesus' voice speaking directly to him. The Holy Spirit also helps us to pray in response, personally conveying to heaven the prayers we offer in Jesus' name. (cf. Romans 8:26-27)

Through the Holy Spirit, Jesus is not restricted to a single group of twelve disciples. He can now disciple an ever increasing number of disciples the world over.

> Because I have said these things, you are filled with grief. But I tell you the truth: It is for your good that I am going away. Unless I go away, the Counselor will not come to you; but if I go, I will send him to you. When he comes, he will convict the world of guilt in regard to sin and righteousness and judgment. (John 16:6-8)

Through the Holy Spirit, Jesus is able to reach the world. Imagine if Jesus had died on the cross, rose again and stayed here on earth. Whether he ruled the church from some central location or continued to walk the streets of our cities, how many could he teach? Through the Holy Spirit, Jesus himself is present in his entire church! His words come alive and he impacts each disciple first hand—not second or third or fourth hand.

So many Christians miss this kind of living faith. For them, Christianity is a second-hand faith; they hear the voice of the church, but not the voice of Jesus. Many experience Christianity as if the Holy Spirit did not exist. They have little personal relationship with Jesus Christ, hardly any visceral response to his authority. They have heard his words but they have rarely heard his voice, so those words have motivated very little "following." They do not understand the intended ministry of the Holy Spirit.

From the very beginning, the biblical understanding of the Holy Spirit's work has been adulterated, confused, and mixed with pagan religious magic. Just read the Corinthian epistles. False teachers arose who tried to turn the Holy Spirit into some kind of esoteric second blessing, a Level 2 of the Christian faith. Creating a caste system of ordinary Christians, and spiritual Christians who had the magical Holy Spirit's anointing—when, in fact, every Christian has the Holy Spirit living within him. That's how he or she came to faith in the first place.

Some are a lot more in synch with him than others, but everyone has the Holy Spirit in him. "Anyone who does not have the Spirit of Christ does not belong to him." (Romans 8:9) "In him you also, when you heard the word of truth, the gospel of your salvation, and believed in him, were sealed with the promised Holy Spirit." (Ephesians 1:13)

That happens to every believer. There is no caste system of spiritual haves and have-nots. Though a great many Christians do not realize it, everyone who has been born again has been given the fellowship of the Holy Spirit to hear Jesus' voice and be discipled by him.

The Holy Spirit's role in our salvation is to make the risen Christ visible to our faith. The gospel calls everyone outwardly, while the Holy Spirit awakens a response. It's not as if he forces anybody to respond, of course. He simply awakens them to Christ and gives them ears to hear Jesus calling them by name. By sending the Holy Spirit to live with us, Jesus says that he and the Father come to live with us as well. Through the Holy Spirit's empowerment and our exercise of faith, Jesus Christ disciples every believer as he discipled the original twelve.

The Holy Spirit makes Christ's Word come alive! Those who are not born again hear the Word of God as nice literature, an admirable but dead book. But those who have the Holy Spirit walking alongside them say things like, "Did not our hearts burn within us while [Jesus] talked to us on the road, while he opened to us the Scriptures?" (Luke 24:32)

The Holy Spirit makes Jesus visible alongside us, as well. When we read God's word and understand what the inspired human authors intended, we know it is the risen Christ who is talking. He is talking to us, and we respond to him.

Living faith is being discipled by Jesus Christ. Through the Holy Spirit, Jesus walks with you 24/7. He walks beside you through your home and your workplace, through your school or playground, in front of the TV and on every date. He commutes with you every morning and shares your vacation. He is with you in crowded restaurants and subways. He'll accompany you onto the battlefield, and stay with you in the hospital when everyone else leaves for the night.

Just as he did with the twelve, Jesus uses all of life to bring his truth home to your heart, to challenge and encourage you and transform you. If you will walk with the Spirit—if your spirit will listen—he will use every activity as part of your training: church services, painting the house, giving a report at work, preparing meals, leading a small group, giving birth, reading a book, listening to music, speaking to friends, helping the weak or needy or the hurting or the helpless, falling in love, breaking up a bad relationship, deciding how to behave sexually and truthfully, responding to trials with discernment and loyalty and wisdom and courage. It will all be part of your discipleship.

As you walk through life, he walks alongside you through the Holy Spirit. He'll teach you. He'll test you with questions. He'll answer questions that you raise. The answers might require years of experience for you to "get it," but he's willing to take that long because, Christian, you are his disciple. His goal is to mold you into his image.

Living faith is discipled by Jesus Christ, personally. The gospel may have made its way to you through a hundred faithful hands but, when you receive it, you receive it directly from Jesus himself. Living faith hears Jesus' voice. His words are all there in the Bible. and his voice is delivered by the Holy Spirit.

What does such living faith look like? …

Disciples of John at Ephesus

> And it happened that while Apollos was at Corinth, Paul passed through the inland country and came to Ephesus. There he found some disciples. And he said to them, "Did you receive the Holy Spirit when you believed?" And they said, "No, we have not even heard that there is a Holy Spirit." And he said, "Into what then were you baptized?" They said, "Into John's baptism."
>
> And Paul said, "John baptized with the baptism of repentance, telling the people to believe in the one who was to come after him, that is, Jesus."

On hearing this, they were baptized in the name of the Lord Jesus. And when Paul had laid his hands on them, the Holy Spirit came on them, and they began speaking in tongues and prophesying. There were about twelve men in all. (Acts 19:1-7)

The Apostle Paul first visited Ephesus briefly on his way from Corinth back to Antioch. He determined to return there and make it his base camp for missions in that region. Paul had left behind in Ephesus married coworkers Priscilla and Aquila to lay the groundwork for the future church.

While the apostle was back home at Antioch reporting about his missionary efforts, a teacher named Apollos came to Ephesus.

Now a Jew named Apollos, a native of Alexandria, came to Ephesus. He was an eloquent man, competent in the Scriptures. He had been instructed in the way of the Lord. And being fervent in spirit, he spoke and taught accurately the things concerning Jesus, though he knew only the baptism of John. (Acts 18:24-25)

Apollos is remembered fondly in the New Testament as a well-educated Christian Jew who was an expert in the Old Testament, persuasive in speech and enthusiastically committed to Jesus Christ. However, "He knew only the baptism of John ... but when Priscilla and Aquila heard him, they took him aside and explained to him the way of God more accurately." (Acts 18:25-26)

The Book of Acts traces the key points of the growth of Christianity, but the Christian movement was spreading all over through hundreds of people. You didn't have to be an apostle chosen by Christ to be excited about the new faith, study everything you could get your hands on and share your enthusiasm with others. Alexandria was the principal seat of learning in the Mediterranean, housing famous libraries. In Alexandria, Apollos heard an outline of information about Jesus and considerable detail about the teaching of John the Baptist.

From John, Apollos learned to understand the great, overarching covenant, or relationship, that God was creating in this world. He learned that God was creating a new kingdom to replace the sinful society we know today, an eternal kingdom based upon repentance and forgiveness of sins, a kingdom built out of God's grace received by faith. From John, Apollos heard that Jesus is the Messiah, the one who enables repentance and achieves our forgiveness. Jesus will return one day to judge all evil and establish God's glorious rule forever. Apollos was able to teach this "way of the Lord" accurately … except for one thing.

Apollos knew that Jesus would establish God's kingdom in fullness upon his return, but he didn't quite get how Jesus is establishing a taste of that kingdom now, through the Spirit he imparts to believers. In theological terms, he only knew of the baptism of John, a baptism of promise in which the power of the Holy Spirit was still a future hope.

Remember, John the Baptist was killed before Jesus completed his ministry. John, and therefore Apollos, didn't realize that the Holy Spirit had already been poured out in great measure through the finished work of Christ. Apollos preached Jesus accurately, except that the gospel he preached was still oriented to the future only. It was oriented toward Christ's return, when he would judge the world. That is when we will serve God with joy and celebrate our forgiveness and be filled with the Spirit of God.

It's not so much that his preaching was wrong; it was actually quite faithful and true. But it wasn't complete. It was missing the dynamic of the Holy Spirit's work in our lives today. Apollos apparently experienced the power of the Holy Spirit. He simply didn't understand it. Priscilla and Aquila respectfully took him aside and explained things. After that, Apollos became even more effective.

Paul returned to Ephesus after Apollos had left for Corinth. Priscilla and Aquila brought Paul up to speed concerning what had happened, so, Paul knew that there might be some whose understanding of Christ was imperfect because of Apollos' earlier teaching. Therefore, when he met groups of disciples such as the twelve in our text, he graciously asked questions to see what they understood.

Like any pastor, I ask similar questions today when folks visit our congregation. I've learned that just because someone has grown up in a church does not mean that he or she has been thoroughly taught even the basics of the faith. I've learned that it is wise to respectfully ask questions to discover a person's spiritual knowledge and experience.

When Paul met a small group that had studied under Apollos, he didn't want to assume they had been inadequately taught, but given Apollos' need for training, neither could he assume that they understood the gospel completely. Perhaps he asked something like, "Tell me about your spiritual journey." "Why is Jesus so important to you?" After a bit, Paul asked, "What is your understanding of the Holy Spirit?" "Did you receive the Holy Spirit when you believed?"

I realize that the King James Version translates the question as, "Have you received the Holy Spirit since you believed?" But that is simply not a proper translation of the Greek. Even the New King James Version corrects that to "when" you believed, not "since." No one receives the Holy Spirit after he believes. Paul clearly taught that it is impossible to believe in Christ and his gospel without at the same time receiving the gift of the Holy

Spirit. "Anyone who does not have the Spirit of Christ does not belong to him." (Romans 8:9)

The answer these disciples gave to Paul's question was telling. "'Did you receive the Holy Spirit when you believed?' And they said, 'No, we have not even heard that there is a Holy Spirit.'" This is a rather bare Greek sentence that requires some interpretation in order to make sense in English. It literally says, "We have not heard whether the Holy Spirit is." It's possible that they meant that they didn't know that the Holy Spirit exists. This would be surprising, however, given the promise of the Holy Spirit in the teachings of John the Baptist. It is more likely that they meant they did not know whether the Holy Spirit is now, that he is a present reality. In fact, some ancient versions of the New Testament literally spell it out this way, "We did not know that the Holy Spirit has been given." Note that there is at least one other verse in the Bible phrased in a similar way. John 7:39 says in the Greek, "the Holy Spirit was not," which in context clearly means, "the Holy Spirit was not...yet given."

Therefore, what these disciples were saying was: "We've heard about the Holy Spirit like we've heard of the new world to come. That's all in our future, right?" For them, the power and presence of the Holy Spirit was still a future hope. This tells Paul that he is almost certainly dealing with disciples trained by Apollos before he was brought up to speed. So, Paul asks a follow-up question that will make the situation plain, "'Then what baptism did you receive?' 'John's baptism,' they replied." Now the apostle knows for sure that he is dealing with people who were only partially instructed by Apollos.

Paul goes on to explain to them that Jesus brought the fulfillment of all the promises John preached. There is still plenty to look forward to in the eternal future, but the Holy Spirit has burst into this world with a foretaste of God's kingdom now.

Apollos' teaching was genuine and true, but incomplete in its understanding of Christ. The disciples he taught were still viewing Jesus through John the Baptist's eyes, eyes that looked ahead and that did not live to see the fulfillment of God's promises. Their new understanding called for a truly Christian baptism, blessed by God with a supernatural sign vindicating that what Paul preached to them was gloriously true!

Christian baptism is virtually the same as that practiced by John the Baptist. John's baptism summarized everything Jesus would stand for. In fact, there is no evidence that the apostles were ever re-baptized in Jesus' name. John's baptism was sufficient when combined with a full understanding of Jesus. However, for people like Apollos and those he taught, John's baptism was not enough because, unlike Christ's disciples who were with Jesus in the Upper Room and heard all about the coming of the Holy Spirit, Apollos did not fully comprehend what Jesus accomplished. Apollos knew that Jesus was the Messiah who would bring in the kingdom, but he didn't realize that in Christ's death, resurrection and ascension, Jesus had already begun to establish his kingdom in this age. Like John, Apollos was still preaching Jesus from the standpoint of the Old Testament, when salvation was still entirely in the future. But in Jesus, God's kingship invaded this rebellious world ahead of time, long before God's rule will be enforced through final judgment and Hell. God's kingship has broken into this world in those who have experienced new life in Christ. Following Christ in this still-fallen world is exactly what the Holy Spirit helps us do.

Of course, the Holy Spirit has been active in redemption since the beginning. Believers in the Old Testament were saved through the Spirit's work.

> The prophets who prophesied about the grace that
> was to be yours searched and inquired carefully,
> inquiring what person or time the Spirit of Christ in
> them was indicating when he predicted the
> sufferings of Christ and the subsequent glories.
> (1 Peter 1:10-11)

The Holy Spirit has been at work in redemption from the beginning, but it truly ramped up when, "through the eternal Spirit [Jesus] offered himself without blemish ... [to] purify our conscience from dead works to serve the living God." (Hebrews 9:14)

This is when the Holy Spirit is described as being "poured out." It's one thing to drink of the Holy Spirit's grace. It's another for him to be poured out like a flood. The Old Testament symbolically looked ahead to a day when a river would pour out of God's altar, making the Dead Sea come alive (Ezekiel 47:1-12). Jesus implied that Ezekiel's prophecy spoke of a pouring out of the Holy Spirit to bring life to a dead world. (John 7:37-39)

Just think of the increased breadth of the Spirit's work after the cross and resurrection. The Holy Spirit's saving work was no longer centered on Israel. At Pentecost, the gospel was opened up to every nation. No longer does one have to become a Jew to embrace the covenant of salvation. The Holy Spirit is awakening faith all over the world. The breadth of his outpouring is staggering.

In addition, the potential depth and intensity of the Holy Spirit's work is equally staggering in the lives of believers.

> That according to the riches of his glory he may
> grant you to be strengthened with power through
> his Spirit in your inner being, so that Christ may
> dwell in your hearts through faith—that you, being

rooted and grounded in love, may have strength to comprehend with all the saints what is the breadth and length and height and depth, and to know the love of Christ that surpasses knowledge, that you may be filled with all the fullness of God. (Ephesians 3:16-19)

Through the Holy Spirit, the presence of God can now be known by repentant, justified and adopted sinners. We can grasp what it means to be loved by him and to love him back, to be his people and for him to be our God. In the Old Covenant, that was mostly a promise, experienced at best by only a few. But now, the Holy Spirit of God dwells in each and every believer in Jesus Christ, and he can fill us to overflowing with Christ. Through the Holy Spirit, we can know what it means for the risen Jesus to live with us and in us, by faith.

Living faith knows the personal discipleship of Jesus Christ— not just of John the Baptist or a good pastor—but Jesus personally. Jesus exists bodily in Paradise right now, but the Holy Spirit enables us to experience Christ's presence anywhere. He manifests Jesus to our faith so that Christ lives with us, here and now.

Being a disciple of Jesus means more than simply looking back on a great Galilean who taught long ago. It means more than looking forward to Paradise one day. For a Christian disciple, the risen Jesus is my Master, right now. He lives with me through the Holy Spirit. I talk to him and, through the Spirit's Scriptures I hear his voice addressing me. Jesus mentors me and inspires me and comforts me and challenges me and teaches me and trains me, just as he did the original twelve. I am a disciple of Jesus, just as Peter and Matthew and Andrew were. I don't have to wait for death or Christ's return to live in the kingdom of God. Eternal life began for me the day I met Christ by faith. Eternal life is not just a dream for the future; it is something I experience today.

I don't think there are still disciples of John the Baptist running around, but this passage does remind me of some in the twenty-first century American church. There is a kind of evangelism that sounds like Apollos' preaching. With commendable fervor, it explains the way of the Lord accurately and with Scriptural depth. It brings people to Christ for salvation, clinging to Christ for the hope of forgiveness and everlasting life. It explains God's grace in terms of Christ's justifying work on the cross, and the promise of glory at Christ's return.

We must be careful though, that we do not neglect the work of the Holy Spirit in our evangelism. I don't mean that we should talk about the Holy Spirit more. The Holy Spirit is intended by God to work unobtrusively in the background. The Holy Spirit testifies about Jesus, not about himself. "When the Helper comes … the Spirit of truth, who proceeds from the Father, he will bear witness about me." (John 15:26)

My point is that the Holy Spirit's witness of Christ is more than his witness to Christ's cross. He also witnesses to the Risen Christ's current reign. Any decision to believe in Jesus is also a decision to follow Jesus. "You are in Christ Jesus, who became to us wisdom from God, righteousness and sanctification and redemption." (1 Corinthians 1:30)

The Holy Spirit not only reveals Jesus as our righteousness and redemption (his past work on the cross), but also our wisdom and sanctification (his present work to disciple us). Many Christians don't seem to really grasp the power of the Holy Spirit to transform us today.

As a seminary student, I heard Francis Schaffer suggest that if God himself cut out every passage in the Bible about the Holy Spirit, it would make virtually no experiential difference to the modern American believer. The Apostle Paul obviously had similar concerns. He said that he kept praying for the Holy Spirit to open our eyes to what we can experience of Christ now.

It's almost—not quite but almost—as if some of us were still seeing salvation through the eyes of John the Baptist. We've got the whole message of salvation; we've got all of it accurately. We come to faith in the Messiah like all the Old Testament saints came to faith, except that we, like John, know that the Messiah is Jesus. Like John, we look ahead to a time when Christ will perfect God's kingdom.

But faith should not be a matter of looking ahead only, as if the Holy Spirit were yet to come to spread God's rule. We can know God's rule today. The Holy Spirit is not waiting for Christ's return to start building God's kingdom. He has already begun, and experiencing his power and joy is a mark of Christian faith.

"So, tell me, Christian, did you receive the Holy Spirit when you believed?" I'm not asking whether you have the Holy Spirit; every Christian does. I'm really asking what you know about him. "Why Pastor, I didn't know that the Holy is … now. I didn't know that I could actually be filled with the Spirit of God in this life."

Christian, open your eyes to what it means to have received the gift of the Holy Spirit! "God's love has been poured into our hearts through the Holy Spirit who has been given to us." (Romans 5:5)

You don't have to wait for Jesus to wrap his physical arms around you to know God's love. I often pray for God to wrap his arms around his children's pain and tears, and I've seen him do it. He does it right then and there as we pray, and the experience is overwhelming. Many people didn't know they could sense God's love like that. God pours out his love into our hearts by the Holy Spirit. (Romans 5:5) He brings that love from the cross to our hearts. Don't wait for heaven to experience that. Don't wait another day.

> You did not receive the spirit of slavery to fall back into fear, but you have received the Spirit of adoption as sons, by whom we cry, "Abba! Father!" The Spirit himself bears witness with our spirit that we are children of God. Romans 8:15-17

You are God's child right now. You are not just tagged to become his child in the future. His Spirit encourages you to lift up your arms to your Heavenly Dad and ask him to pick you up. Even if the Divine King is on his throne administering royal business, he will still pick you up on his knee. And sitting on God's knee, you will see his government of the world and his provision for your life from a different perspective, one that can easily look up to see his smile.

> There are varieties of gifts, but the same Spirit ... To each is given the manifestation of the Spirit for the common good. (1 Corinthians 12:4,7)

You don't have to have an ordination service to be gifted by God to serve him. The Holy Spirit has already equipped you to be a blessing. Just do it; just bless others any way he has equipped you to do it. You don't have to sit on the sidelines, watching others experience the power of God in ministry. That power is yours. Use it. Just serve with what you have. The one who fed five thousand with five loaves and two fish can do amazing things with what you offer him.

> The kingdom of God is not a matter of eating and drinking but of righteousness and peace and joy in the Holy Spirit. Whoever thus serves Christ is

acceptable to God and approved by men. (Romans 14:17-18)

Using your spiritual gifts is just the beginning. Gifts are but tools. You can serve God now, not only in Heaven or when Christ returns. You can serve God, whether at home or at work or at school as a beacon of righteousness, an anchor of peace, and a fountain of joy. You can serve God because the Spirit of Christ is actually living in you and walking alongside you.

> Praying at all times in the Spirit, with all prayer and supplication. (Ephesians 6:18)

> We do not know what to pray for as we ought, the Spirit himself intercedes for us with groanings too deep for words. (Romans 8:26)

The Holy Spirit enables you to speak with God intelligently, even when you don't know exactly what you are talking about. God has planned to move heaven and earth through your prayers, so pray!

> Eager to maintain the unity of the Spirit in the bond of peace. (Ephesians 4:3)

Churches do not have to split. Christians do not have to be so embedded in their own wants that they use the church and throw it away when they are done. We can maintain and keep our unity. We can maintain the truth in a godly peace forged by the Holy Spirit.

> And do not get drunk with wine, for that is debauchery, but be filled with the Spirit, addressing one another in psalms and hymns and spiritual songs, singing and making melody to the Lord with your heart, giving thanks always and for everything

to God the Father in the name of our Lord Jesus Christ. (Ephesians 5:18-21)

We can be so aware of God's Spirit that we are filled to overflowing with Christ. That doesn't mean that we talk a lot about the Holy Spirit; it means that we are so filled with his presence that we do everything alongside Jesus and in Christ's name. Our whole lives—not just our worship, but our whole lives —become music to God, and Jesus becomes palpably present in every relationship.

Living faith believes that I am a disciple of Jesus. The disciples that Paul found in Ephesus received the gospel, but they thought of themselves as Old Testament-style believers. They knew about Christ accurately, but they didn't realize that God's kingdom begins with our faith, not with our death or Christ's return. Make no mistake, Christian. You *did* receive the Holy Spirit when you believed. Don't live like someone who only has Old Testament promises.

Living faith looks like the disciples of John at Ephesus, discovering that Christ's Spirit enables them to walk with Jesus today.

Spiritual Growth Is From The Inside Out

> Likewise, my brothers, you also have died to the law through the body of Christ, so that you may belong to another, to him who has been raised from the dead, in order that we may bear fruit for God. For while we were living in the flesh, our sinful passions, aroused by the law, were at work in our members to bear fruit for death.
>
> But now we are released from the law, having died to that which held us captive, so that we serve in the new way of the Spirit and not in the old way of the written code. (Romans 7:4-6)

The Apostle Paul describes two ways people can relate to the Lord, using the analogy of marriage. The first kind of marriage describes the way we must relate to God before we appreciate and embrace the gospel. At that time, we relate to God through his commandments, or Law. That is to say, our relationship with God was only as good as our own goodness. In that marriage, we feared God's Law. The Law exposed our failings and condemned us. Our spiritual experience was one of apprehension and hiding from God. When the Law exposed us, we had to feign repentance and promise to do better, knowing that we would only fail again and go through the same agony over and over, with little hope of ever pleasing him. A sad marriage, indeed.

But faith in Christ changes all that. One implication of "dying" with Christ is that the old marriage with God is dissolved (a marriage is over when one spouse dies). The reborn Christian remarries God, but this time the relationship is not established by our righteousness through God's Law, but rather, through Jesus' righteousness which is ours through faith. Now, our relationship with God is as good as *his* goodness, not ours. In this marriage,

Christ is our focus, not the Law alone. We do not fear him; his love and grace and goodness are our salvation. Now, our spiritual experience can be one of delight. A great marriage, indeed.

The key to spiritual growth is keeping in mind that we relate to God through Christ, using the Law to remind us of our true identity and destiny, rather than using it to condemn our many faults. When we continue to relate to God in the old way (as many Christians do) it leads to frustration and failure as we mistakenly assume that our relationship with God is only as good as our goodness, not his.

We must try hard to appreciate what Paul is saying here. We originally came to Christ because in one way or another the Law of God shone into us from the outside, whether brightly from God's Word, or dimly through our own conscience. Its holiness and righteousness were alien to the self-obsessed core of our being. It exposed the graffiti scribbled all over our dingy souls. It exposed antagonism to God's authority and created tremendous external pressure. The Law condemned us and, by God's grace, it showed us the need for repentance and faith. Once we learned of God's offer of forgiveness and grace in Christ Jesus, we grasped it gladly.

But Paul says that once that is accomplished, our relationship to the Law is like a previous marriage that was terminated by death. When we died to the Law through Christ, our old marriage ended. Now that we are married to Jesus, we don't relate to God through the Law anymore, we only relate to God through Christ. What this means is that spiritual growth cannot come from using the Law in the same way we used it before we knew Jesus. The external pressure of God's Law helped me find Christ, but it cannot help me grow once I've found him.

Think about it. The pressure of guilt and shame and failure is no longer relevant to the believer in the same way, because it has all been absorbed on the cross of Christ. The old guilt-producing pressure has no leverage for someone whose guilt is completely covered. How could I be motivated by guilt, when all my guilt has forever been removed?

What causes Christians to grow is not external pressure, but inner faith energized by the Holy Spirit who made us new creatures in Christ. "But now we are released from the law, having died to that which held us captive, so that we serve in the new way of the Spirit and not in the old way of the written code." "For at one time you were darkness, but now you are light in the Lord. Walk as children of light." (Ephesians 5:8)

We *are* light, so *be* light. That's the New Testament logic: be what you have already become in Christ. Motivation for change does not have to be created; it already exists in every born again believer, and needs only to be directed and encouraged.

To illustrate his point another way, Paul speaks later in Romans 7 of two levels of the human soul. Down deep, at the core of our being, is what Paul calls in verse 22 "the inner man." Solomon called this inner core our "heart" when he said, "Keep your heart with all vigilance, for from it flow the springs of life." (Proverbs 4:23)

There is a fundamental wellspring of who we are underneath all of our surface behaviors, values and attitudes. The inner man, or heart, refers to the basic predispositions of our character, particularly our predispositions toward God as to whether to trust, worship, honor and obey him—or alternatively, to distrust him, worship ourselves and do what we independently think is best.

Around this inner core is what Paul calls "the flesh" (often translated "sinful nature"). The way Paul uses the term, it includes more than our literal body, but also every mental and emotional faculty we have to interface with the physical world. It refers not only to our physical tendencies, but to our mental and emotional habits as well. It is filled with all the values and attitudes we have constructed (before coming to faith) out of a heart that was born predisposed against God's authority. It is made up of all the habits of behavior we have built up, as our old heart followed the direction of the world and the devil. No wonder Paul says that nothing good lives in his flesh. (Romans 7:18)

The way that the Holy Spirit brings a person to life through faith in Christ is to divinely transform his or her heart, or core, so that it miraculously becomes predisposed to trust, worship and obey God. "I will give you a new heart, and a new spirit ... I will put my Spirit within you, and cause you to walk in my statutes and be careful to obey my rules." (Ezekiel 36:26-27)

Not only does such a new heart quickly embrace the gospel with mustard seed faith, but it also yearns to grow, transforming attitudes, values and behavior in what the Bible pictures as bearing the fruit of godliness.

Paul explains this by saying that the Holy Spirit, in essence, has taken the Law once written externally in stone and written it internally on our hearts. (cf. 2 Corinthians 3) This transforms the way a Christian uses God's Law. It is no longer a threat from the outside. It is now a precious guide on the inside toward what we long for more than anything else: godliness.

Therefore, the motivating power for growth and change in a born again believer does not come from the external guilt raised by God's Law. Instead, it comes from the faith-based desires welling up from our new heart, our new wellspring of life. Spiritual growth is no longer a matter of becoming someone different than we are. It is matter of rejecting the old ways which are no longer consistent with the person we have become in Christ, and embracing the new thoughts, emotions and behaviors that match our new life. To put it simply, spiritual growth happens from the inside out.

Why is all this important? Because living in faith that we change from the inside out frees us from the agonizing cycle of self-hatred in our walk with God. We learn the difference between hating sin, and hating ourselves.

The Apostle Paul described the struggle for godliness this way,

> I do not do what I want, but I do the very thing I hate. … I have the desire to do what is right, but not the ability to carry it out. For I do not do the good I want, but the evil I do not want is what I keep on doing. (Romans 7:15, 18-19)

Many Christians stop there, as it were, experiencing the struggle as a hatred of ourselves. "I am so evil. I am such a failure." "There is no grace or power in my life." "God must be disgusted with me." "I've got to pay for my failures and make myself better if I hope to have his blessing."

But Paul doesn't go there. In fact, he goes in a shockingly different direction. "Now if I do what I do not want … it is no longer I who do it, but sin that dwells within me." (Romans 7:16-17) Did that register? To make sure we hear it, he says it again.

> The evil I do not want is what I keep on doing. Now
> if I do what I do not want, it is no longer I who do it,
> but sin that dwells within me. (Romans 7:19-20)

Paul takes responsibility for his ongoing sin, but he doesn't think of that sin as belonging to his new nature and identity. Instead, it expresses his old, untamed habits of mind and body. Paul is no longer fighting God. God and Paul are now on the same side, working together to fight the old, ungodly habits that still influence Paul's behavior.

What this means is that, as a Christian, the sin which I struggle with now is no longer the real me. From God's perspective, the real me, the person God sees in Christ, is reflected by my new heart. That's where his Spirit lives, in the "inner man." All the rest is old habits, ugly graffiti, gouges in my soul that need to be filled in, sanded down, and repainted.

Paul did not hate himself. He did not get angry with himself. Paul was frustrated by the sin that still vexed his soul. Paul hated the sin that had been carved and spray painted on his soul over the years. He hated it and worked every day to sandblast it or wash it off. But he did not hate himself. He was married to God through Christ. How could he hate what Christ loves and cherishes?

> I have been crucified with Christ. It is no longer I who live, but Christ who lives in me. And the life I now live in the flesh I live by faith in the Son of God, who loved me and gave himself for me. (Galatians 2:20)

Hate the sinful lies, values, desires and habits that still deface your soul. Hate them with a passion. But hate them because they are now alien to you. If God sees you as a new person in Christ, then see yourself that way. Hate sin as you would a fungus, a parasite or some previously cultivated disability that keeps you from being all you are meant to be. Work to get rid of it, to cleanse, mend and remove. "Let us also lay aside every weight, and sin which clings so closely." (Hebrews 12:1)

But Christian, do not hate yourself. The old you that was truly worth hating justly died on the cross, the object of all the hate God Almighty can muster. In its place, God the Holy Spirit has created something new, something he loves. "You have been born again, not of perishable seed but of imperishable." (1 Peter 1:23) God's seed of a new life is in you (1 John 3:9) at the center of your being, and it's growing.

Living faith looks for spiritual growth from the inside out, as we purposefully and steadfastly nurture our new inner desires. Growth doesn't happen when I respond to God's Word in fear or in self disgust, as if it were still an external threat. Growth happens as I feed my faith and focus on God's Spirit in my heart. It happens as I take the time to celebrate how I am free from just condemnation and am alive to God in a glorious relationship that I can never lose. I reject my old ways of thinking and feeling because I don't want them anymore. I want something better. I want all that God's wonderful Law describes—not because it threatens me, but because I find it written on my heart.

Living faith struggles less with stifling old passions and focuses more on exploring new ones. It spends less energy pretending to obey God and more energy enjoying his good and perfect will. It ceases to be overcome by evil as it learns to overcome evil with good (Romans 12:21).

What does such living faith look like? …

Mary Magdalene

> And Jesus answering said to him, "Simon, I have something to say to you." And he answered, "Say it, Teacher."
>
> "A certain moneylender had two debtors. One owed five hundred denarii, and the other fifty. When they could not pay, he cancelled the debt of both. Now which of them will love him more?" Simon answered, "The one, I suppose, for whom he

cancelled the larger debt." And he said to him, "You have judged rightly."

Then turning toward the woman he said to Simon, "Do you see this woman? I entered your house; you gave me no water for my feet, but she has wet my feet with her tears and wiped them with her hair. You gave me no kiss, but from the time I came in she has not ceased to kiss my feet. You did not anoint my head with oil, but she has anointed my feet with ointment. Therefore I tell you, her sins, which are many, are forgiven—for she loved much. But he who is forgiven little, loves little." And he said to her, "Your sins are forgiven." (Luke 7:40-48)

Mary Magdalene illustrates how Jesus' attitude toward women differed from that of Socrates, Aristotle, the Jewish rabbis and the Qumran community made famous by the Dead Sea scrolls. For all the others held women in relatively low esteem, while Jesus welcomed women followers. Mary Magdalene is mentioned as one of the faithful few at the cross; she was there to see where they laid his body; she came to anoint the body on Sunday and she was the very first person who saw the risen Lord.

Is she the prostitute mentioned in the text quoted above? Immediately after the story of the prostitute, Mary Magdalene is mentioned by name as a woman who found freedom in Christ and who followed him with the disciples. Of course, that does not prove they were the same person. Even so, I personally think that they were. The one small bit of extra evidence that convinces me will become clear at the very end of this chapter.

At any rate, for the sake of discussion, we'll let Mary Magdalene represent the whole class of people whom Jesus delivered from desperate circumstances. For we read of "some women who had been healed of evil spirits and infirmities: Mary, called Magdalene, from whom seven demons had gone out …" (Luke 8:2)

Demon possession is a difficult subject for the modern mind because it involves a view of reality that has room for spirits, human spirits and other spirits both good and evil. Demons are another name for what the Bible sometimes calls "angels." Angels are not human, of course; they are another class of beings altogether who exist as spirits. They were created to serve God and at least some watch over us.

The Bible says some angels fell into sin before the human race did. These fallen angels, led by one called Satan or Lucifer, feel entitled to rule this world. They are called demons and they do not watch over our welfare. They effectively manipulate the common human passion for self rule, and undermine any who are converted to seek God's rule once again. The Old Testament points out how angelic beings can so convincingly tempt us with lies that we will follow those lies even to our own destruction. For example, lying spirits goaded King Ahab into a battle that cost him his life. (1 Kings 22)

In the New Testament, Jesus underscores how Satan is the greatest tempter of all, distorting the truth. These distortions lead to horribly self-destructive behavior. The New Testament mentions violence, cursing, cutting oneself, throwing oneself into fire. Since Satan is the leader of this angelic rebellion, any demonic activity may be referred to as a satanic activity or the work of Satan.

Satan began with lies about God in the Garden of Eden. (Genesis 3) "Did God really say that? Does God really have a right to tell you how to live? God is not sovereign and all-wise. You can and you should run your life on your own terms. You weren't created with a purpose. You should define your own purpose." With such attractive lies, Satan leads us into a lifetime of confusion and misery. Since we were made to be in God's image, distorting truth about God will inevitably distort our understanding of ourselves.

Confused, distorted thinking then inevitably leads to confused, distorted living. We still have all the natural and good drives that God gave us, but no confidence that God's commandments are the best way to satisfy those drives. Our spiritual immune system compromised, we become vulnerable to all kinds of temptations to seek fulfillment in strange ways. Temptations like isolating sex to physical excitement only, thus disabling our capacity to enjoy relationships as originally intended. Temptations like using drugs to chemically simulate a mirage of peace and happiness, instead of cultivating an inner character which encourages happiness. There are many ways in which distorted thinking leads to distorted living.

When Mary Magdalene encountered Jesus, she was in bondage to such distortion in seven desperate ways. We don't know what seven they were, but in multiple specific ways her identity was smeared and blurred. She worked against herself, basing her life on false assumptions that led her into destructive and self-destructive behaviors.

Of course, not everyone acting out self-destructive behaviors is possessed by a demon. Only the most radical and bizarre behaviors in the Bible were described as "possession," while there are many, many lesser ways that malevolent spirits tempt us to obsess over falsehood, trapping us into serious bondage. The Bible calls Satan the spirit at work in our disobedience, the ruler of the kingdom of the air. (Ephesians 2:2) It tells us that the whole world is under the control of the evil one. (1 John 5:19) When we yield to satanic temptations, his poisonous lies harden into the foundation of our thoughts and feelings. Then, on top of those feelings and thoughts we build a superstructure of behaviors that frame a crippled lifestyle.

How sabotaged and self destructive such lifestyles can become! For Mary Magdalene, life was dominated by seven demons. How can such a person find the power to be transformed? Imagine a tower of rock, built up, grain by grain, on a foundation of lies. And imagine wanting to tear down that tower of misery to erect something better. How do you tear it down? Verbally bellowing against the top with the Law of God is not going to reduce it. The Bible says that the Law of God is excellent as a divine guide and it does a great job of exposing our sin, but it has no power at all to effect change.

Consequently, Mary Magdalene was not changed by listening to people condemn her or counsel her with the Law. Jesus had to first cure her of her demons. He had to first cleanse the inside of her soul from lies before she could become a genuine disciple. He had to demolish the foundations of falsehood before the unhealthy behavior could begin to crumble.

Look at the example of the weeping woman of Chapter 7. We'll just call her "Mary" for convenience. Jesus is invited to dine by a Pharisee, someone with the reputation for being a self-righteous religious conservative. On the whole, the Pharisees did not think much of Jesus. They didn't like the way he freely associated with known sinners. Maybe that is why this host is barely welcoming (he provides no customary water for Jesus' feet and no kiss of greeting.)

Many are surprised to learn that such meals were not necessarily private affairs. They were often a relaxed, semi-formal opportunity for the community to meet a guest of distinction. It was not unusual for folks to collect in hopes of seeing or overhearing the honored visitor. People could come in off the street to respectfully listen, and perhaps ask questions. Even so,

Simon the Pharisee was not expecting to see Mary. Mary was, according to the text, "a sinner"—probably a euphemism for prostitute. (I don't know in what connection Simon knew Mary, though he obviously recognized her.) When you host a public party for a visiting religious figure you don't expect to see a local call girl show up.

They ate reclining at a table, each lying against the left arm with his head over the table. Mary, therefore, approached Jesus' feet. She carried a bottle of expensive perfume, which she undoubtedly intended to pour on Jesus' head according to custom. There are other examples of Jesus being anointed on his head in a similar manner. But she lost it. She began to cry and tears spilled down on Jesus' feet. She was so embarrassed that in a spontaneous display of humility, she unbound her hair, knelt and used her hair as a towel to wipe off her tears. Too overcome to do anything else, she just continued to clasp his feet and pour out her perfume there.

She is the only person mentioned in the Bible to ever pour perfume on someone's feet! You washed feet, you didn't put perfume on them or hug them. That wasn't her plan, it just happened that way. It was a completely unique, touching faux pas that endeared her to Jesus.

The Pharisee was inwardly critical of both the woman and Jesus—against the woman because she was known for her sinful lifestyle, and against Jesus for being too dumb to know what this woman was. All that the typical Pharisee knew to do with sinners in bondage was to preach at them, or about them, reciting God's commands against adultery and publicly reflecting on their wickedness.

Of course, like so many disintegrated people, Mary probably already knew that she was a mess. Lies at the foundation of her life supported a miserable tower of bondage. Perhaps she bought the lie that the attention of lovers would make up for a lack of affection in her childhood, or that supporting herself away from parents was worth any indignity. Whatever lies lay at the foundation, the life built on those lies was lonely and dangerous and vulnerable—every day harder to look into the mirror, every night a longer debate about whether another day was even worth it.

Of course, the Pharisees did well to preach the Law to Mary. She needed to be told that God designed something better than this. But after dozens of sermons comparing her to Jezebel, they really didn't have that much more to offer her. She learned that God had every right to hate her and be disgusted by her, which was true. But that's all she learned. So she concluded that God had given up on her. And if God had given up on her, what hope did she really have? Another drink please and make it a double. If you're trapped in sinful habits, it's too late, too late to be blessed and too late to change. That was what she got from the Pharisees.

But Mary wasn't there because of what she had heard from the Pharisees. She was there because of what she had heard from Jesus. At some point, within some crowd, Jesus had seen her pain and touched her life with the sanity and peace of God's love. She heard his teaching that God was even more holy and good than the Pharisees realized. God was not only good enough to hate sinners, but he was also good enough to find a way to love them. He told people to stop believing the half truths promoted by Satan and discover in him who God really is.

In word, in deed and in person, Jesus presented a fuller, richer and a truer vision of Almighty God, a much bigger picture than that of the Pharisees. The truth is that God is so big that he can deal with sin; he can kill it and swallow up the death it brings. God is so awesome that he can do what seems unthinkable: he can remain holy, yet still find a way to love the unholy. No one who heard Jesus could understand that fully until after the cross, but many got the gist of it early.

Mary was one person who got the message. She could not have told you exactly who Jesus was; she didn't understand the Trinity. She could, however, see that Jesus knew God in a way no one else did. And if Jesus said that God could destroy sin and swallow up the misery of it, then it must be true. By God's grace, Mary became alive through faith. And when she saw the living object of her faith at that dinner, she just broke down and cried—tears of repentance and regret, tears of gratitude and love, tears of joy and hope. Through Jesus, she had learned the truth about God and the truth had set her free.

The point of Jesus' discussion with Simon was that Mary's actions demonstrated that she had discovered a grace his host knew nothing about. She was a changed woman, changed not by altering her behavior, but by Jesus altering her vision of God. All the bindings of sin were unraveling from the inside out.

As we grow up, the devil capitalizes on all the abuse we received from people he had already ruined before us. Not that we are all "possessed by demons." Such language is reserved for the worst cases. But Satan successfully tempts all of us to believe distortions of the truth. Cut off from God by sin, we frantically try to define ourselves and we will use anything to do it. We'll use the opinions of parents and the pontifications of professors. We'll even use deodorant commercials. We'll use anything, all the while building a confused tower of fear and desperation.

How can I be freed from all this? Calling for change from the outside is appropriate and even necessary, but it is hopelessly ineffective by itself. I may even come to the point of believing I should change, perhaps for my health, or for social or religious advantage. I might even clean up my act for a while or to a point. But I simply cannot succeed as long as I believe that God is dead or sick or is my enemy. As long as I believe in my heart that God is unworthy of my trust or is simply not interested in the likes of me, then I will have no choice but to live in fear and hopelessness and desperation.

No choice, that is, until one day I hear a person who understands God's revelation differently than the Pharisees. Someone new, someone unique. And I find myself saying what countless others have said: "Never have I heard a man speak like this before." His name is Jesus. Jesus said that God is so good that he is willing to forgive—not politely, not grudgingly and not as some cosmic wimp—but mightily, so that sin is killed by his forgiveness, rendered dead and unable ever again to either anger him or enslave us. That message gains its full power from the cross, for that is where Jesus demonstrated and accomplished the mighty love he talked about.

Christ reveals God's true nature. In Jesus, God loved us to death. I don't just mean that he loved us enough for him to die; I mean that he loved us enough for us to die. The moment I see that, the lies in the foundation of my soul crack and crumble. And with their collapse, down comes my bondage.

Years ago, I visited the Bay of Fundy in New Brunswick. The tides there are among the most powerful in the world. Twice a day they change forty to fifty feet. They create some of the most unusual geologic formations; small towers of rock just separated from the main cliffs. The wind could blow on the top of those rocks for millions of years without wearing them down, but for a relatively short time, geologically speaking, powerful tides have come in and out, wearing down the foundations of those towers. Looking like huge mushrooms, the bases of these "flower top rocks" are quickly wearing away. Before long, each one will come crashing down.

Grace is like that. You can shout the Law at people who are locked in the lies of Satan, and the best you can accomplish is to raise guilt. Guilt is appropriate for guilty people. But it is not enough. It makes us realize that we need to change, but it gives no power to do so. If all a person has is guilt, he or she descends into despair or hypocrisy.

However, the grace of God comes in with the sound of many waters and hits the foundation, those lies about the Living God that you and I have built our sorry lifestyles upon, and it quickly wears those lies away. When the thinning foundation cracks, then the whole tower of sin and fear and hopelessness collapses with it and Christ can begin a glorious rebuilding.

Jesus cured Mary Magdalene of seven demons. What all the well meaning sermons from the Pharisees couldn't accomplish, Jesus achieved by showing her who God is and changing her on the inside. After that, she just wanted one thing: to be Jesus' disciple. All she wanted was to mold her life around the Living God she had found in him—the prostitution, the degradation all gone. Now she wanted to live like a daughter of the King. Because she had become a daughter of the King.

I can't imagine her agony at the cross. Except for young John, all the men had fled, but she stayed and watched him die. She helped bury him. She went back on Sunday to finish the job, but the body was gone. She collapsed, her eyes blurring with bitter tears. Jesus had cast out seven demons. He gave her new life. Now, they had taken away his body and she could not even give him the dignity of a decent burial.

"Woman, why are you crying? Who is it you are looking for?" Thinking she was talking to the gardener, she said, "Sir, if you have carried him away, tell me where you have put him, and I will get him." That's when Jesus said one word: "Mary."

Overwhelmed, she did what she had done once before at the house of a Pharisee …

Living faith looks like the woman who was changed from the inside out, in pure joy clasping Jesus' feet.

All I Have To Do Is Fear God

> My son, if you receive my words and treasure up my commandments with you, making your ear attentive to wisdom and inclining your heart to understanding; yes, if you call out for insight and raise your voice for understanding, if you seek it like silver and search for it as for hidden treasures, then you will understand the fear of the LORD and find the knowledge of God. (Proverbs 2:1-5)

Solomon was one of the most successful men in history. Others have gained more territory and spent the lives of thousands in great campaigns. But Solomon took a ragtag tribal confederation and turned it into a prosperous, healthy nation in one generation, expanding its borders and skyrocketing its international prestige, all without going to war. Solomon was a Renaissance man 2,500 years before the Renaissance. The touch that Midas proverbially had with respect to gold, Solomon had with respect to everything. Business, religion, civil service, art, military preparedness, poetry, diplomacy and science all flourished in his generation. He was the key leader in each endeavor (1 Kings 4:29-34), and was unashamed to say that his success was due to faith in the God of Abraham, Isaac and Jacob.

One of the things people liked about Solomon was that he had a habit of telling stories and making up one-liners—not jokes exactly, but little morsels of life dipped in a tasty sauce that made them good to chew.

For example, when he solemnly convened a court, he might say, "When the tempest passes, the wicked is no more, but the righteous is established forever." (Proverbs 10:25) Or when he gathered informally with his cabinet, he might open a meeting with, "Where there is no guidance, a people falls, but in an abundance of counselors there is safety." (Proverbs 11:14) Or maybe he'd turn to a friend at a fancy state dinner and whisper, "Like a gold ring in a pig's snout is a beautiful woman without discretion." (Proverbs 11:22)

Solomon had a proverb for every situation—3,000 have been preserved. The biblical compilation records quite a sampling. Many of these tasty tidbits were about God's character; some were about relationships or economics. All were about life and being successful at life.

In Chapter 2 of Proverbs, Solomon describes godly success in several ways. God guards those who walk in integrity. (vs, 7) God protects those committed to justice. (vs. 8) Later, in verse 11, it is "understanding" that guards and "discretion" that protects. The point seems to be that if you search for it, your heart will find wisdom. (vs. 10) God will give us the understanding and insight we need to be protected from danger, whether expected or unexpected. He will enable us to know just what to do, and when and how. He enables us to do it all effectively, winsomely, with joy and satisfaction.

But if wisdom is the beginning of success, what is the beginning of wisdom? Our text answers that by declaring that if we search for wisdom with all our heart, "then you will understand the fear of the LORD and find the knowledge of God."

Solomon's most famous proverb is," The fear of the LORD is the beginning of wisdom." (Proverbs 9:10) According to Solomon, then, all success begins with the fear of God. It doesn't matter whether you are talking about love or or government or music or business or science. If you want to be truly successful, what you have to do is fear God.

What does it mean to "fear God"? It is a subtle concept with different shades and colors. For the wicked—by which we mean sinners who have not repented and sought grace for forgiveness and change—for the wicked fearing God means being afraid of him because of his judgment. Solomon says, 'The way of the LORD is a stronghold to the blameless, but destruction to evildoers." (Proverbs 10:29) "Everyone who is arrogant in heart is an abomination to the LORD; be assured, he will not go unpunished." (Proverbs 16:5)

The day of judgment that will end this phase of history is so terrible that when it comes, those who are not sheltered by God's grace will beg mountains to fall on them (Revelation 6:16). Better to be buried alive than be exposed to God's wrath.

Outside of God's grace, sinners should be terrified of God. Yet the artificial distance from God caused by unbelief means that the ones who ought to be terrified of the Lord, are not. Solomon's father David taught him, "Transgression speaks to the wicked deep in his heart; there is no fear of God before his eyes." (Psalm 36:1)

Redeemed sinners, believers in Christ, have no reason to be afraid of the Lord. In the New Testament, the Apostle John says to believers,

> We may have confidence for the day of judgment …
> There is no fear in love, but perfect love casts out fear. For fear has to do with punishment, and whoever fears has not been perfected in love.
> (1 John 4:17-18)

In other words, being terrified of God's judgment is inappropriate for a Christian because Christ has taken our punishment, once for all. If a Christian is still afraid of God's judgment, he has some growing up to do in his faith, because being afraid in that way is completely unnecessary.

Yet, while the believer is not afraid of God, Solomon says that he or she is exactly the person who fears God. Therefore, the fear of God must mean something more than being afraid of him.

I learned of a fear that is different than being afraid on a trip I took to New York City while in elementary school. I remember standing at the very base of the Empire State Building and looking up. It was my first experience of open-mouthed awe. On the one hand, I felt a twinge of being afraid. What if it fell on me? What if something fell off the building and landed on me? But on the other hand, I was excited. I reveled in something so incredibly, unimaginably big. I wanted to go all the way to the top so the view could blow me away.

I had a similar feeling the first time I saw the Atlantic Ocean as a child. It could suck me under or I could get lost in its vastness—but how exciting to sail away and discover new places! I still get the same reaction every time I look up at the stars at night. The thought that I'm wheeling about in orbit around the sun at 67,000 mph scares me a little, but the dance of the planets and moons and galaxies is far more thrilling.

Overwhelming size or power is either threatening or exhilarating. A big roller coaster rivets your attention, gets adrenaline pumping, heart racing.. But are you terrorized? That depends on whether you got on willingly or not. If you were forced on so as not to disappoint a child, you may be ready to lose your lunch, but if these things make you feel like a kid, then you're having great fun.

What does God's authority feel like? That depends. If I see him as a Judge, the thought of being accountable to him makes me sweat. But if I see him as a Coach, then every encounter is an opportunity to show him what I've learned to do and receive invaluable training to accomplish even more. The two reactions are completely different, yet both could be described by the word "fear" because whether dealing with a Judge or a Coach, I am not in control. And it's impossible to be entirely comfortable when I'm not in control.

Solomon linked the fear of God to the knowledge of God. The more we think about the Almighty, the more we feel out of control. We experience that apprehension either by being intensely afraid, or by feeling intensely awestruck and exhilarated.

Niagara Falls is a great place to experience this phenomenon. When you first come upon the Falls and see them laid out before you, it's impressive—the sound, the rising of the mist. It looks just like the postcards, pretty impressive. But if you get up-close and personal to the Falls, you feel a whole lot more than just "impressed." Approach the base of Horseshoe Falls, where 600,000 gallons of water crash into the rocks every second, where the water creates a downdraft of air upwards of 70 miles an hour, and you start to feel small, out of control. It's scary. How that scariness comes across as you approach the Falls would depend on your relationship to the water. If you are bobbing in the Niagara River, 10 seconds from going over the edge in a helpless plunge, your fear becomes abject terror, for you will be crushed to death. But if you are on a tour boat at the base or on a firm walkway designed for safety, you'll probably have the time of your life. You will be unforgettably inspired as you feel the vibration and the power surging around and through you. It will create one of your best memories.

That's the way it is with God. He is more overwhelming the more we become aware of him. But how we are overwhelmed depends on our relationship with him. Am I approaching judgment as a naked sinner, or am I approaching glory dressed in the righteousness of Christ? The closer we get to the power of God, the more extreme our reaction, whether it's uncontrollable terror or boundless excitement. The soul-riveting exhilaration of a believer drawing near to the Almighty is what the Bible calls "the fear of God."

When you understand it properly, the fear of God is one of the most potent and positive concepts in biblical faith. In fact, the fear of God is simply a visceral way of talking about faith when it is being exercised. Religion can be a tame and distant thing, but real faith is always close to the edge. Religion is at best impressive, God on a post card, "Hmmm, very nice!" Personal faith, on the other hand, gets so near to God that it makes your mouth dry because you know you are not in control. God loves you. God cares for you. But God could do anything. God could do anything around you. God could do anything with you. He could do anything to you. He could do anything without you. He could do anything through you.

Religion educates our faith and directs it; it increases the knowledge of God. But when we respond to that knowledge by drawing near and living with such a God, life gets spicy. It doesn't matter what you're doing. It doesn't matter where you are. You could be at school, at work, at home. If you are going to respond to God right now above everything else, you're getting close to the edge. How are you with heights?

And the more faith you exercise—the more you embrace the truth about the sovereign and holy Lord in the moment—the more out of control you are. You know he is going to do whatever he wants, and you know that you are going to do whatever he wants. The closer anyone gets to the white hot presence of the Holy One, the scarier it is. For the unbeliever, the approaching blast generates more terror than he knew he could feel. For the believer, however, it's the white knuckled excitement of strapping yourself into a 150-foot rocket with 6 ½ million pounds of explosive thrust that will fly you to the moon!

Solomon says in every situation, if I want God to be with me, if I want that marvelous combination of confidence and humility that I need to succeed, if I want genuine divine oversight of my life, all I really need to do is fear God. Whatever else may be called for, I cannot go far wrong, and I will probably end up right on target, if I just fear God and respond to him right now. In business, in love, in education, in politics, in ministry, am I willing, right now, to be overwhelmed by someone infinitely more powerful and worthy than I? Am I willing to trust in his competence and his affection for me revealed in Christ? Such willingness climbs aboard that towering rocket and blasts off to make kingdom history.

The fear of God realizes that nothing in your life is safe. Fearing God sees a Lord too big to say "No" to, and trusts him too much to question him. When that is true, then nothing in life is safe. Your career isn't safe because you would be willing to change jobs. Your money isn't safe because you would be willing to invest it or share it. Your extramarital affair isn't safe because you would be willing to give it up. Your political opinions, your retirement plans—all subject to change as you study God's Word and grow in the knowledge of what he wants you to do.

Nothing in your life is safe … but *you* are safe because you are God's friend.

The Bible says that to fearing God primes you for success in anything.

> Come, O children, listen to me; I will teach you the fear of the LORD. What man is there who desires life and loves many days, that he may see good? Keep your tongue from evil and your lips from speaking deceit. Turn away from evil and do good; seek peace and pursue it. (Psalm 34:11-14)

Blessed is everyone who fears the LORD, who walks in his ways! You shall eat the fruit of the labor of your hands; you shall be blessed, and it shall be well with you. Your wife will be like a fruitful vine within your house; your children will be like olive shoots around your table. (Psalm 128:1-4)

The angel of the LORD encamps around those who fear him, and delivers them. Oh, fear the LORD, you his saints, for those who fear him have no lack! The young lions suffer want and hunger; but those who seek the LORD lack no good thing. (Psalm 34:1-10)

Ultimately, the more we fear God, the more we are like Jesus. That was a theme in one of Isaiah's prophecies about him,

the Spirit of the LORD shall rest upon him, the Spirit of wisdom and understanding, the Spirit of counsel and might, the Spirit of knowledge and the fear of the LORD. And his delight shall be in the fear of the LORD. He shall not judge by what his eyes see, or decide disputes by what his ears hear. (Isaiah 11:2-3)

There has never been anyone better than Jesus at trusting God and putting his will first. What was the result? You may think, at first, "The cross!" But no, it was the empty tomb and a crown of glory.

Living faith knows that all I have to do is fear God. When that dominates my fear of anything and everything else, then I am primed for success.

What does such living faith look like? …

Jehoshaphat

> And they rose early in the morning and went out into the wilderness of Tekoa. And when they went out, Jehoshaphat stood and said, "Hear me, Judah and inhabitants of Jerusalem! Believe in the LORD your God, and you will be established; believe his prophets, and you will succeed."
>
> And when he had taken counsel with the people, he appointed those who were to sing to the LORD and praise him in holy attire, as they went before the army, and say, "Give thanks to the LORD, for his steadfast love endures forever." (2 Chron. 20:20-21)

Long before I ever read the Bible or heard of Jehoshaphat, I saw war movies. I remember being fascinated by how British relief columns were sometimes led by a group of pipers, that is, bagpipers. This Highland Regiment tradition goes back to the Middle Ages, involving such battles as Waterloo, the Somme, Dunkirk, El Alamein, Sword Beach, right up to the Falklands and Desert Storm. In WWI, these kilted pipers often joined in the battle unarmed, earning the German title of "Ladies from Hell." An interesting name, since they represented a reliance on divine help.

On this side of the pond, we are more familiar with a British alternative that began in the 1700's, when Hanoverians reorganized the English Army and required troops to march in step. Only Scots used the bagpipes. The English elected to import from Europe an alternate form of music: fife and drum. Fife and drum were used mainly to practice, move and position troops. But when battle commenced, they would still march out in front to taunt the enemy with a show of faith in God's favor.

Of course, it was fife and drum that was used in the American Revolutionary Army. In fact, "The Spirit of '76" is embodied in a painting of two drummers, one old and one very young, marching with a wounded man playing a fife. Fife and drum continued to be used until extended artillery and increased mobility made them obsolete.

The tradition behind all this began long before our Revolution, long before the Hanoverians and even long before the pipers of Scotland and Ireland. It started when King Jehoshaphat of Judah had to decide what, or whom, he really feared. That decision became part of his enduring legacy, a legacy that has inspired millions.

King Jehoshaphat inherited a strong commitment to godly religion from his father, Asa. King Asa led a religious revival in Judah, tore down competing idols, sacrificed thousands of sheep in worship, renewed the covenant with public oaths and music. Because of that, the Lord God blessed him.

But King Asa had a way of keeping his faith in a religious box. When it came to dealing with the "real world," he laid the box aside and preferred to trust in more worldly forces. In order to stave off an attack from the northern tribes, he entered into an unholy alliance with Aram. It seemed a brilliant move, but God sent a prophet condemning the king's action because he chose to fear his enemies more than his God. Asa threw that prophet in jail. After that, things went downhill.

> In the thirty-ninth year of his reign Asa was afflicted with a disease in his feet. Though his disease was severe, even in his illness he did not seek help from the LORD, but only from the physicians. (2 Chronicles 16:12)

After two years of suffering, he died. That was Asa's mixed legacy to his son.

From Asa, Jehoshaphat inherited a legacy of strong religion with roots going back to David.

> The LORD was with Jehoshaphat, because he walked in the earlier ways of his father David. He ... sought the God of his father and walked in his commandments, and not according to the practices of Israel. (2 Chronicles 17:3-4)

But religion is not exactly the same as fearing God, is it? Religion instructs and celebrates the truth. It takes something more to live it out. Just like his father, Jehoshaphat left his faith in the Temple when it came to politics. This time, it was a marriage alliance with Ahab to the north which sucked him into a war he wanted no part of. Jehoshaphat barely survived that war, and he witnessed what happened to men like Ahab who rebelled against the Lord. Just as with his father, the Lord sent to Jehoshaphat a prophet.

> Jehu the son of Hanani the seer went out to meet him and said to King Jehoshaphat, "Should you help the wicked and love those who hate the LORD? Because of this, wrath has gone out against you from the LORD. Nevertheless, some good is found in you, for you ... have set your heart to seek God." (2 Chronicles 19:2-3)

So far, Jehoshaphat was turning out just like his Dad. A man trained to be faithful in his religion and blessed by God because of it ... yet, a man whose faith went no further than his religious activities, one who could trust more in worldly conniving than in the love, protection, grace and power of his God. What would

Jehoshaphat's legacy turn out to be? Would he die like his father, too stubborn or too afraid to seek the Lord, trusting only in worldly resources? Or would his legacy be something different?

Jehoshaphat determined that his legacy would be different. He decided to fear God, actually trust and obey him, outside the worship of the temple.

> Jehoshaphat lived at Jerusalem. And he went out again among the people, from Beersheba to the hill country of Ephraim, and brought them back to the LORD, the God of their fathers.
>
> He appointed judges in the land in all the fortified cities of Judah, city by city, and said to the judges, "Consider what you do, for you judge not for man but for the LORD. He is with you in giving judgment. Now then, let the fear of the LORD be upon you. Be careful what you do, for there is no injustice with the LORD our God, or partiality or taking bribes." (2 Chronicles 19:4-11)

Reading the law had been done before; holding revivals in which the covenant was renewed with singing and sacrifices, that had been done before. But this was radically different. Instead of using political cronies, Jehoshaphat took the men who knew God's Law best and made them judges. He told them to make God's Law the practical law of the land, not only in the outlying areas, but in Jerusalem as well. In other words, Jehoshaphat was determined that the Law of God should extend to the King, too.

This was a remarkable thing. How many leaders seriously make themselves accountable? Jehoshaphat practiced fearing God. He practiced turning his religion into obedience. He had already made the same kinds of mistakes his father had. He had already received the same kind of warning from God. He decided that he wanted to be a better king. He wanted a better legacy.

And, one day, Jehoshaphat faced the challenge that would determine that legacy. Three of Israel's ancient enemies to the East banded together for a surprise attack. It was a surprise because these groups hated each other as much as they hated Israel. But they had somehow taped together a temporary alliance to destroy their common ancient enemy. It was so much of a surprise that the enemy wasn't discovered until they had reached En Gedi on the western side of the Dead Sea, only 15 miles away from Jerusalem as the crow flies.

There was simply no time to muster an army. If you adjust for technology, this would be like looking up at the sky on December 7th at Pearl Harbor to see 183 Japanese planes approaching. Jehoshaphat simply had no time to organize an effective response. All he had time to do was to inquire of God's prophets. What should he do? Should he hole up in the fortress of Jerusalem to save the Temple and let the oncoming army completely obliterate the countryside, or should he go out with a woefully inadequate home guard and face them on the field?

Jehoshaphat led a very moving public prayer to the Lord, ending with, "O our God, will you not execute judgment on them? For we are powerless against this great horde that is coming against us. We do not know what to do, but our eyes are on you." (2 Chronicles 20:12)

God's response was to raise up a prophecy through one of the Levite musicians.

> Listen, all Judah and inhabitants of Jerusalem and King Jehoshaphat: Thus says the LORD to you, 'Do not be afraid and do not be dismayed at this great horde, for the battle is not yours but God's.
> Tomorrow go down against them … You will not

> need to fight in this battle. Stand firm, hold your position, and see the salvation of the LORD on your behalf … Do not be afraid and do not be dismayed. Tomorrow go out against them, and the hand the LORD will be with you. (2 Chronicles 20:15-17)

Here was the king's answer. Don't hole up, but instead go out with the men you have. God will fight this battle. All you have to do is show up. All you have to do is fear God. Don't fear them, fear God.

Jehoshaphat decided to fear God. The next day, the king personally led out the home guard, hopelessly outnumbered, to face the approaching army.

God had used a musician to inspire his heart. So at the last minute, he got an idea.

> And when he had taken counsel with the people, he appointed those who were to sing to the LORD and praise him in holy attire, as they went before the army, and say, "Give thanks to the LORD, for his steadfast love endures forever." (2 Chronicles 20:21)

Jehoshaphat was the king of God's people. It was not enough just for him to fear God; the entire army would fear him, too! "And when they began to sing and praise, the LORD set an ambush against the men of Ammon, Moab, and Mount Seir, who had come against Judah, so that they were routed." (2 Chronicles 20:22)

The text goes on to explain that the tenuous alliance among these three nations fell apart at the last minute. Two factions ganged up on the third and after that, they turned on each other. By the time the small Israelite army arrived, the only enemies remaining on the field were already dead.

Jehoshaphat's legacy was profound even in his own day.

And the fear of God came on all the kingdoms of the countries when they heard that the LORD had fought against the enemies of Israel. So the realm of Jehoshaphat was quiet, for his God gave him rest all around. (2 Chronicles 20:29-30)

At his death, it was said that he did "what was right in the sight of the Lord." And even long, long after his reign, his unique musical maneuver became the standard way for Western armies to declare that they feared God more than they feared their enemy.

When it comes to true success in this world, whether in small decisions or in our overall legacy taken as a whole, all we have to do is fear God.

We aren't talking about our essential salvation here. While it is true that saving faith always bears external fruit, God does not require us to leave a stellar legacy in order to be saved. Simple faith, even if undeveloped, even if only the size of a mustard seed, is all that is required. Our salvation depends on Jesus' legacy, not ours.

But we can also build a legacy of our own, a legacy of faith based on openly fearing God. "For God is not unjust so as to overlook your work and the love that you have shown for his name." (Hebrews 6:10)

The phrase "fear God" uses the older meaning of the word "fear." Fear used to mean "healthy respect," in the sense that you want a child to learn a healthy respect for powerful things like fire, or the sea, or the force of Law. The fear of God refers to a fundamental and all-surpassing respect for the Almighty. It means that you count God as the most important factor in any situation, in any confrontation, in any decision. To treat God as less powerful than other forces, to treat his will as less important than that of other people, is to not fear him or respect him as we ought.

A believer should never be afraid of God; he is our Friend, Father and Savior. But we should always fear him in the old sense. For us, his will is more important than the desires of any man or woman. His approval is the most desired outcome in any situation. His power upholds, rules and overrules every other factor. Fearing God is faith in action. It is faith taken outside of religion into the real world.

The tragedy of mankind is that our world does not fear God; the world never does. It does not take him seriously. It confines God within religion.

As a result, people of the world fear other things. They fear political, military and economic power. They fear the disapproval of peers. They fear missing out on something others may have. When God is replaced at the foundation of life by something else, reverent fear collapses and twists into a negative, terrifying thing. Fear takes on its more modern meaning of being afraid. As people's understanding of what makes the world go around turns from God to themselves or the society they create, fear turns from worshipful respect and inspiring admiration into anxiety and terror. Instead of being confidently drawn forward by the fear of God, the world is driven in terror by its fear of man, driven by the need for power—I can't lose face, I can't lose this vote, I dare not lose anything. Driven by the need for prestige—a corner office, titles, a plaque, an Oscar, a gold watch. Driven by the need for the perfect body, driven by the need to experience everything, whether healthy or unhealthy, all for fear that I might miss something. Without the fear of God, the world wastes away in anxiety and dread. Just like Jehoshaphat's father.

Jehoshaphat stared out following his father, keeping his faith boxed in by his religion. But after making some early mistakes, he chose a different way. He chose to practice fearing God in the real world by arranging to hold himself accountable to obey God's laws. Fearing God takes practice, and the practice is daily obedience.

Because Jehoshaphat had practiced obedience in order to learn the fear of God, he was ready when the enemy was at the gates. He calmed himself and sought God's Word. When he discovered God's promises, he treated them as the most important facts before him—more important than his small military reserves, more important than the approaching deadly alliance just hours away.

And when Jehoshaphat took his place at the head of his makeshift army, he realized that someone else was the real Hero of Israel, and he wanted that Hero to be made visible for all to see. So that day, it wasn't the king who led; it was God who led, manifested in the music of praise. And it was God who was glorified that day, the day Jehoshaphat crafted his legacy of faith.

What will it take for us to be successful, Christian? God's love for us is not the issue; it is ours in Christ and it is perfect. It's our growing love for God that is at issue, whether we actually trust him outside the walls of the church. It is the overall legacy that we will leave behind that is at issue. Will our faith make God more visible in this world? Will we treat him as the most important factor in our decisions, in the way we conduct ourselves, in the way we meet the challenges that confront us?

Many in the church can identify with Asa and Jehoshaphat. We started off with a religious heritage gained from our parents. Then we made some mistakes and confined our faith in a religious box. But God's Word has been faithful. It has corrected us, challenged us and encouraged us.

So what shall be our response? Like Asa, shall we throw the prophets in jail, shut them up, restrict our faith to religious services, and trust only in the world's remedies while life rots away? Or, like Jehoshaphat, shall we train ourselves to fear God?

Make no mistake, fearing God takes practice. It means becoming accountable to obey God on a regular, day to day basis. You don't learn to fear God in a crisis—crises bring out what has already been built up inside. We learn to fear God by thoughtfully, intentionally obeying him day after day, after day.

We learn to fear God by becoming accountable to God's Law in our own little kingdom. Rather than just critiquing others while considering ourselves exempt from God's revealed will, we insist that his authority extends to us, too. We practice fearing God by simply obeying him outside the walls of the church—in our personal habits, saying "no" to ungodliness, and in our personal commitments, saying "yes" to unselfish investment. Every day that we neglect conscious obedience to God, we allow the fear of man to sap our inner strength. While each day of joyful accountability muscles the soul with powerful confidence in the Almighty.

It's the crises of life that reveal how well we have practiced. Every life has crises, conflicts, turning points, challenges that reveal just what we truly believe. They arise whenever our well being is seriously threatened. They usually come on suddenly, when our greatest nemeses gang up on us and it seems like everything we've worked for is in danger of collapse: the loss of a job, or even a career, the breakdown of a family, loss of health or mobility, the estrangement of a child, the death of a soul mate, or the death of a dream—even our own impending death. What to do? Try to tough it out relying on whatever worldly schemes and resources we can muster? Curl up behind thick walls and hide, hoping it will all go away? Or …

"You know, I've been practicing the art of living my life in the fear of God, limiting myself over here, extending myself over there in accordance with his written Word, giving him first place. What does he say I should do now? What promises in the Scriptures are relevant to my situation? What commands? What examples? What encouragements? I don't have to be reckless and I don't have to hide my head in the sand either. There is a third option, one that I have been practicing for a long time. I can fear God. I can fear my God and refuse to fear anything else."

When you do that, Christian, you solidify a godly legacy. You assure that your life is going to be successful, and not just in the short-term. You are determining how you are going to be remembered. You are determining how God will remember your life here.

I don't know what fearing God will look like for you. Saying "no" when your boss insists that you falsify a tax report—saying "no" because you fear God more than you fear him. Maintaining your confession of faith in the face of a hostile, mocking college professor—maintaining your confession because you fear God more than you fear her. Choosing to use the Sabbath to rejoice in your Lord, rather than to honor the scheduling desires of others—because you fear God more than you fear social pressure on you and your kids. Facing your social responsibilities with honor, or facing cancer with unshakable hope.

I don't know what fearing God will look like for you as you build your legacy, but I think I know what it will sound like. It will sound like the distant advance of ancient harps, or bagpipes, or fife and drum. It will sound like the music of praise as you face a seemingly unbeatable foe, treating God as the most important factor in the battle—not knowing, but just about to discover, that your battle has already been won.

God Is Always Right

> Trust in the LORD with all your heart, and do not lean on your own understanding. In all your ways acknowledge him, and he will make straight your paths. (Proverbs 3:5-6)

One of the most persistent and enduring images in the Bible is that life is like a journey. Whereas Eastern philosophies tend to view life in terms of repeating cycles, the Bible views world and personal history in a more linear fashion. Life has a beginning and life has a goal, something to which it is moving. Life has purpose, a purpose defined not by us, but by our Creator. The adventure of life is discovering or lining up our sense of purpose with God's purpose for us. In the Bible, a successful life chooses paths that follow God's design. An unsuccessful life goes off course and becomes lost.

Using that analogy, life is a series of traveling decisions, choices of which path to take when you come to a fork in the road. Most of the time, one choice will be better than the other. But we cannot see the future; we cannot look down the road very far—hence the adventure of making decisions. Sometimes our decisions are not the best. We find ourselves on roads that are in ill repair, or going through dark and dangerous places. We need help, therefore, in choosing our paths and recovering our way.

Virtually everyone wants divine guidance on the journey. Ancient cultures had their oracles who searched for divine signs in scattered bones and used tea leaves—some extra help from the gods, a little edge in making good decisions or dealing with the bad ones. The modern world has its own superstitions designed to give the illusion of divine guidance. Most of us know our zodiac sign, and millions of horoscopes are consulted every day, along with tarot cards, Ouija boards, psychic hot lines and fortune cookies. You can even have your palm read over the internet! These attempts at divine guidance parallel the irrational ways that people think about their gods.

Solomon says that divine guidance is truly possible because the Living God is, in contrast, quite rational. Believers in the covenant God of the Bible are not dependent on horoscopes or hunches because the Lord has revealed his mind. He has revealed his thoughts and purposes in a rational way. He has gone to great trouble to intervene in human history, to shape and mold it, revealing his plans in space and time through a clearly defined covenant. Ultimately, he personally fleshed out this covenant by entering this world in human flesh—all that we might know him.

Solomon says that the God of the covenant will help his people choose the best way, which is the way that best pursues his purposes. What God has revealed about himself, about us and about the world is sufficient to always help us choose the best way. Much later, Jesus will tell us that he has given us his Holy Spirit to help us understand how God's revealed truth relates to our situation and how we can apply it effectively. God will even intervene when we choose the wrong path. He is masterful at finding those who are lost on paths that have nothing to do with his purposes. He is great at salvaging our worst course deviations, bringing some good out of our mistakes and getting us back on track in record time. Solomon makes it very clear that the Living God will guide his people. He'll make their path straight.

The problem, then, is not that God is slow to guide. Rather, we tend to be slow to follow.

Solomon warns us not to lean, meaning rely, on our own understanding. All decisions rest on something. In general, we lean our decisions on our best understanding, our best intellectual assessment of the situation using all our education, reasoning and abilities. We rely on past experience, extrapolating future results from past encounters and observations. Sometimes we mix all those things together into something we call "intuition," homogenized from all our inner thoughts and feelings, a deep rooted sense of direction that bubbles up from our subconscious.

Because it seems to come out of nowhere, Christians sometimes assume that their own intuition must be God speaking to them. "You know, I think God must be speaking to me, telling me to do thus and so." No conscious reason—it's just an inner feeling.

Of course, you don't have to be a Christian to have such feelings. Millions of people feel "led" by ancestors, by departed loved ones, by angels, or by their god. It's a common practice to take one's own instincts as divine guidance.

Similarly, some Christians use our text in Proverbs 3 to justify following their own intuition as if it were God's guidance, as if "not leaning on our own understanding" meant avoiding any conscious reliance on reason, and the purest faith would shut down our intellect entirely. ("Use the force, Luke.")

That is exactly what this passage is not saying. How often Solomon tells us in the Book of Proverbs to grow in our conscious understanding of God, and to value such wisdom like gold and silver. Solomon prizes the experience of old age and urges us to explore our purposes so we can aline them with the Lord God. It's true that our intuition is important, because it flags concerns and convictions we have not yet put into words. It is no substitute, however, for conscious understanding of God's will. Solomon consistently urges us to intelligently understand what God has revealed to us. Surely he is not backtracking in this one verse to tell us that we need not bother to think.

Solomon does not bid us to abandon understanding, but rather not to rely on our own understanding. We began our study in the first chapter of this book learning that we cannot define God out of our own head. Solomon assumes that here. We cannot rely on our reason or feelings or intuition alone and apart from God's historic revelation of himself. We need Scripture to correct what we thought we knew and inform us of things we could never know unless God told us. This exercises our intellect and our emotions by guiding them with Scripture.

And I think Solomon takes that notion one step farther. Not only must our intellect and emotions be guided by revelation, but we must also never assume that process is finished. We must not pause in our journey on the road to wisdom, lean only on what we already know and go no further. We must never assume that our quest to know God's mind is over, that we have learned all there is to learn, and that our understanding is now equal to the Almighty's. Solomon urges us to persevere in our quest to learn from and submit to God, always reflecting back to him our best understanding to see if it can be improved.

Given a fork in the road, perhaps we already know enough to know which way to choose. Maybe we can reason it out or draw from our experience with God. Maybe the sum total of our wisdom bubbles up with wise intuition, which upon reflection we can trace back to Scripture. That's wonderful; that's what God wants. He wants us to become more like him.

Solomon's point, however, is that we should not rest on what we already know. The next fork may present subtly different choices, choices that require fresh insights from God's Word. We will need those fresh insights in order for him to direct our paths. Don't rest on what you already know as if that's all there is to know. We must always be learners, and must always allow God's revelation to challenge and direct us.

In other words, whenever there is any discrepancy between our own current understanding and God's revealed Word, then there is no question about which to lean on. God is always right.

You and I may be right a lot, but God is always right. We should approach every situation assuming we have more to learn from him and be willing to choose his revealed will even when it goes against the current state of our intuition. We need the conviction that God is always right.

This conviction does not come easy to us. We have a deep seated tendency to trust our own assessment over God's. We would rather interpret our inner voice as God's voice, rather than do the hard work of studying his revealed Word and sometimes make the difficult choice to trust God's wisdom over our own.

Do we not often give more weight to our reasoning than to God's reasoning? His Word teaches something about marriage or the Sabbath or tithing or whatever it might be, but when what he says is not what we want him to say, we find intellectual arguments to get around the meaning of his words. The Pharisees did that all the time. They could take any Old Testament Law and twist it seven ways so that it applied to everybody else but them. We all do the same thing from time to time, and when we do we are leaning on our own understanding instead of assuming that God is always right.

Sometimes, we give more weight to our experience than to God's experience. Mark Twain once said, "We should be careful to get out of an experience only the wisdom that is in it—and stop there; lest we be like the cat that sits down on a hot stove lid. She will never sit on a hot stove lid again—and that is well; but also she will never sit down on a cold one anymore." In other words, we tend to overplay our experience. When we get burned in a relationship or burned in a job, we will hopefully learn something worth learning. But sometimes we apply that lesson to every other relationship or job, even when the situations are entirely different. God, however, has helped his people through every conceivable situation, millions of times. His experience is far more trustworthy. But, like Mark Twain's cat, we want to interpret our limited experience in universal terms. We know it all. "No Lord, you couldn't possibly want me to do thus and so. I've tried that before, and it didn't work—or I've watched others try it, and it didn't work for them." And so we lean on our own limited understanding, refusing to move on and learn something new, refusing to believe God is always right.

When you think about it, it is the essence of sin to give our desires and preferences and even our tastes greater importance than God's revealed plans and purposes. We act as though it were up to us to determine what makes us happy, when he is the one who designed us. "What the Bible says about this couldn't possibly make me happy; therefore, I will choose to believe that God's will is something that makes more sense to me." We often lean on our own understanding rather than trust that God is always right.

The bottom line is that we sometimes baptize our intuition and christen it, "Divine Guidance." After rationalizing our questionable logic, and weighing our experience far beyond what it is worth, and sneaking in our own clandestine desires under the table, we fashion an intuitive sense of what we want and choose that path, regardless of what God's Word says about it.

Truly, our intuition is very important. It's a precious thing. It's a growing thing. God wants it to be like his. We will often sense the truth of a situation before we can put it into words that apply the Scriptures. But the fact remains that it's our intuition, not God's. When we are tempted to say something like "I'm going to do this because I feel that God is leading me to do this," we must be certain to first submit our feelings to God's written revelation.

Otherwise, we will cut short our journey toward wisdom. Leaning on our own understanding can be dangerous.

Why, then, do we do it? Solomon tells us that the issue is trust. "Trust in the LORD with all your heart, and do not lean on your own understanding." The root of all sin and all error, the reason we get lost and choose horrible paths for ourselves, is our refusal to trust God. The Bible says that sin entered the world because our first parents believed the lies of Satan about God's character. That distrust of their Creator hardened in their hearts as their souls took shape, and that distrust has been passed down to every single human being (with only one exception). It is, therefore, much harder to trust God than you or I may think. We are born with a built-in predisposition to choose our own paths. We would rather deal with life on our own. We are dealing with an instinct introduced into the human soul by the devil.

In fact, when a person begins to trust God again, the change is so radical the Bible calls it conversion. Conversion is a response to sovereign grace smashing into our train wreck. The Lord lifts us out of the wreckage and brings us home to himself. That was the message of John the Baptist, announcing the coming of Christ.

> The voice of one crying in the wilderness: "Prepare the way of the Lord, make his paths straight. Every valley shall be filled, and every mountain and hill shall be made low, and the crooked shall become straight, and the rough places shall become level ways, and all flesh shall see the salvation of God." (Luke 3:4-5)

Jesus is famous for saying, "I am the way, and the truth, and the life. No one comes to the Father except through me." (John 14:6) Jesus' truth and life are the way out of the collapsed rubble of our lives, the way back to God.

Has that ever happened to you? Has Jesus ever cut his way to you, calling "Follow me; I'll get you out of this"? Have you ever turned from your hopeless entrapment and followed him? Solomon knew that the Lord made a highway for Israel out of Egyptian slavery, and realized that God does the same thing for everyone in his covenant of grace. Solomon urges you to practice the trust that began when God saved you. Once the Lord has cut a path to get you out of danger, don't stop. Don't say, "Lord, thanks a lot. I can take it from here. I can lean on my own understanding now."

No, God is always right. "In all your ways acknowledge him." Apply the same gospel and the same trust you had at your conversion to every decision you have to make. "Therefore, as you received Christ Jesus the Lord, so walk in him, rooted and built up in him and established in the faith, just as you were taught, abounding in thanksgiving." (Colossians 2:6-7)

Let your understanding grow. Continue to believe and act according to what God has revealed—even when your thoughts aren't there yet, because his thoughts are higher than your thoughts—even when your intuition isn't there yet, because his ways are higher than your ways. Trust him. It's trusting in your own thoughts and intuitions that got you lost to begin with. Jesus cut a road out for you. Trust God now and don't stop following, leaning only on the understanding you have picked up so far. Add to it. Assume there is always more to learn. Acknowledging God in all our ways means trusting that God is always right in every decision you ever make.

Prayer is a good place to begin. Prayer is how you tell God you trust him and that you will follow him if he shows you how. Don't put off praying until after you have already made up your mind about what to do. You don't have to already know the best path, or be able to tell God exactly what he has to do for you. In prayer, don't lean on you own understanding. Rather, acknowledge God in everything. Explain to the Lord your best take of the situation, and then ask him to perfect your understanding. Open your heart to correction and deeper insight. Above all, tell God that you trust him—or if you don't trust him just now, confess to him that you don't but you deeply want to.

And along with prayer, meditate on God's Word. Biblical meditation is not Eastern meditation, in which you empty your mind. Biblical meditation is filling your mind with what you've learned from the Bible, chewing on it, turning it over, examining it from every angle, trying to fit it into your current situation. Biblical meditation is like digging for gold or silver ore. It's a lot of work and it takes a lot of time. What you discover has to be processed and purified in the heat of trial and sometimes error.

Here is where the Holy Spirit really shines. He comes alongside to guide us to understand the same revelation he originally inspired. The less you know of God's Word, quite frankly, the fewer insights he can give you. But take heart, because you probably know more than you think. You know the Golden Rule, some of the Ten Commandments and the Sermon on the Mount. You know the simple gospel that in Jesus, God became man to save you. You may even know the Lord's Prayer. You already know a lot. The Holy Spirit takes the truth of whatever of God's revelation you have stored in your mind, and he illumines it, shines light on it. He helps you refine it. He helps you believe it. He helps you apply it.

The Holy Spirit will work with you now, and he will keep working with you over the years to get it right. As a result, you understand God's mind better now than you did five years ago, and you are going to understand it five years from now better than you do at this point. You actually develop an ongoing, lifelong conversation with God. As you read his Word, he reveals truth; he speaks to you his mind. As you pray concerning every decision and every situation, you tell God you trust him and want to trust him better. You review with God what you know, but you don't just rest on what you know. You ask God for more. And the Holy Spirit answers your prayers by giving you new insights and applications from the truth you have packed away in your heart. Your understanding of God's mind grows, but you are never satisfied, you never rest, you never simply lean on what you already know. You ask God the Holy Spirit for more and more and more insight … and he gives you more and more and more insight!

To keep yourself honest, it's always good to consult often with godly friends because they are often more objective about your challenges, just as you are often more objective about theirs. If you really are gaining insights into God's mind, they will probably be able to affirm it.

And when you do know God's mind in any matter, choose it, embrace it, act on it. You may sense down deep in your soul that it is right and good; it may feel very comfortable intuitively. But even if it rubs your intuition the wrong way, choose God's understanding, revealed in Christ and his Word and his Spirit; choose it over yours. Live by the conviction that God is always right.

How seriously should I take this conviction? Well, how much do you want God to guide you? How much do you want to prosper? "The way of the wicked is an abomination to the LORD, but he loves him who pursues righteousness." (Proverbs 15:19) How much do you want to avoid the pain and expense of messing up and having to retrace your steps over and over again? "Teach me your way, O LORD, and lead me on a level path." (Psalm 27:11) How much security do you long for? "The highway of the upright turns aside from evil; whoever guards his way preserves his life." (Proverbs 16:17)

God Almighty will make your paths straight to whatever degree you are willing to trust in him with all your heart, not leaning on your understanding. To whatever degree you acknowledge him in all your ways, through submissive prayer, honest meditation, and choosing his will as you best understand it.

That kind of trust leads to safe and straight paths. I'm sure Solomon remembered the prayer of his father, David,

> He made my feet like the feet of a deer and set me secure on the heights. He trains my hands for war, so that my arms can bend a bow of bronze. You have given me the shield of your salvation, and your gentleness made me great. (2 Samuel 22:34-37)

And one more thing: practicing trust in God also helps you deal with wrong decisions, too—times when you haven't acknowledged him and have gotten into serious trouble. Remember that the Lord God knows when we are ready to truly repent, turn around and trust him again, and he will lead us out.

After Israel sinned so grievously against the Lord and was exiled to other nations across a vast desert, they repented. Separated from their homeland by a burning desert, they prayed to God, acknowledged him and sought to follow him afresh. The Lord's response? "Prepare the way for the people; build up, build up the highway; clear it of stones." (Isaiah 62:10)

> The wilderness and the dry land shall be glad; the desert shall rejoice and blossom like the crocus; it shall blossom abundantly and rejoice with joy and singing ... And a highway shall be there, and it shall be called the Way of Holiness ... And the ransomed

of the LORD shall return and come to Zion with singing; everlasting joy shall be upon their heads; they shall obtain gladness and joy, and sorrow and sighing shall flee away. (Isaiah 35:1-10)

God can make such a highway for you in your wilderness. No matter how badly you have sinned, no matter how much time you have wasted, God can cause gladness to overtake you so that your sorrow and sighing flee away …

If you're willing to trust him. Are you? Are you willing to stop leaning on your own understanding, as if you knew it all? Are you willing to admit it was your immature rationalizations that got you into this mess? Are you willing to acknowledge God in all your ways? Affirming that God is right in those very matters where you have substituted your intuition for his Word? Are you willing to make whatever changes you need to make?

And then, are you willing to trust him enough to accept his forgiveness? Are you willing to believe that you are completely clean and forever free? Are you ready to take his path and walk away from your guilt?

"Trust in the LORD with all your heart, and do not lean on your own understanding. In all your ways acknowledge him, and he will make straight your paths." This is a fundamental conviction concerning divine guidance, directing us in every decision and helping us whenever we get lost. God is always right.

What does such living faith look like? …

Joseph

Now Joseph was handsome in form and appearance. And after a time his master's wife cast her eyes on Joseph and said, "Lie with me."

> But he refused and said to his master's wife, "Behold, because of me my master has no concern about anything in the house, and he has put everything that he has in my charge. He is not greater in this house than I am, nor has he kept back anything from me except you, because you are his wife. How then can I do this great wickedness and sin against God?"
>
> And as she spoke to Joseph day after day, he would not listen to her, to lie beside her or to be with her. (Genesis 39:6-10)

A famine was coming, an unexpected famine proceeded by years of prosperity, something like the stock market crash of 1929. A seven year famine was coming like an undetected, slow moving Tsunami that would soon swallow the eastern Mediterranean with hungry death. In great cities, thousands would perish.

In Beersheba of southern Canaan, there was little vegetation in the best seasons, so the family of Abraham didn't stand a chance. Yet, they had to survive. They had to. God chose that family to function as a conduit of salvation. The Old Testament is their story, their genealogy, their history. The Old Testament tells how God preserved this family, who would later grow into a nation. As this terrible famine began to cook in Earth's atmosphere, the Lord instituted a plan to preserve his covenant people—a plan that involved a beloved son of Jacob, the man who was renamed "Israel." It was God's purpose to raise up his son Joseph as a "type," or model, of Christ, whose greater salvation would later fulfill all the promises of this great covenant of grace.

Joseph knew the Lord had called him to something special and given him prophetic insight into God's mind, but there is no indication that Joseph understood any of the details of his future role. Quite the contrary, for him life seemed to spin completely out of control. The favor that he received from God and from his father Jacob led to the worst kind of sibling rivalry. Your brothers and sisters may sometimes have a hard time tolerating you, but hopefully they would not sell you into slavery. That's what Joseph's brothers did to him. They almost killed him, but decided instead to sell him to a passing caravan bound to Egypt. There, he became a slave in the household of Potiphar, chief of Pharaoh's guards.

Joseph simply could not control the events of his life. The only way he could live out his faith was to always take the next obvious step of obedience. So, Joseph concentrated on obeying God on a day-to-day basis. In Potiphar's house, that meant focusing on becoming the best servant he could possibly be. He became such a faithful servant, in fact, that Potiphar entrusted to him all his possessions.

That's when things got complicated. Remember the line from *The Graduate*, "Gee, Mrs. Robinson, if I didn't know better, I'd think you were trying to seduce me." Potiphar's wife was bored; with her husband gone so much, she wanted to play. The text reads as if she was used to getting her way, too, so it probably wasn't the first time. What a temptation for a healthy and single young man, the fun of sex and the implied promise that it would do his career no harm.

How would giving himself to his boss's wife impact God's design for his life? Joseph didn't know. I suppose he could have moped and thought that if being an Egyptian slave was the best God had for him, what difference would it make? But he didn't. He assumed that God was still leading him and the only way to follow was one step of obedience at a time. And in this instance, the next step was obvious. "How then can I do this great wickedness and sin against God?"

The result of his purity was that Potiphar's wife had Joseph thrown into jail. How would rotting in jail get Joseph any closer to God's purposes for him? He didn't know, so he decided to keep following God one step at a time. He couldn't chart any course for the future, so he tried hard to obey God every day, every single day, just where he was. He became not only a model prisoner, but an exceptionally helpful and useful one. He used his considerable management skills so well that he became the warden's helper, a person of considerable internal freedom and influence.

It was in his capacity as warden's helper that he heard two fellow prisoners discussing their dreams. Joseph was gifted in interpreting dreams, and he explained to them that one would be released and restored to favor, the other beheaded. And that is exactly what happened. (The interpretation of dreams was a form of prophecy.)

Two years later, the surviving man was released and returned to his service to Pharaoh. He saw that his Master was deeply troubled by one of his own dreams. The King was convinced God was speaking to him, but he didn't know what God was saying. The former prisoner remembered Joseph, so he was brought from prison. Joseph interpreted the dream to reveal an approaching famine of huge proportions, and how Egypt could prepare for it. Joseph became the early warning system for this tsunami of a disaster. Pharaoh appreciated Joseph's interpretation so much that he gave him almost unlimited authority to implement it. Before long, Joseph became one of the highest officials in the administration.

This is more than just a curious story. At the end of this completely unpredictable turn of events, Joseph was in the perfect position to save his Hebrew family from starvation and thus preserve the progress of God's salvation.

God's wonderful plan for Joseph did not come to pass because Joseph devised a clever scheme to pull it off. Rather, one small step at a time, in every decision of obedience, whether small or great, Joseph lived by the conviction, "God is always right." If Joseph had chosen to sleep with Potiphar's wife, his position in that family would have remained secure. Joseph might have had a nice life and never have been thrown into prison. But prison was the only place he could have become known to the man who later recommended him to Pharaoh. If Joseph had tried to figure out how God wanted him to be happy, instead of simply assuming that God is always right, he would have unknowingly traded a place in the Egyptian court for a little illicit sex and security. More importantly, he would have forfeited his role in saving his Hebrew family so that one day, Jesus Christ would be born.

This story reminds us that God has a plan, a calling for each of his children in Christ. His plan for us may not be as grandiose as Joseph's, but it is equally divine in its design. He has a plan for how each of us can be blessed to take part in what God is doing in this age. "For we are his workmanship, created in Christ Jesus for good works, which God prepared beforehand, that we should walk in them." (Ephesians 2:10)

It is part of Christian faith and hope that not only can God bless me, but the blessing he has in mind is not a small self-centered thing designed for my enjoyment alone. It is something bigger than I. It's a way to glorify him by blessing others.

God has designed specific ways that my life can shine. That level of blessing is not for us to define, for we did not create ourselves. God created us for his good pleasure. He designed our personalities and best strengths. He placed us in the family and the century he wished, thus defining our opportunities.

How will all this work out? How will my strengths and my opportunities flow together into the best ways that I can glorify God? We don't know that until the situations present themselves. God knows, but he's not telling. "The secret things belong to the LORD our God, but the things that are revealed belong to us and to our children forever, that we may do all the words of this law." (Deuteronomy 29:29)

God does not reveal to most of us, ahead of time, the exact part he has written for us to play in bringing him eternal glory. The works he has prepared in advance for us to do—whether raising a nation from calamity, or raising a ministry in a local church, or raising one single child for Christ who will go on to do other things for him—we will know what God has designed us for only when we see it.

Discovering your own, unique calling is one of the great adventures for the believer. It is the adventure of divine guidance. Not that you will be forced to play your own glorious role. It is our choice whether or not to do these good works. If we refuse, God will find another way to glorify himself in our generation. Remember Esther …

> If you keep silent at this time, relief and deliverance
> will rise for the Jews from another place, but you
> and your father's house will perish. And who
> knows whether you have not come to the kingdom
> for such a time as this? (Esther 4:14)

The good works God has designed for us to accomplish are dependent on our spiritual gifts and talents, our place in history, our family and church, and the issues of our day. The scope of these works may not be as grand as Joseph's, but they are all wonderful because they glorify God.

How do we find and accomplish these works? How do we find the path that leads to the fulfillment of God's design for us? This is what guidance is really all about.

But many people aren't the slightest bit interested in that kind of divine guidance. They have no idea that God would enable them to accomplish things that he has planned, things of eternal value. Most folks have been sold a bill of goods by a world that has no room for God. This world takes the good and pleasant things of life and tears them out of their divinely ordained sockets and makes them ends in themselves. The sex discussed in our text is an obvious example. The world rips it out of its socket of life-long committed love and building a family, and makes it an end in itself. God is all for sex. He invented it! He is all for education, a good job, influence, a good salary. But none of these good things make for an adequate substitute for God's plan and God's glory.

> Thus says the LORD: "Let not the wise man boast in his wisdom, let not the mighty man boast in his might, let not the rich man boast in his riches, but let him who boasts boast in this, that he understands and knows me, that I am the LORD who practices steadfast love, justice, and righteousness in the earth. For in these things I delight, declares the LORD." (Jeremiah 9:23-24)

Even Christians make the mistake of seeking good things for their own sake, without regard for God's plan for them. Christian kids can leave home thinking that the goal of life is to get a good job so they can have lots of things, even though Jesus said,

> Do not be anxious about your life, what you will eat or what you will drink .... Is not life more than food, and the body more than clothing? (Matthew 6:25)

Many can't understand what Jesus is talking about because they assume that God's guidance is supposed to advance *their* agenda, instead of *God's*. We want God to guide us to goals we devise, rather than simply obey what God has commanded, and watch him lead us to the goals he designed.

How easy it would have been for Joseph to exchange God's perfect will for something that either felt good or seemed safe. He could have had sex with Potiphar's wife and maintained a cushy job for years. He certainly would have avoided jail ... and along with it, any opportunity to become second in command in Egypt, with the power to save his family and keep the promise of salvation alive for millions, including you and me.

You may ask, "Pastor, how could Joseph have known all that God would do in that prison?" The answer is that Joseph could not have known. He wasn't supposed to know ahead of time. The secret things really do belong to the LORD our God. It is only the things he has revealed that belong to us, so that we can focus on obeying everything we know to be his will. Joseph didn't have to know God's secret plans to bless him. All Joseph had to do was to follow his Lord one step of obedience at a time, simply doing what God has said is his will.

The point, of course, is not that if we make one little mistake, one sin, we lose God's perfect will; it doesn't work that way. The point is that our small, daily choices to follow God are what guidance is really all about. Not focusing on what we can't know, but focusing on what we already know that God wants. Not seeking guidance as much as assuming it—trusting God to guide us.

Only later, after we have followed God in obedience in a hundred small ways, perhaps over many years, can we begin to see the pattern, begin to see how God has led us. It was not until God had exalted Joseph to immense power in Egypt and used him to save thousands of Egyptian lives, not until Joseph saw his brothers who sold him into slavery arriving for food, not until then did he realize what God had done. He said to his brothers,

> Do not be distressed or angry with yourselves because you sold me here, for God sent me before you to preserve life. For the famine has been in the land these two years, and there are yet five years in which there will be neither plowing nor harvest. And God sent me before you to preserve for you a remnant on earth, and to keep alive for you many survivors. So it was not you who sent me here, but God. (Genesis 45:5-8)

How did Joseph get to this place? Was it by adopting his own goals for life and doing whatever it took to achieve them? Rather, it was by believing at every step that God was guiding him to something good, and moving toward that goal by assuming in every specific decision that God is always right.

God has placed a treasure on the path of righteousness that he has laid out for each of us. For some it is a large treasure, for some it is smaller. In each case, however, it is something of everlasting value. If I disregard God's clearly marked path and set off on my own to follow worldly dreams of conquest, I will find nothing which I may ultimately keep. But if I simply stay on God's path, I will find an eternal treasure suitable for me.

What is God's path? It is called his Law: the Ten Commandments, the Sermon on the Mount, all the teachings of Scripture. It's all the will of God that the Holy Spirit prompts me to love in my heart. Like the command to avoid adultery, these things have been revealed. These same things will guide each of us along our own personal path; for I will apply them in my family, my career and my ministry and you will follow them in your family, your career and your ministry. As we travel, you and I will be tempted with sin—tempted not only in the sense of pursuing evil, but also tempted in the sense of swerving off the path in search of treasure, off the way that leads to fulfilling our purpose of glorifying God with the lives he gave us.

If Joseph had chosen sin when he was tempted, he would never have been cast into jail where God had the treasure waiting. Joseph didn't know where the treasure was. He wasn't expected to know, but he did know how to find it. He just had to assume, in every decision, that God is always right.

In this, Joseph was a model of Christ, wasn't he? It was God's plan for Jesus to be the Savior prophesied in the Old Testament. To accomplish that, all Jesus had to do was to obey his Father. Who would think that becoming a hero involved a cross? But Jesus kept his focus on doing his Father's will. "My Father, if it be possible, let this cup pass from me; nevertheless, not as I will, but as you will." (Matthew 26:39)

Earlier, Satan tempted him to consider attractive shortcuts. But in the end, Jesus knew that the only question was whether his Father was right. As a man, Jesus would find his glory by letting obedience lead him to it. "Although he was a son, he learned obedience through what he suffered." (Hebrews 5:8)

> And being found in human form, he humbled himself by becoming obedient to the point of death, even death on a cross. Therefore God has highly exalted him and bestowed on him the name that is above every name, so that at the name of Jesus every knee should bow, in heaven and on earth and under the earth, and every tongue confess that Jesus Christ is Lord, to the glory of God the Father. (Philippians 2:8-11)

For all eternity, Jesus will glorify God more than anyone else because, when the hard decision had to be made, he didn't exchange his Father's will for a fabricated substitute. He chose to believe that God is always right.

Christian, guidance is what your life is about, every day. You may be fooled into thinking that you only need guidance when you want to get from A to B, or when you pick out a goal for yourself and you want God to help you get there. But that is not what guidance is. Joseph teaches us that guidance is not something we initiate. It's not a heavenly GPS service we use to punch in a destination and get driving instructions. Guidance is something God initiates. God initiated it when, in his workmanship, he created you in Christ Jesus to do good works, which he prepared in advance for you to do. We are guided by God when, through consistent obedience, we accomplish those good works.

"The LORD is my shepherd … He leads me beside still waters … He leads me in paths of righteousness for his name's sake." (Psalm 23:1-3) You don't have to convince or cajole your shepherd to guide you. You don't even have to ask him to guide. That's what he does. Sheep don't have to tell the Good Shepherd where to go. Jesus' sheep follow him down paths of righteousness.

Beware the temptation to dwell on how you wish God would bless you, because it is so easy then to exchange God's treasure for something so much less. It's a temptation to trade what God has planned to accomplish through you to his glory, for whatever you feel would make you happy. Imagine if Joseph had done that! Ask any young man with raging hormones what he feels like he wants, and you may not get a particularly spiritual answer. Joseph didn't fall for that trick. He didn't try to negotiate what he wanted in life. He knew what he wanted; he wanted what God wanted for him. God is always right, and Joseph was determined to follow him regardless of the immediate consequences.

Imagine life as a game show. Door Number One is labeled "God's design" for how you can be a great blessing. Door Number One remains covered. To claim it, all you have to do is walk over and open it up, and then it's yours. However, the world throws back the curtain of Door Number Two to reveal ... a new car! It gleams with a powerful engine, sporty lines, and an estimated retail value of $56,500. You can have it simply by choosing to ignore the path of righteousness and take a different path. Walk over there and take the keys.

I bought a new car a few years back. Transportation is necessary and new cars can be fun. But would I really want to trade all that God has prepared for me by ignoring his revealed will in order to grasp such a thing for free? True, Door Number One is covered. It might lead to prison or some other form of difficult obedience. Yes, it might. But if it does, then that's where I will find my treasure.

Christian, don't fall into the temptation of trading away God's design for something less. How about this: instead of occasionally seeking God's guidance to help you get from A to B, why not assume God is a Shepherd who is guiding you every day, even right now? To where? That's a secret. That's a secret thing in the Shepherd's mind. But he has revealed all we need to know in order to follow him there. God is guiding you, Christian. He hasn't specified to you the exact destination and he hasn't warned you of some of the difficult terrain, but the next step is right in front of you. If you honestly allow his word to saturate your soul, you know what the next step is. The next step may not be glamorous. How glamorous was it for Joseph to work at being an excellent Egyptian slave? How glamorous were his years in prison, working hard to be an excellent prisoner?

Joseph could have left the path for something much more glamorous. Instead, he found the good works God had prepared for him to do just by believing God is always right.

Christt Is Worth It

And they sang a new song, saying, "Worthy are you
to take the scroll and to open its seals, for you were
slain, and by your blood you ransomed people for
God from every tribe and language and people and
nation, and you have made them a kingdom and
priests to our God, and they shall reign on the
earth." (Revelation 5:9-10)

The Lord God gave the Apostle John a visionary look at the
future. Not newsreel footage of future events, and not a crystal
ball to allow John to see whatever he wished or answer personal
questions. But rather, a vision of unforgettable images depicting
God's plan for this world.

Chapters 4-5 of Revelation are a vision of heaven, reminiscent
of Daniel's less detailed vision of the Ancient of Days. (Daniel
7:9-10) John sees God in terms of a great rainbow-surrounded
throne. This is not a vision of God in the abstract. It is a vision of
God accomplishing his purpose and plan for the world—a plan
God is holding in his hand. "I saw in the right hand of him who
was seated on the throne a scroll written within and on the back,
sealed with seven seals." (Revelation 5:1)

This image is grounded in the first century AD. Today, such a
vision would not picture a scroll but some other information
device, a book or electronic tablet. This scroll contains so much
information that it is written on both sides. A scroll sealed with
seven seals suggests a legal instrument, an official decree. This is
God's detailed plan and purpose for mankind.

The Bible teaches that mankind is the pinnacle of God's
creation. In design, very good, each human being a creature of
inestimable worth. But the Bible also teaches that mankind is
tragically, insufferably fallen—prone to trade the glory of God for

a whim, guilty of every conceivable sin and without the integrity even to honor our own conscience. "Your iniquities have made a separation between you and your God, and your sins have hidden his face from you." (Isaiah 59:2)

Human existence has become an exquisite agony. We have the aspiration to reach for the stars. But if we ever reached them, we would bring with us the same greed, war and lust we pursue here.

Human life is not what God originally intended it to be. He designed us to transform this planet into a place of ever-increasing beauty and productivity, where human death is unknown. That is not what it has become. As Moses once sang,

> You sweep them away as with a flood; they are like a dream, like grass that is renewed in the morning: in the morning it flourishes and is renewed; in the evening it fades and withers.
>
> For we are brought to an end by your anger; by your wrath we are dismayed. You have set our iniquities before you, our secret sins in the light of your presence. For all our days pass away under your wrath; we bring our years to an end like a sigh. The years of our life are seventy, or even by reason of strength eighty; yet their span is but toil and trouble; they are soon gone, and we fly away. (Psalm 90:5-10)

In the right hand of him who sat on the throne, John saw God's answer to our exquisite agony. Written on that scroll was the way out of sin and death. Written on that scroll was all the judgment of God, a judgment perfectly measured to obliterate sin from the earth forever. And God's blessing was also written. The scroll detailed a salvation that shields sinners from the judgment they deserve, and transforms them into people who build a world according to his design.

Every religion seeks some way out of the mess we are in. But no religion devised by man can bring together God's judgment and his blessing. Without judgment, sin wins, but without blessing, sin takes us down with it. Written on a sealed scroll, this vision portrays the merging of judgment and blessing, of righteousness and mercy.

The plan is in God's hand. But who can accomplish it? A call goes forth for a human being to accomplish God's will on earth as it is in heaven.

> And I saw a mighty angel proclaiming with a loud voice, "Who is worthy to open the scroll and break its seals?"
>
> And no one in heaven or on earth or under the earth was able to open the scroll or to look into it, and I began to weep loudly because no one was found worthy to open the scroll or to look into it. (Revelation 5:2-4)

English mythology pictures this vision in terms of a sword in a stone. My first introduction to the Arthurian legends was The Once and Future King, T. H. White's adaptation of Sir Thomas Mallory's tales. The way T. H. White puts it, a young squire accompanies his master to London, where a sword is magically embedded with the inscription: "Whoso Pulleth Out This Sword of the Stone and Anvil, is Rightwise King Born of All England." The greatest knights of England were unable, unworthy to pull it free.

The dramatic scene in heaven is similar, except that before the throne of God Almighty, the issue is a bit larger: Who is worthy to lead a redeemed humanity? Who can execute a judgment that burns out sin completely, yet without singeing a hair of any who belong to the Lord God? This is exactly the impossible promise God made long ago.

> Fear not, for I have redeemed you; I have called you by name, you are mine … when you walk through fire you shall not be burned, and the flame shall not consume you.
>
> For I am the LORD your God, the Holy One of Israel, your Savior … Because you are precious in my eyes, and honored, and I love you … bring my sons from afar and my daughters from the end of the earth, everyone who is called by my name, whom I created for my glory, whom I formed and made. (Isaiah 43:1-7)

Who can deliver sinners through a judgment hot enough to destroy them? "And one of the elders said to me, 'Weep no more; behold, the Lion of the tribe of Judah, the Root of David, has conquered, so that he can open the scroll and its seven seals.'" (Revelation 5:5)

There is one human being worthy to break the seals and open the scroll. Worthy to bring God's people through the fires of his holy justice unharmed. Worthy to pull the sword out of the stone.

In an earlier chapter, we explored how Jesus is both divine and human, the Lord God incarnate. We are not surprised, then, to see him identified by two striking images. The first, a lion. "The Lion of the tribe of Judah, the Root of David, has conquered, so that he can open the scroll and its seven seals." (Revelation 5:5) When Abraham's grandson Jacob blessed his sons, he said,

> Judah is a lion's cub; from the prey, my son, you have gone up. He stooped down; he crouched as a lion and as a lioness; who dares rouse him? The

scepter shall not depart from Judah, nor the ruler's staff from between his feet, until tribute comes to him; and to him shall be the obedience of the peoples. (Genesis 49:9-10)

Judah was blessed to become the ancestor of a great ruler. He would not only rule the twelve tribes of Israel, but "to him shall be the obedience of the peoples". A true LionHeart. Much later, the Apostle Paul spoke of him to Gentile audiences:

The times of ignorance God overlooked, but know he commands all people everywhere to repent, because he has fixed a day on which he will judge the world in righteousness by a man whom he has appointed; and of this he has given assurance to all by raising him from the dead. (Acts 17:30-31)

Jesus is the universal ruler appointed by God to execute divine judgment over the entire world. Jesus will judge the world with God's righteousness.

But how will this Lion spare God's people from the condemnation they deserve along with the rest of the world? This brings us to the second vivid image: a lamb.

And between the throne and the four living creatures and among the elders I saw a Lamb standing, as though it had been slain, with seven horns and with seven eyes, which are the seven spirits of God sent out into all the earth. (Revelation 5:6)

When John looked to see this Lion, what he actually saw standing before the throne was a Lamb. This unusual Lamb has seven horns representing all authority in heaven and on earth. He has seven eyes representing the Spirit of God in all his awareness, knowledge and presence.

But the most striking thing about the Lamb is that his throat is cut. The Lamb looks as if it had been slaughtered, yet is alive; a clear reference to the death of Jesus on the cross and his subsequent resurrection. It is through this death, a death which has been overcome, that he has accomplished God's plan. Christ is *qualified to accomplish* God's will because of who he is, God incarnate. He *actually accomplished* that will through what he did in his death and resurrection.

> And they sang a new song, saying, "Worthy are you to take the scroll and to open its seals, for you were slain, and by your blood you ransomed people for God from every tribe and language and people and nation, and you have made them a kingdom and priests to our God, and they shall reign on the earth." (Revelation 5:9-10)

Jesus Christ is worthy to open the scroll because he was slain. His death was redemptive. It was substitutionary, meaning that he died in the place of others. He went through the fires of divine judgment on their behalf. In God's eyes, it's as if everyone "in Christ" by faith went through those fires. But because he went through them as their substitute, none of them will be burned. He's done the seemingly impossible. He's executed judgment and brought blessing, both at the same time! "Steadfast love and faithfulness meet; righteousness and peace kiss each other. Faithfulness springs up from the ground, and righteousness looks down from the sky." (Psalm 85:10-11)

Those who are redeemed in this way come not only from Israel, but from "every tribe and language and people and nation." He has made them a new kingdom, one without national boundaries but defined instead by a common priesthood and service to the Living God. Christ founded the only kingdom destined to remain and continue, when all other nations dissolve in the unstoppable cleansing fire of God's judgment.

"And when he had taken the scroll, the four living creatures and the twenty-four elders fell down before the Lamb, reach holding a harp." (Revelation 5:8) It is fitting that the praise of the church is mentioned first, because the Lamb's work delivers us from sin and death and hell. But the scene unfolds like the climax of a movie, ever widening, as the roar of applause and shouts of praise crescendo.

> Then I looked, and I heard around the throne and the living creatures and the elders the voice of many angels, numbering myriads of myriads and thousands of thousands, saying with a loud voice, "Worthy is the Lamb who was slain, to receive power and wealth and wisdom and might and honor and glory and blessing!" (Revelation 5:11-12)

The view pans out to millions of angels, a heavenly host we know so little about. They see God accomplishing his will through creatures of dust, by becoming one of us. They see Christ transform humility and humiliation into glory, and they explode in overwhelming praise.

> And I heard every creature in heaven and on earth and under the earth and in the sea, and all that is in them, saying, "To him who sits on the throne and to the Lamb be blessing and honor and glory and might forever and ever!" (Revelation 5:13)

We forget how much the other creatures of our world have suffered because of us, and how much all creation has longed for someone to open that scroll and make things right again.

As T. H. White told the story, the young squire named Arthur forgot to bring his master's sword for the tournament. The inn was locked, but he noticed in the empty churchyard a strange sword stuck in an anvil. It had words inscribed that he did not think to read. He thought he would borrow it for his master's use, so he went over to take it …

> There was a kind of rushing noise…all around the churchyard there were hundreds of old friends. They rose over the church wall all together…there were badgers and nightingales and vulgar crows and hares and wild geese and falcons and fishes and dogs and dainty unicorns and solitary wasps and corkindrills and hedgehogs and griffins …They loomed around the church wall…and they all spoke solemnly in turn…"Come along, Homo sapiens, for all we humble friends of yours are waiting here to cheer."
>
> [He] walked up to the great sword…. put out his right hand softly and drew it out as gently as from a scabbard. (The Once and Future King)

Imagine the cheer in John's vision as all the earth's creatures proclaim Jesus the rightwise King of a new, eternal kingdom where righteousness reigns!

The overwhelming worthiness of Jesus is the mainspring of a Christian's life. It gives energy far beyond mere religious habit or self-control. It motivates sacrifice and holiness and immense joy.

But ironically, as in our text, it is a conviction forged from tears of despair. We are born into a world of hurt, and start out believing we can fix it. We believe we can make life what it ought to be, if not for the whole world, then at least in my little corner of it. Surely, I can fulfill my dreams if I try hard enough. I can unroll my life like a scroll decreeing one blessing after another. I can wrench my life from the hand of God, break any seal and create a personal paradise out of this wilderness.

Every time you have lifted your hand to oppose evil or reduce suffering, you have attempted to break one of those seals. From the day you opposed an elementary school bully or first tried to raise money for a good cause, to whatever you do today to craft political solutions or soothe the loneliness of old age. As you battle for the souls of your children and, indeed, fight desperate battles for integrity in your own soul, you are trying to dig your fingernails under the first seal. You are trying to release a divine plan to stamp out evil and establish righteous peace. You know it has to be done, you have to try.

Each time you have attempted to make life what it ought to be, every time you have tried to build joy and satisfaction for yourself and others, you have hopefully placed your hand on the hilt of the sword to draw it out. From sacred wedding vows, to the miracle of giving birth, to crafting memories, to building a career, to pursuing a cause that makes some lasting difference in this world, you and I have strained to budge that sword. We've tried to bring God's will to pass, to stamp out evil and the misery it generates and make the world what it ought to be.

But, "who is worthy to open the scroll and break its seals?" Each one of us has tried and we have failed. We have sensed that the worthiness is not in us. We've tried to accomplish with brute strength and force of will what only holiness can achieve. Sooner or later, we drop exhausted to the ground, and the tears are real. "No one in heaven or on earth or under the earth was able to open the scroll or to look into it."

It is a hard thing to face reality and realize that you are not worthy to open the scroll. You can't turn the world into a paradise. You can't build a tiny corner of paradise. You can't even keep death from your own doorstep. You feel it brush you at the funerals of family and friends. You realize that even if you came close to accomplishing your dreams, they will die with you, giving way to the equally transient efforts of others.

What makes a person finally realize that he or she cannot open the scroll? For me, it was the intellectual impact of seeing my worldview disintegrate. For others, it's the shock of having a key relationship break, or a goal fall apart to which you gave your all. For some, it's when death taps them on the shoulder with a very serious disease. For others, it's just accumulated weariness. However it comes, the utter despair of finally realizing that you cannot make life right is a blow to the spirit. I remember it very well. As John saw this vision, he found it so vivid that he could not help weeping all over again. He tasted the bitter realization that the human race is not going to make it.

The one who weeps like that is ready to hear the gospel. "Weep no more; behold, the Lion of the tribe of Judah, the Root of David, has conquered, so that he can open the scroll and its seven seals.'" Behold the worthiness of Jesus Christ! The paradise we cannot build, he can build. The sin and misery we cannot overcome, he can overcome. Through his death and resurrection, he earned the right to break the seals. Already, the scroll is unrolling. Already the judgments of God are tasted in this world, each new calamity another warning to repent. Already the blessings of God are tasted in this world, as a new kingdom of priests rises to live in harmony with God and each other.

Jesus has purchased a kingdom with his own blood and he is calling it together. And at his return, Christ will accomplish fully everything that we could not accomplish, creating a world without violence and hunger, filled with people without vanity and weakness.

Living faith in the worthiness of Jesus Christ puts an end to our weeping. The truth of who Christ is, what he has done, is doing and is going to do sets us singing. "Worthy is the Lamb who was slain, to receive power and wealth and wisdom and might and honor and glory and blessing!"

What does such living faith look like? ...

Stephen

> Now when they heard these things they were enraged, and they ground their teeth at him. But he, full of the Holy Spirit, gazed into heaven and saw the glory of God, and Jesus standing at the right hand of God. And he said, "Behold, I see the heavens opened, and the Son of Man standing at the right hand of God."
>
> But they cried out with a loud voice and stopped their ears and rushed together at him. Then they cast him out of the city and stoned him. And the witnesses laid down their garments at the feet of a young man named Saul. And as they were stoning Stephen, he called out, "Lord Jesus, receive my spirit." And falling to his knees he cried out with a loud voice, "Lord, do not hold this sin against them." And when he had said this, he fell asleep. (Acts 7:54-60)

A week before I originally outlined this chapter, the superintendent of the Air Force Academy acknowledged to a group of Jewish leaders that religious intolerance had permeated the school. A report of the Americans United for the Separation of

185

Church and State declared that "the promotion of a culture of official religious intolerance is pervasive, systematic and evident." Ninety percent of the students at the Academy identify themselves as Christian. It is common knowledge that many born again Christians are on staff and administration. These evangelicals were charged with promoting a culture of intolerance toward non-Christians. Some examples included two cases of non-evangelicals being dissuaded from attending the academy because of religious pressure, discrimination in granting passes to off-campus religious activities and one case of an improper rotation of a non-evangelical chaplain to Japan. CNN cited students putting up posters of Mel Gibson's movie *The Passion* in the cafeteria, using email to promote the movie and attempting to proselytize other students by sharing the gospel with them—implying or stating outright that Jesus is the only way to God. One official said he was confident he could stamp out this problem in six years.

In response, it occurs to me that abusive religion is more about abuse than it is about religion. Discrimination about granting passes, for example, would be characteristic of prejudicial leadership rather than spiritual doctrine. The subsequent official investigation found that no outright or intentional religious discrimination had taken place at the Academy, but I certainly agree that truly abusive practices should be exposed and disciplined wherever and whenever they occur.

Notice, however, that CNN took matters a very different and dangerous step further by declaring that the simple affirmation that a particular religion is actually *true* is abusive.

Our society's concept of tolerance and intolerance is radically changing. To "tolerate" comes from the Latin *tolerare*, to endure pain, or to put up with the existence of something one does not like or agree with. Conversely, discriminating against or demeaning people who don't agree with you has always been intolerant.

Refusal to allow the co-existence of those you do not agree with is intolerant. Some of the charges against evangelicals at the Air Force Academy seemed to fall into that category, which is why an investigation was in order. The logic of the complaint against them was that intolerance should not be tolerated. That makes sense.

But a student simply sharing his or her personal faith that Jesus is the only way to God is not intolerant behavior. Sharing an opinion does not refuse to allow the coexistence of other opinions. That does not treat people of other beliefs with disrespect or challenge their right to hold their opinions. Rather, it is the refusal to allow the expression of deep personal faith which is, in fact, intolerant.

Our contemporary conflict is reflected in the New Testament's experience of Stephen. Consider his strong Christian opinions …

> You stiff-necked people, uncircumcised in heart and ears, you always resist the Holy Spirit. As your fathers did, so do you. Which of the prophets did your fathers not persecute? And they killed those who announced beforehand the coming of the Righteous One, whom you have now betrayed and murdered, you who received the law as delivered by angels and did not keep it. (Acts 7:51-53)

Stephen believed in Jesus Christ, and to believe in Jesus is to accept a biblical view of ourselves and of history that is not flattering. When Stephen was challenged to explain the personal faith behind his healing ministry, he did so honestly. He didn't hide that which would offend the sensibilities of his accusers.

The result was violent. "They cried out with a loud voice and stopped their ears and rushed together at him. Then they cast him out of the city and stoned him."

So, who in this story is intolerant? Who is unable to allow the existence of another point of view? Stephen, who honestly and clearly speaks his mind, or the Sanhedrin and their mob who illegally stone him to death in a fit of anger? Having a point of view that challenges others does not make Stephen intolerant. Intolerance is the Sanhedrin and their supporters not allowing anyone to challenge them. That is why I'm concerned in our day when "intolerance" is used to describe deeply held *personal* opinions, while not used to describe *official* attempts to "stamp them out."

Having said that, the Bible seems more concerned about raising up a faith able to endure intolerance rather than one concerned only with avoiding it. Living faith can be willing die for the gospel.

Stephen could surely have avoided this terrible end so very easily. Stephen could have throttled back his rhetoric and public ministry of healing. That may sound unspiritual, but if you knew that you would be shot if you went to the hospital one more time to heal cancer patients, wouldn't you be tempted to stay home? Or Stephen could have simply declined to talk about his faith. If saying that Jesus healed these people was offensive because Jesus had recently been crucified, then maybe he could just say "God did it," and let it go at that. Or when brought before the Sanhedrin, he could have denied false charges and downplayed his faith. He would have gone home that night to his wife and kids.

But Stephen did none of those things. He didn't stop doing good. The good he did, he did in Jesus' name. When they asked him what he believed, he told them clearly and unambiguously, knowing full well, I think, that it could cost him.

Stephen reminds us that genuine suffering is a price Christians must often pay to believe in Jesus. That's not the sort of thing you hear much about today. We rather focus on how Jesus meets our deepest needs (because he does). We stress the abundant life that is ours in Christ (because it is sweet). But the Apostle Paul also taught, "It has been granted to you that for the sake of Christ you should not only believe in him but also suffer for his sake." (Philippians 1:29)

Perhaps one reason we avoid this teaching is because it has at times been misused in the past, as if there were something good or meritorious in suffering itself. We reject such deformed thinking, but may in the process neglect the significance of suffering altogether. Some believers in history have thought suffering to be virtuous in itself, and therefore created their own suffering, such as whipping themselves or wearing canvass. Some aspired to develop wounds in their hands to imitate the wounds of Christ, just for the privilege of suffering similar wounds.

But the Bible does not teach the value of suffering for its own sake. For example, in an earlier-quoted Philippians passage about the necessity of Christian suffering, the context is about maintaining unity and love while enduring the opposition of intolerant folks outside the church. When the Bible commends suffering, God is not recommending self-inflicted pain; he is admiring calluses that come from hard work toward worthwhile accomplishments. The point is not to artificially seek rough skin. The point is to do the hard work that makes one's calluses a mark of character.

If a Christian follows Christ in this world, then he or she will of necessity have to endure or suffer in the process. The Christian will have to tolerate difficulty and pain. The reason is perfectly simple: in a world where every path is imperfect and twisted, with so many potholes and so much broken glass, the journey to do good is costly. If the world were perfect, love would be easy and fun. But as it is, love is often costly and painful. In a world with so many sharp edges, it is costly to love a child from infancy to adulthood, to love one spouse until death parts you, to love a country enough to defend it or to correct it, to love business superiors who will use you as soon as care for you, to love the church that will one day be a spiritual cathedral when it is still something of a warehouse of hurting and healing souls. Love is costly. Therefore, while suffering for its own sake is foolishness and self-deception, to suffer the cost of love is a noble thing. The calluses of love are marks of faith.

Stephen's soul was covered with the calluses of love. We first meet Stephen in the previous chapter, where we read of an ethnic problem in the early church. As widows came to Christ, they left the charity of the Temple and became dependent on the new Christian church structure for support. Among these Jewish widows were women of local descent who spoke Hebrew, and also women whose cultural roots were Greek or Hellenistic. This is a clear example of the ethnic division that made up the new movement. Apparently, the Hellenistic widows believed that they were not being treated equally with the locally raised Hebraic widows. It is important to understand that the problem was not simply an administrative one of collecting and distributing food. It was that, but it was also an ethnic problem involving possible discrimination.

The apostles were determined to neutralize any potential discrimination in the church. Their solution was to ask the congregation to elect seven men, called "servants" (*deaconos* in the Greek) to solve the problem. It's obvious that they could use good administrators. But the official qualifications were "seven men of good repute, full of the Spirit and of wisdom." (Acts 6:3)

How interesting to note that the first deacons all had Hellenistic names (Acts 6:5), implying that seven members from the minority were elected to solve the problem. One of them was Stephen.

Successfully bringing these two divergent ethnic groups together was the first crucial challenge faced by the new church. Had they failed, had ethnic pride and hypocrisy won the day, the church would have been critically hamstrung. As it was, the result was truly impressive. "The word of God continued to increase, and the number of the disciples multiplied greatly in Jerusalem, and a great many of the priests became obedient to the faith." (Acts 6:7)

Try to imagine, given our own experience of racial tension, the work required to successfully deal with this challenge. Imagine the patient teaching that had to be repeated over and over. Imagine the long hours invested in listening—listening to stories of injustice, bitter memories, anger against "those people," anger against specific individuals. Imagine Stephen mastering his own prejudice, and then dealing with prejudice against him as he reaches out to Hebraic families. Imagine Stephen dealing with charges of ethnic treason from his own Hellenist friends. How many long days did he invest, days of repeated kindness and generosity? How many hours, how many nights absent from his own family? Imagine the practical challenge of setting up policies and procedures for a massive new spiritual community and training people to run it well. The debates, the appeals, the tears, the use of humor—all that it takes to win over one person at a time to love "the other side." So much labor that when he was done, many Temple priests—from the same group that had so recently felt threatened by Jesus—came to faith because they had never seen this kind of reconciling love before.

Stephen's soul was full of beautiful calluses. Every day during those months he devoted himself to mending the congregation, efforts so important that God blessed them with miraculous signs and healings. Every day, Stephen chose to give a little more of himself, a little more of his life to Christ. These were not religious gestures of devotion. Stephen literally gave away a little more of his life each day by paying the price to love.

In his service to Christ, Stephen got used to the self denial required in order to love people. Not all relationships require self sacrifice, of course, but those that don't are not in the category the Bible describes as "love." In this world, among fallen people, love is costly. The cost is in caring, and in hours of time and money, and prayer on your knees, and perseverance when progress is slow, and forgiveness when you are the convenient brunt of another's frustration.

What inspires this love is Christ, himself. The Holy Spirit "opens our eyes" to reveal Jesus to our spirit. This begins when the Holy Spirit makes Jesus visible to us on the cross. Of course, the cross is a one-time, historical event. Christ died for our sins once and for all; he doesn't die over and over each day. The Holy Spirit opens our eyes to the cross by enabling us to appreciate the historical cross afresh every day. As we taste his past suffering love for us, we are motivated by a profound gratitude to imitate him.

Then, the Holy Spirit enables us to see the risen Christ at our side today. The risen Jesus is located in heaven, but through his Spirit, he is genuinely present with us wherever we are. When we are faced with the challenges of loving and ministering to another person, the Holy Spirit enables us to see Jesus at our side. We see Jesus reaching out across some chasm ripping people apart. We see him in front of us reaching out, and then turning back to urge us to follow him. "Come on, just one more step; take one more small step of love. Go just a little further with me than you've ever gone before. I know it hurts. I know the cost of suffering, but the cost is worth it. I know that, too. You were worth it to me."

The suffering inspired by faith is about learning to love each other alongside of Jesus Christ, because he is worth it. As Paul put it, "I rejoice in my sufferings for your sake, and in my flesh I am filling up what is lacking in Christ's afflictions for the sake of his body, that is, the church." (Colossians 1:24) While nothing was lacking in Christ's cross to save us, there is still plenty of suffering we are privileged to share as he brings God's love to others.

I can't quite imagine being in mortal danger because of my faith, remaining true to preaching and living the gospel even though the people around me will not tolerate it. Being willing to die seems such a giant step up for my faith. For Stephen, however, it was different, because every day for some time, Stephen had been taking small steps of self-sacrifice to follow Jesus. Over the months before, Christ had reached out to bring healing, forgiveness and reconciliation to church factions lost in suspicion and bitter hatred. Day after day, Jesus stood just a step or two ahead, "Come on Stephen; take just one more step with me. Absorb with me just a little more of the cost of love." And Stephen responded with his eyes on Christ, "Yes, Lord, you are worthy of one more step."

So, when it finally came to it, Stephen made the surprising discovery that dying for Christ was no longer a huge leap. It was just one more, one last, step. And once again, he could take that step because he could see Jesus just out in front. "Full of the Holy Spirit, [Stephen] gazed into heaven and saw the glory of God, and Jesus standing pat the right hand of God. And he said, 'Behold, I see the heavens opened, and the Son of Man standing at the right hand of God.'" And as he took that last step to come alongside his Lord, he found himself naturally repeating Jesus' own sentiment from the cross, "Lord, do not hold this sin against them."

God have mercy on his church when we are intolerant of others. God have mercy to chasten and teach us better when we kill people over land we call holy, conduct inquisitions of torture, cover up sex crimes, make coworkers or neighbors or fellow students feel socially unacceptable because they do not share our faith.

But may we never collapse under the intolerance of others who will not share the world with people who believe as we do. Who today tell us to shut up, and tomorrow may decide to silence us.

> Since we have the same spirit of faith according to what has been written, "I believed, and so I spoke," we also believe, and so we also speak, knowing that he who raised the Lord Jesus will raise us also with Jesus and bring us with you into his presence … So we do not lose heart. Though our outer self is wasting away, our inner self is being renewed day by day. For this light momentary affliction is preparing for us an eternal weight of glory beyond all comparison. (2 Corinthians 4:13-17)

Living faith believes Christ is worth it, despite the "light and momentary affliction" that may arise out of it.

Remember, Stephen is not dead the way the unbelieving world thinks of death. His spirit is literally alive and doing quite well, thank you. He awaits the literal resurrection of his body, when loving will no longer be painful. Considered up to the present day, how much of Stephen's existence was spent in costly love? Assume he was fifty years old when he was killed. Alive now in heaven, he has so far existed over two thousand years. This means that his life of loving suffering was only 2.5% of his whole existence—that percentage shrinking all the time. In other words, up to now, Stephen has spent 2.5% of his life bearing the pain of love and 97.5% of it in bliss with Christ—and true glory is still to come at Christ's return! That's why Paul said, "I consider that the sufferings of this present time are not worth comparing with the glory that is to be revealed to us." (Romans 8:18)

There are probably many things, many decisions and actions that Stephen would wish he could erase or do differently over his lifespan in the first century, but the suffering required to love the widows of the church and start the congregation off to a glorious future, and that last hour of faithfulness under a hail of stones— I'll bet those are exactly the days and moments that he treasures most right now. Because, in the end, it is God who will write the history books, and God who will determine what deserves to be remembered. Already, millions upon millions have thrilled to Stephen's faith. It is that kind of suffering with Christ that will be remembered forever, when all the other stuff is long forgotten.

God uses such faith to turn around and transform even those most resistant to the gospel. Like the Temple priests who became Christians upon seeing Stephen's work. And like the young student who held the coats of those who stoned Stephen to death. A young man who later became known as the Apostle Paul. His participation in Stephen's murder never left his mind. He later wrote,

> I thank him who has given me strength, Christ Jesus our Lord, because he judged me faithful, appointing me to his service, though formerly I was a blasphemer, persecutor, and insolent opponent ... Christ Jesus came into the world to save sinners, of whom I am the foremost. But I received mercy for

this reason, that in me, as the foremost, Jesus Christ might display his perfect patience as an example to those who were to believe in him for eternal life. (1 Timothy 1:12-16)

In his own day, Stephen's life touched hundreds of people for Christ. But through Paul's conversion, the impact of Stephens' death is incalculable.

Living faith embraces the cost of loving alongside of Jesus Christ. Others may not always tolerate such faith, but we Christians are called to tolerate the cost of loving them, anyway. After all, Jesus stands just ahead of us, reaching out to them but looking back to us saying, "Come on, just one more step. Follow me." When all other motivations fail, it's that vision of Christ that enables us to take the next step, even if it's our last one.

Living faith looks like Stephen, gazing into heaven, sustained on earth by the One who is worth it.

I Can Make This World A Better Place

> Awake, O sleeper, and arise from the dead, and
> Christ will shine on you. (Ephesians 5:14)

In the days of the early church, the church's hymnbook was the Old Testament Book of Psalms, but Christians also began to sing new songs. The new music would sound dry and dusty to us today, but at the time it was cutting edge, a creative stretch to the traditional mindset. In the text introducing this chapter, Paul quotes a bit from what may have been one of those songs, "Awake, O sleeper, and arise from the dead, and Christ will shine on you."

It's a song about resurrection, but not Christ's resurrection or even the resurrection of the body at the last day. The verses that precede it deal with how we should live today. Paul characterizes the Christian life as an experience of light in darkness. "At one time you were darkness, but now you are light in the Lord. Walk as children of light (for the fruit of light is found in all that is good and right and true)." (Ephesians 5:8-10)

Then he quotes a new Christian song to poetically celebrate the "resurrection" or awakening of the soul, when a believer comes to faith and begins to live in the light of Christ's glory. It's a song about what Jesus called being "born again." Saving faith comes from a soul that has been raised by God from the dead—reborn, made alive.

The Bible says that humanity died spiritually long ago. Since then, we are born with souls that are alive to this world, but not alive to God. When it comes to God, our souls are born dead, or unresponsive. Whatever inner sense is needed to perceive God accurately is a sense that is dead in us, all of us. We can see the world, but we cannot see the Creator. He is dark, unknown and unknowable. We can imagine God, but we cannot see him or know him.

Plunged into spiritual darkness, life is a mystery. A mystery sometimes grand and glorious, but often fearful and dangerous. We set up whatever small campfire that either reason or superstition can ignite in order to push the darkness back a few yards and avoid losing ourselves in the shadows. But our little games in the fire circle—accumulating bric-a-brac, scratching out and defending our personal space—sustain lives that do not know what or why life is.

And then, Jesus touches the soul. He calls our name, and we awaken! "Awake, O sleeper, and arise from the dead, and Christ will shine on you." When a person is born again by an act of God on his soul, it's like waking up from a lifetime of sleep. The ever-present darkness is gone. The campfire of desperate philosophy and superstition smolders unattended because everything is bright. Not only do we see Christ shining before us, but in his light we also see the whole world for the first time. The church's song sings about rising from the dead, waking up to a new morning. The whole world is illuminated by Christ.

Faith in Christ makes life make sense. Faith in him not only explains the world as it is now, but it also reveals to us how things ought to be, how they were designed to be and shall be again one day—and therefore, how they could be now, at least in part. Faith in Christ colors every thing and every person with meaning and significance. Jesus reconciles born again individuals with God and begins to weave relationships between believers. You begin to see how every person and every thing in the universe is part of his design—how it all ought to work, how it is broken, and how it can be fixed.

When you are born again, all of life becomes part of a new spiritual calling to serve and glorify God, a calling that extends far beyond religion to everything you are. You don't just see the sun streaming through a beautiful stained glass window at church; you leave the church to find the sun shining everywhere.

Paul goes on to immediately write, "Look carefully then how you walk, not as unwise but as wise." (Ephesians 5:15) When your soul rises from the dead, you want to get on with the business of living. You want to take care of how you live, not in the sense of being tentative or fearful, but in the sense that you want to go after life thoughtfully, wisely and well. You're tired of wasting time and energy and resources. Everything is too important now, too precious to waste. God is involved in everything you touch and that touches you. The fallen world wants to waste its precious time with petty schemes and trivial pursuits that mean nothing in the long run. You don't want to waste any more of your life that way. You want to make the most of every opportunity to live as God intended you to live. You want to cast off the petty selfishness that has shaped so much of life thus far. You want to use every day, every relationship, every role you have to glorify God.

"Therefore do not be foolish, but understand what the will of the Lord is." (Ephesians 5:17) Sometimes, we look at "the Lord's will" as the magic answer to a specific problem, but Paul comprehends the idea much more broadly to describe God's design for living. God's will is for us to shine in a way the brings the blessings of faith into the fallen world's darkness. That's why Paul goes on from here in Ephesians to talk about the primary roles of family and career through the end of Chapter 5 and into Chapter 6. A risen soul wakes up to find that Jesus has transformed every personal role into a grand new spiritual calling. It's not just prophets, priests and kings who have callings from God. When Christ calls your soul to life, you receive a divine calling that embraces everything you are.

This is the way to understand Paul's comments about marriage later in vv. 21-33. Because our society is undergoing a revolution concerning gender roles, we tend to view Paul's comments about marriage as focused on that topic. It is more helpful, however, to remember the point Paul is developing. Awakened souls are called to bring the light of Christ into their marriage to make it a model of Christ and the church.

> Husbands, love your wives, as Christ loved the church and gave himself up for her, that he might sanctify her, having cleansed her by the washing of water with the word, so that he might present the church to himself in splendor, without spot or wrinkle or any such thing, that she might be holy and without blemish. (Ephesians 5:25-27)

Marriage is a divine calling involving a man and a woman committed to glorifying Jesus Christ together. The husband's role is explicit: do whatever he can and pay any price to make his wife spiritually radiant. That's part of his divine calling.

> Wives, submit to your own husbands, as to the Lord. For the husband is the head of the wife even as Christ is the head of the church, his body, and is himself its Savior. Now as the church submits to Christ, so also wives should submit in everything to their husbands. (Ephesians 5:22-24)

Wives are told to submit to how the husbands are called to lead. Just as the church must submit to having our feet lovingly washed by the Savior who calls his church to be the light of the world, wives are called to submit to their husband's encouragement to shine in faith.

We live in an age that seems to know nothing about this kind of unique relationship. Our society has almost completely lost the concept of marriage as a holy calling for two people to radiate the love and righteousness of Jesus. In our society, marriage is a social contract made between two people for mutual convenience and pleasure, resulting in a tug of war over who is in control. The church often has little to add to this besides innocuous platitudes, and when evangelicals do wish to press a point, we tend to harp on a husband's "authority" over his wife.

Against all this, Paul declares that when you wake up in Christ, you see marriage in a different light. Rather than a tug of war over authority, it becomes a shared divine calling that involves not two people but rather two people and God. It becomes the principle testing ground, laboratory and workshop of faith. Marriage becomes a holy calling when Christ wakes us from the dead. Husbands are called to lead in submitting to Christ; wives are called to follow their husband's lead and do exactly the same thing.

Paul then extends his application to parenting.

> Children, obey your parents in the Lord, for this is right. "Honor your father and mother" (this is the first commandment with a promise), "that it may go well with you and that you may live long in the land." (Ephesians 6:1-3)

Teaching children to honor parents kindles a trust and obedience that can one day develop into a mature and healthy faith in God.

Teaching children to obey in a healthy way makes it easier for them to take God seriously and treat him as preeminent. Any home that builds itself around its children is working to ruin them, because this world was not built for them. Rather, it is built for the Living God. Children will only discover what their lives are about by exalting God.

"Fathers, do not provoke your children to anger, but bring them up in the discipline and instruction of the Lord." (Ephesians 6:4) Proper spiritual training in the home is empowering and delightful. As children bond to parents, they learn how to bond with the Lord. Children learn from their parents how to rest in God's acceptance and rely on his good will and competence.

Good parental training can inspire love and confidence, and we dare not neglect it because we are too busy. Any home that builds itself around parental convenience is working to ruin its children, because the world was not built for parents. Rather it is built for the Living God. That's something parents need to revel in and teach their children to celebrate.

When you wake up and see that all things exist from, by, and for the Lord God—when you lose everything in that way—you are primed to get it all back the way you were meant to have it. In Christ, the Lord God wants to share everything with us, everything there is. But on his terms, terms in which genuine love and righteousness are the norm. The parent/child relationship is where we can begin to learn all that.

Finally, Paul applies our new calling to our careers.

> Bondservants, obey your earthly masters with fear and trembling, with a sincere heart, as you would Christ, not by the way of eye-service, as people-pleasers, but as bondservants of Christ, doing the will of God from the heart, rendering service with a good will as to the Lord and not to man, knowing that whatever good anyone does, this he will receive back from the Lord, whether he is a bondservant or is free. (Ephesians 6:5-8)

Forms of slavery were, perhaps, the most difficult careers, so it is helpful that Paul tackles that in his illustration. Paul says that our careers become part of our spiritual calling when we treat our jobs as opportunities to explore and accomplish God's will. Remember, "God's will" is more than just a sporadic answer to questions we think to ask. God's will is his design for living as a human being. God's will is what we wake up to when Jesus raises our spirits to life. God's will is righteousness and integrity; God's will is mercy, kindness and compassion. God's will is loyalty and good will and patience. Because our spiritual calling embraces our careers, God's will is to do good to and for our employer, regardless of how he/she treats us. We are not just working for the boss anymore; in all things we are working for Jesus Christ!

> Masters, do the same to them, and stop your threatening, knowing that he who is both their Master and yours is in heaven, and that there is no partiality with him. (Ephesians 6:9)

Christians in authority also have a holy calling. Christian masters are to "do the same," treating Christ as their boss, too. No matter how much authority a Christian has in any organization, he/she is never higher than middle management, with Christ as the President and CEO who sets the workplace policy which they must carry out.

Apparently, faith in Christ changes every human institution in which Christians participate. Different societies do things differently, but Christians should have a positive impact in each one. If Christ is shining on us, we bring his light to wherever we are. The new life God gives me isn't left on a coat hanger in church; I wear it all the time, in every role I have—church, family, work, community—everything.

We know that we have been called to life by God when our spirit wakes up to live alongside the living Jesus Christ. We know that the world will not be fully mended until Christ is finished calling people to himself. But we have received a holy calling to bring blessing through every role we have. As a result, it's not just that God is planning to renew the world on the Last Day. We are also working right now to replicate his design in our corner of the world, inevitably making it a better place. In a sense, Christians naturally materialize some of the world's future glory ahead of time. Why? Because that is the kind of people we are becoming as Jesus shines on us. Dogs dig, cats clean their fur; people awakened by Christ's Spirit embrace a holy calling to reshape their world and make it a better place. It's who we are. If that's not you, then ask God to wake you up!

When I was born again, I awakened to a life in which every role is part of a great spiritual calling. My calling is a wheel in which many spokes radiate out from God's life in me, including church, marriage, parenting, career and citizenship. I used to pursue all these roles in the dark, doing pretty much as society told me, or as I pleased. Not much purpose, no coordination, going through life in a daze, waiting for the next thing to happen. Then Jesus woke me up! "Awake, O sleeper, and arise from the dead, and Christ will shine on you." I realized that the whole thing, life itself, has a purpose. Glorifying God is why I was made! Through Jesus, God woke me up. He didn't want me to sleep through the renewal of all things. I'm to be a part of it all. So now, everything in my life is part of my calling.

My marriage is now a place where I cultivate God's glory in this world. It's where I learn about love and forgiveness and fairness. It's where I learn to manage money, and to express God's compassion and justice. In my marriage, I will make this world a better place.

His kingdom will start growing in my home. Raising the child God entrusts to me is a huge part of my calling. I won't just have kids to satisfy my desire to make people in my image. Raising children is where I get to see people I love begin to take on God's image. Here is where the glorious gospel prepares my child to shine. Here is where we learn to bow together before the Almighty. Here is where we learn that there is no limit to God's love. Here is where we learn that no sin can destroy us if we'll repent, turn around, and come home. In my parenting, I am making this world a better place.

I'm also going to reflect Christ in my church, in the love and ministry we craft together. I'm going to reflect Christ in my career and in my influence as a citizen. In everything, I'm called to reflect Christ's light around me and make a better place of this world.

For this is a world with little love and even less righteousness, a world where people hide their brokenness beneath pleasantries. I am called to reflect Christ to people so broken that I can get scraped just by brushing past them. Into this darkness I am called to bring light, bringing into my sphere of influence Jesus' wisdom, integrity, mercy and love.

God has one of his agents working in the places I travel every day … and it's me! I'm making the world a better place right there, bringing the fragrance of heaven under everyone's noses, doing whatever I can to help others prosper in ways that really count.

"Awake, O sleeper, and arise from the dead, and Christ will shine on you."

What does such living faith look like? …

Zaccheus

> Jesus entered Jericho and was passing through. And
> behold, there was a man named Zaccheus. He was
> a chief tax collector and was rich. And he was
> seeking to see who Jesus was, but on account of the
> crowd he could not, because he was small in stature.
> So he ran on ahead and climbed up into a sycamore
> tree to see him, for he was about to pass that way.
>
> And when Jesus came to the place, he looked up
> and said to him, "Zaccheus, hurry and come down,
> for I must stay at your house today." So he hurried
> and came down and received him joyfully. And
> when they saw it, they all grumbled, "He has gone
> in to be the guest of a man who is a sinner."
>
> And Zaccheus stood and said to the Lord,
> "Behold, Lord, the half of my goods I give to the
> poor. And if I have defrauded anyone of anything, I
> restore it fourfold."
>
> And Jesus said to him, "Today salvation has come
> to this house, since he also is a son of Abraham. For
> the Son of Man came to seek and to save the
> lost." (Luke 19:1-10)

Rome had an interesting way of collecting taxes. It farmed the
collection of taxes to locals who bought the role at a fixed yearly
price. This price represented the tax Rome anticipated from a
given district. What the local "tax farmers" actually bought for
this price was the right to levy taxes in a district—taxes on all
goods bought or sold or transported through the territory.
Therefore, tax districts tended to center around key trade
intersections. There were three such districts in Israel, centered at
Caesarea, Capernaum and Jericho. (You might remember that

Jesus encountered a tax collector at Capernaum named Levi, whose name he changed to Matthew when the man became his disciple.) Administratively, each district was managed by a chief tax collector who bought a district from the tax farmers and then sublet taxation rights to local tax gatherers.

How were tax rates computed? That's the interesting part. Rome didn't care. All they cared about were the fixed prices paid by the tax farmers. There were no fixed tax rates. They were set by the local tax collectors so as to meet their quota. In practice, this meant that each tax collector levied whatever the local traffic would bear. If you didn't like it, you could do business in another district. Tax collectors were hated because they were virtual extortionists. They were official leeches who used their authority to bleed an area dry, charging as much as they could without actually putting people out of business. The local merchant had no recourse because tax collectors were backed by Roman authority.

Another reason they were hated is that they were locals who worked for Rome in this despicable fashion. They were Jews who got very rich by oppressing their brothers. They were despised as traitors and excommunicated from the synagogues.

Jericho was the hub of a lucrative trade district linking Damascus, Tyre and Sidon to the north, with Egypt to the south and Caesarea and Joppa to the West. The text tells us that Zacchaeus was the chief tax collector of Jericho. In terms of money, therefore, Zacchaeus was probably the most wealthy Jew in town. In terms of social standing, however, he was at the bottom. His very name dripped of hypocrisy; Zacchaeus means "righteous one," but there was nothing righteous about this traitor to Israel. Every business felt his oppression. Every family loathed him as he walked by in his ill-gotten splendor. Zacchaeus had sold his soul for gold; the city knew it and he knew it. He was even unwelcome in the synagogue. I'm sure he socialized with other unpopular powers that be, but no decent citizen would spend time with him or his family.

When we think of lost souls, we sometimes think of the "down and out," the poor, the homeless, the helpless ones stewing in their own ignorance and addictions. Zacchaeus is an example of the "up and out" lost soul. He had everything money could buy. But he had no real friends, nobody close who was not there to leach off of him. His family was isolated, he was isolated.

I'm sure this was not the kind of life he had envisioned in the synagogue as a boy. There, he learned who God is and how we are supposed to be like him. He learned that God loves righteousness and hates wickedness. He also learned of the gracious and loving covenant made for those who trusted and followed God. But somewhere along the way, he had chosen a different path. God had not deserted him, but he had deserted God. As a result, life had turned out both better and worse than he had expected. He had become somebody important, but no longer knew who he was. He was lost; he needed God and he knew it, but he had chosen to leave God behind and it was too late to go back ... or was it?

Word had it that Jesus was coming through Jericho on his way to Jerusalem. Everyone had heard of Jesus: his miracles, his power over demons, his power to put people in touch with God again. All kinds of people. Zacchaeus was the most powerful man in Jericho and pulled a lot of strings. Any other important visitor, any other mover and shaker of society would have stopped at Zacchaeus' house so they could grease each other's palms. How ironic that the holy man he most wanted to meet was the person he was least likely to meet, because the chief tax collector was the most infamous sinner in Jericho.

Still, Zacchaeus had to at least see the man. The problem was that Jesus was always surrounded by crowds wherever he went, crowds that moved with him through town. Zacchaeus was a short fellow, and it would be humiliating to try to press through the crowd. No one would make way for him out of courtesy. So, Zacchaeus went ahead and climbed a tree to station himself where the procession would pass. There he waited. Eventually, the crowd turned the corner and approached. The figure in the center was Jesus. The tax collector must have focused very intently on the one man who could help him, yet whom he could not reach.

"Zacchaeus, come down."

"What? Is he calling my name?"

"Zacchaeus, come down, I must stay at your house today."

"This holy man wants to stay with me? He called me by name. He knows who I am and he still wants to visit? He still wants … me?" As he climbed down, he could probably hear the townsfolk murmuring. "Of all people, Jesus wants to spend time with that one!" "Why does he want to waste his time with such a sinner?" The crowd parted as the master approached the base of the tree.

Sometimes, you see an unexpected opportunity open up right in front of you, perhaps an opportunity for a job or a relationship, and you know that the future direction of your life depends on what you do next. This was one such opportunity, an opportunity straight from God himself. Zacchaeus looked at Jesus and saw in him another chance to reach out for God's blessing, another chance to become the kind of person God wanted when he made this man called "Zacchaeus," the righteous one. Christ offered another path, another way, another life. He was another path, another way, another life. It isn't obvious whether the next statement was declared instantly or after an evening with Jesus, but the tax collector's choice was crystal clear: "Look, Lord! Here and now I give half of my possessions to the poor, and if I have cheated anybody out of anything, I will pay back four times the amount."

A simple gesture of kindness and grace from Jesus enabled this man to repent. A perfect illustration of how real repentance works. "God's kindness is meant to lead you to repentance." (Romans 2:4)

I wonder if most of us really understand repentance. Surely, turning around and changing your mind about life involves sorrow for the past, and we can easily imagine that in quiet moments, Zacchaeus would grieve over his lost years.

At its root, however, true repentance is more about joy than about grief. It is like choosing to walk out of prison when God unlocks the door. Are you sad to have wasted time in prison? Are you ashamed that you deserved to be imprisoned? Of course. But sadness is swallowed up when the door swings open. You are pardoned and you go free.

In that moment under the tree, Zacchaeus turned a corner. New motivations spawned by gratitude welled to the surface. The calcified shell of selfishness broke apart and Zacchaeus began to breathe the free air of generosity, the desire to make the world he formerly pillaged a better place. In that moment, the whole direction of his career changed. Zacchaeus publicly admitted what the whole town knew was true: he had been a cheat and a liar. Before any policy manual is rewritten, Zacchaeus is changing the way he does business.

"From now on, I'm not going to cheat anyone, ever again. From now on, I'm going to be the man God meant me to be: Zacchaeus, the righteous one. I'm taking responsibility for my past misdeeds and focusing on how I can contribute to this district."

This is more than just turning over a new leaf; this is accepting responsibility for all the old leaves too. In Leviticus and Numbers, the Old Testament demands a twenty percent penalty when you cheat or extort someone. Exodus demands paying back double for theft. Zacchaeus is paying back twice that, four times his theft. In the Old Testament, the purpose of a generous restitution was not just to punish, it was to rebuild damaged relationships. The idea was to pay back beyond what was fair, in order to reconcile with the offended party. Zacchaeus not only wanted to take responsibility for his sins, he wanted to reconcile with the people he had sinned against.

Consider the implications of this pronouncement from the chief tax collector. His policy would set a new set of standards for the entire region! Zacchaeus was redefining the taxation business in his district.

Zacchaeus found himself caring for people other than himself. He publicly committed half of his possessions to help the poor. The Old Testament commanded generosity, but this was more than generosity; this was caring. It was also freedom, freedom to embrace life from God's perspective. For the first time in his adult life, Zacchaeus tasted hope, and as he savored that hope and made immediate plans to share it, hope ripened into joy.

Zacchaeus decided to turn his life around. That's repentance. As it always does, godly repentance brought great joy as Zacchaeus rediscovered who he was meant to be. Zacchaeus rediscovered who he was meant to be because Jesus told him. "Today salvation has come to this house, since he also is a son of Abraham." A son of Abraham! A believer in the covenant, one who believed in God's grace and who discovered his identity in God's design. As a son of Abraham, Zacchaeus was a child of God, created to live in God's image.

And one final thought Jesus shared with everyone who would ever read his story … "For the Son of Man came to seek and to save the lost."Salvation is what happens when a lost person is found. The Bible says that we are all lost. We are not sure where we came from. We do not know why we are here. We do not know where we are headed or how to get to where we ought to be. Whether we are down and out, or up and out, or just out of it, the Bible says we are all lost.

The need to find God is universally felt. The Apostle Paul preached,

> God made from one man every nation of mankind to live on all the face of the earth, having determined allotted periods and the boundaries of their dwelling place, that they should seek God, and perhaps feel their way toward him and find him. (Acts 17:26-27)

Jesus is all about God coming from heaven to find us. We cannot know God's mind because we are too jaded to trust him, and since we cannot trust him, we will not submit to his design for life. Jesus, however, reestablishes trust as faith recognizes that he died in our place. Jesus satisfied the demands of God's Law on our behalf, so his Spirit can use the new trust generated by faith to cultivate God's Law in us. When Jesus finds us, we discover who we are, who we were meant to be, and why God created us in the first place. Renewed trust in God enables us to embrace his design for life.

In Jesus, I find that I was created to glorify God by making his invisible character visible in this world, cultivating a human influence on this earth as beautiful as the planet itself is among the stars. Jesus did not secure my forgiveness so I could continue to be the selfish pig I was when he found me. His goal is to transform me into the noblest creature in the galaxy.

Zacchaeus is a great example of how salvation changes my identity and makes me want to get on with a life that is truly alive. I don't want to wait for eternity to begin so I can live differently. I am different right now, and I want to make this world a better place right now. That's the kind of person Jesus has made me to be.

Our God-given place in this world is sometimes called "the Cultural Mandate." It is one of two pillars that support the identity of a Christian. The other is the Great Commission, which assigns me a role in helping Christ build his church (the subject of the last chapter). The Cultural Mandate is God's overarching purpose for humanity—overarching because it began at our creation and will follow us forever. It's our assignment to enhance the Earth's beauty and productivity in every way possible. If we had not sinned, it would be all we would ever be. One day, it will be everything we do. Right now, we experience it in the roles God has given us.

Lost people who are found by Jesus Christ will look at their careers differently, just as surely as Zacchaeus did. No longer is a "secular" job disassociated from faith; secular jobs are no longer unspiritual. We have become spiritual, alive in God. Therefore, we bring spirituality to everything we touch.

Appreciating this requires that we distinguish the spiritual from the religious. Religion is essential and wonderful, but unless you are a religious professional, your job is not part of your religion. It is not a place to publicly pray, sing, preach, baptize and celebrate communion. Those things are not part of your job. But your job is spiritual in that you can walk with God at work. You can follow and glorify him. You can make his presence and his character visible at work. You can bring good will with you in a thousand ways. That is your proper role—not as defined by the workplace, but as defined by your Creator.

Like Zacchaeus, you will be especially sensitive to eliminate any impression of hypocrisy. Remember that the name Zacchaeus means "righteous one." You also bear a name, the name of "Christian." Once you have been found by Jesus, you will not want to bear his name in vain. Your standards of integrity will shoot up very high. You will modify your own job description to include high standards of integrity, honesty and appropriate loyalty, as well as kindness, compassion, gentleness and generosity. You will endeavor not only to "do your job," but actually make a worthy contribution both to your employers and to all the people your career impacts.

You will begin to hold yourself accountable for past misdeeds. That's how you will know that hypocrisy has been forsaken. You will own up to past wrongs at work, and accept responsibility for them. You will confess them and make appropriate restitution. And when you are done, your integrity will become unassailable, for there are no skeletons left in your closet.

You make restitution for your past misdeeds not only to protect your name, but also to rebuild relationships you have damaged. Just as Zacchaeus paid back four-fold what he stole, you find ways of going an extra mile or two to demonstrate that you not only take responsibility for past failures, but are also sorry and want to rebuild good and working relationships.

If you have a position of leadership, you will find that changes in your life ripple out to all the folks you work with, perhaps even over your entire profession. Your policies of integrity and kindness become the policies of those under you. Zacchaeus' change of heart impacted every tax collector in the Jericho district. I wouldn't be surprised if some chose to leave the business, but those who remained would bless every business owner and every family in Jericho. That, in turn, would make Jericho more attractive to business, creating a positive cycle of blessing.

Your career is only one place that is affected when Jesus finds you. You have many opportunities to improve the world at large.

Of course, the world at large is a big, precious, dirty and dangerous place. You will not solve all the problems of this world. Jesus declared, "The poor you always have with you," implying that there is no way to change the underlying godless, broken nature of the world in its present form. This world is in rebellion and will stay that way until Jesus returns to defeat it.

However, even if you cannot change the fundamental nature of the world, you can make it a better place. Why would you want to? Because that is the kind of person you become when Jesus finds you. You were created to care for the continents and oceans. You were created to care for the animals and birds and fish. You were created to care for the people, your brothers and sisters in Adam, who live here. They are your responsibility, and it glorifies God, it makes his care visible, when you care for them. Zacchaeus celebrated his new life by giving half his possessions to the poor. Jesus hadn't told him he had to do that. Zacchaeus wanted to do it. He wanted to become what God made him to be and cease trying to be something else. If Jesus Christ could call him out of his isolation into friendship with God, then Zacchaeus could become a friend to all whom God cares for.

I suspect that Zacchaeus was the biblical model for Ebenezer Scrooge, especially since Dickens wrote about both. Hollow men obsessed with wealth, who had gained the world but lost their souls. Men touched by the Spirit of One whose birth we celebrate at Christmas, men whose hearts were opened by Christ. Did you know that in Dickens' original story, one of the first things Ebenezer Scrooge did after his transformation was to go to church? You don't see that in most of the movies. And like

Zacchaeus, he changed the way his business was run. Like Zacchaeus, he gave generously to help the poor. And although contemporary renditions delete this point, Dickens said that Ebenezer Scrooge committed himself to a pure life that was pleasing to God.

An unspiritual mindset might think that a "pure life" looks as unappetizing as the earlier Ebenezer, withered and life-denying. But that isn't true. Repentance and faith in Jesus Christ open the soul to great joy. Remember how the story ends?

> "A merry Christmas, Bob!" said Scrooge, with an earnestness that could not be mistaken, as he clapped him on the back. "A merrier Christmas, Bob, my good fellow, than I have given you for many a year! I'll raise your salary, and endeavor to assist your struggling family … Make up the fires, and buy another coal-scuttle before you dot another i, Bob Cratchit."
>
> Scrooge was better than his word. He did it all, and infinitely more; and to Tiny Tim, who did not die, he was a second father. He became as good a friend, as good a master, and as good a man, as the good old city knew. (A Christmas Carol)

That is repentance. That's what it's like when a lost person is found by Jesus Christ. He or she naturally begins to make this world a better place.

Christian, you have a purpose in life. More urgently, it is defined by the Great Commission, but more importantly, it is defined by the Cultural Mandate, God's original charge to create a human family that exercises creative, responsible, loving dominion over the earth. This purpose for us will be ours long after the Great Commission is finished. Christian, you can make the world a better place through your career—in the way you do your job, in the way you reconcile and befriend the people you work with, in the way you influence your whole profession in godly ways that improve the lives of others. You can even make a difference in society at large. Even if you can't mend the underlying fabric of society, you can patch it in many ways. You can help the poor, the refugee, the abandoned and abused. You can protect the innocent from evil oppression. Use your imagination, use your resources, use your education and your opportunities. Use your heart and discover your calling to be the most noble creature in the galaxy.

The motive for all this is always the same; it is the joy of being found by Jesus Christ. Maybe you've become lost in an enslaving job or a chaotic society. Maybe you've managed to gain a little more of the world by spending pieces of your soul. And then perhaps you decide to come to church because you know Jesus passes by there and you'd like to catch a glimpse of him. What's that? Is he calling my name? He wants to come to my house?

Jesus will transform your inner life and completely redirect your eternal future. And you will know that is true as you find yourself making this world a better place.

Everyone Is Important

"Which of these three, do you think, proved to be a neighbor to the man who fell among the robbers?" He said, "The one who showed him mercy."

And Jesus said to him, "You go, and do likewise." (Luke 10:36-37)

The story of the Good Samaritan was Jesus' way of demonstrating how the religious leaders of his day underestimated the requirements of God's Law. They thought they were taking God's commands more seriously than Jesus, but the only reason they thought so was that they had a relatively surface understanding of what God had in mind. They imagined that their good works fulfilled God's will, but could only do that by dumbing down God's Law to something sinners can manage.

This came up in a discussion between Jesus and a biblical (Old Testament) scholar. The scholar said he could merit eternal life by loving God above all, and loving his neighbor as himself. Jesus said that was a good answer, assuming the man actually lived that way. Had the scholar lived that way? His uncertainty became evident when he asked Jesus to define what God meant by "neighbor."

The scholar was employing a technique of contemporary Rabbis. Limit the application of God's Law to something we can manage In this case, put boundaries around the people we are responsible to care for—not this kind of person or that sort of situation. and certainly not them, and not when it means doing that.

In order to fulfill the Law of God, I would have to first dumb it down, shrink it to the level of my actual behavior so I could pretend that God commands only what I am prepared to give. If I'm good at it, then my version of God's Law will simply describe what I'm already doing. Sure, I love my neighbor just as God tells me to, but those people in need, you see, are not my neighbors; they don't live in my community. They don't speak my language. We would not naturally socialize. According to my interpretation, my boundaries, my limits, of course I love my neighbor!

Jesus, however, would not get drawn into that kind of silliness. Instead, he did what he usually did. He told a story, a story designed to challenge our assumptions and expose the Law's true dimensions. He spoke of a man lying in need on the side of the road. We know nothing about this man, and that lack of detail is significant. His anonymity is an important part of the story. We know nothing about who he is or what he is. We don't know his religion, occupation or character. His possessions and even his clothing are stolen. He could be a prince or a priest or a pauper. We don't know.

But we do know something of the people who pass by. The first two are members of the religious establishment. Jesus specifically says that both of these men saw the victim but ignored him. They knew the Golden Rule (Jesus paraphrased that from Leviticus), but they refused to treat this fellow as their neighbor. After all, they didn't know the man or know anything about him. They passed by on the other side of the road, determined to remain uninvolved.

The last person who came by is identified as a Samaritan. Samaritans lived to the north of Jerusalem. They were racial and religious half-breeds, considered by the religious establishment to be spiritually second class. But this Samaritan turns out to be a first-class human being and helps the man in distress. He gets involved at personal cost. In effect, he helps the man the way he would wish someone would help him if he were robbed and left for dead.

Notice how Jesus has subtly reversed the scholar's entire perspective. The scholar wanted to discuss the limitations of our responsibility, the social claim some people have on our help (and others don't). But Jesus makes the victim anonymous, focusing not on the social claims of the recipient, but instead focusing on the character of the person giving aid.

In other words, "who is my neighbor?" is the wrong question. The right question is "what does it mean for me to be a neighbor?" The right question does not explore who I should love. The right question explores whether or not I am a loving person. It goes to my heart, my motives, and my character. Because that is what the Law is about: the character underneath of my behavior. Thus, Jesus, exposes the expert's shallow understanding of the Law.

Living faith loves our neighbor as ourselves. It does not filter the "neighbor" category in order to whittle it down to something more manageable. It keeps the focus on our character, not the kind or sort of person in need. Living faith produces a conviction in me that everyone is important, and that we should treat each fellow human being as we would wish to be treated if we had a similar need.

"Everyone is important" is a principle of faith that flows out of the biblical understanding of what it means to be human. Human beings are special because every human being is a creature—a created being—crafted in the image of God. "God created man in his own image, in the image of God he created him; male and female he created them." (Genesis 1:27)

The biblical view of reality is that there is a hierarchy of creation—a hierarchy of beings.

> O LORD, our Lord, how majestic is your name in all the earth! ... You have set your glory above the heavens. When I look at your heavens, the work of

your fingers, the moon and the stars, which you have set in place, what is man that you are mindful of him? ... You have made him a little lower than the heavenly beings and crowned him with glory and honor. You have given him dominion over the works of your hands; you have put all things under his feet, all sheep and oxen, and also the beasts of the field, the birds of the heavens, and the fish of the sea. (Psalm 8:1-8)

God is at the top, the eternal, majestic, uncreated Spirit. Then comes angels. Angels are created spirits; they can appear in bodily form, but they are not truly physical. Then comes humanity. Human beings are created spirits too, but fundamentally integrated with a physical body. Humanity rules over the other creatures who exist only in physical form.

Thus, human beings are the image of God in the physical world. Our created spirits are like God's Spirit in miniature. Our bodies give us a perfect interface with the physical world we are charged to rule in a way consistent with God's character, design and sensibilities.

We've already studied how this world is fallen and how sin has broken and damaged all of us. But even though God's image is tragically damaged in us all, his image is still what we are. And that is how we must treat one another. We instinctively know this about ourselves, which is why we care so much for ourselves. Jesus builds on that by teaching that we must learn to care for others the way we care for ourselves. Why? Because, every human being is the image of God, just as we are.

This leads to an amazing implication: how we treat any person demonstrates the level of our respect for God, himself. Consider carefully the logic of this Old Testament command, "From his fellow man I will require a reckoning for the life of man. Whoever sheds the blood of man, by man shall his blood be shed, for God made man in his own image." (Genesis 9:5-6) Why does God hold people mortally accountable for murder, rape, or other capital crimes? Not only because we are violated. It's because his image is desecrated. Therefore, how we treat other human beings—regardless of their relationship to us—is an open indication of what we think of our Creator. For anyone who respects God, that makes everyone important.

Certainly, this realization raises many questions. How do I balance caring for strangers with caring for my family? How is love best expressed? Do you always give what people request or should you try to give them what you believe they need? How do we love people that we do not admire? How do we oppose ungodly behavior, while at the same time expressing a profound respect for the personhood of those involved?

Jesus' teaching raises lots of questions that are not addressed in this simple story, non-trivial questions we must use the rest of Scripture to answer. But Jesus' point is clear: whatever guidelines we use, we must never filter out individuals or classes of people as if they were not in God's image. We may never cut out some people, or some types of people, from our sphere of concern. The specific identity of my neighbor is always a secondary concern to my love for the Lord, whose image that person reflects.

Living faith treats every human being, regardless of who and what they are, as a precious, valuable, important person. Admiration is a different sentiment; admiration is something earned. But respect for someone's personhood expresses my Christian faith. Whether or not they believe they were created by my God, I believe it. Whether or not they honor him, I will honor him by honoring them.

This is a hard teaching. We have all picked up some pretty strong filters while growing up. Christians must help one another deactivate those filters and work hard to teach this conviction to our children, not just by what we say but also by what we do.

Everyone is important, including the unborn and the aged, or people of different races and social status. Everyone is important, including the nominal believer and atheist and agnostic, or the Jew or Muslim or Hindu or whatever. Everyone is important, including the flagrantly immoral, the ones who glory in their perversions. Everyone is important, including illegal immigrants, the handicapped, those mentally and physically challenged, afflicted ones who no longer recognize their own children, everyone from the boss to the temporary help. They are not all saved, not all godly. They are not all like us, but they are all important. We do not need to admire them or emulate them. When necessary, we must vigorously confront or oppose them. But we must always try to help them when they are in need. We must love them with dignity because whether they know it or not, they are in the image of our God.

Living faith is willing to adopt such a lifestyle. It is willing to plunge into all the tough, inconvenient questions such faith raises. It stops asking, "Who is my neighbor?" and starts pondering the sort of neighbor I'm going to be.

What does such living faith look like? …

Dorcas

> Now there was in Joppa a disciple named Tabitha, which, translated, means Dorcas. She was full of good works and acts of charity. In those days she became ill and died, and when they had washed her, they laid her in an upper room.
>
> Since Lydda was near Joppa, the disciples, hearing that Peter was there, sent two men to him, urging

him, "Please come to us without delay." So Peter rose and went with them. And when he arrived, they took him to the upper room. All the widows stood beside him weeping and showing tunics and other garments that Dorcas made while she was with them. But Peter put them all outside, and knelt down and prayed; and turning to the body he said, "Tabitha, arise." And she opened her eyes, and when she saw Peter she sat up. And he gave her his hand and raised her up. Then, calling the saints and widows, he presented her alive.

And it became known throughout all Joppa, and many believed in the Lord. (Acts 9:36-42)

Every church has within it some individuals who especially inspire the faith of others, whose words—and perhaps more often, whose deeds—shine with living faith in a living Savior. Such people are often not the pastors, whose duty it is to proclaim the truth clearly, regardless of how much or how little they have absorbed personally. The people who most inspire faith are those who live it best, whose faith is simple and deeply felt, people who actually live by the basic convictions of the gospel. They live, for example, assuming that God is who he says he is and God is in control, that the world is not what it should be but God will make all things right.

They also believe that everyone is important.

Tabitha was one such person. Since no family is mentioned, she probably was a widow. However, since she could afford to buy materials and spend every day making garments to give away, we also assume she was one of the few widows with access to family money. Tabitha's grace was reflected in her name, which is Aramaic for "gazelle." In Greek, the name is translated as Dorcas. Dorcas was "a disciple ... full of good works and acts of charity." Hers was not the gift of speaking; hers was the gift of doing, or helping. She communicated the grace of God in the church through her actions. She made clothing for fellow widows who could not support themselves.

Perhaps you are aware that the experience of widows in the ancient world was often desperate. If there were children to care for her, or if she inherited a substantial sum from her husband, she would be all right. But remember, women did not generally run businesses by themselves in that society. There was no insurance. There was no Social Security and no government housing or help with heating. In the ancient world, unattached widows were completely vulnerable and commonly destitute.

In the new Christian church, members who were widows were fed by a collection regularly taken up by all believers. That is, in fact, how the office of deacon originally arose, to take care of that offering. But what about clothing? That's where Dorcas stepped in. Every day, she spent her personal savings making clothes so that the other widows in the church at Joppa would not have to wear rags. Dorcas clothed them with dignity. After her death, when Peter arrived in Joppa, "All the widows stood beside him weeping and showing tunics and other garments that Dorcas made while she was with them."

Dorcas had a living faith that everyone is important. Not just natural family and relations, not just personal friends and people you were expected to care for, but everyone. Dorcas was not able to provide for all the needs of all the widows in Joppa, of course, but she did what she could for the widows who came in contact with her through the church. And to them, she came to exemplify what living faith in Christ is all about. She believed in Jesus, that he died for her sins and rose again from the dead so she could find a new life that would carry on into eternity.

Christ's passion to restore God's design changed how Dorcas thought and lived. It taught her that everyone was worth her love. Her freely given, hand-made clothing proclaimed that faith. And every single day, when each of the dozens of widows arose and put on a fine robe—as fine as other women who had families that loved and respected and cared for them—they would remember that they were loved and respected and cared for, too. Not only by Dorcas, but by the risen Christ who lived in her.

I suppose there are many reasons why living faith in Christ inspires such love. Genuine Christians tend to feel an overwhelming sense of gratitude to God for Jesus. Nominal Christians, people who simply like church and want to be generically religious, can confess that Jesus died for their sin very dispassionately, but those whose re-born spirits really believe that God took flesh in order to absorb his own wrath on their behalf, take that rather personally. God's grace naturally draws forth a profound gratitude that needs to be expressed somehow. We long to love God back.

But what can we do for God? Jesus answers that question by pointing to other believers and saying, "As you did it to one of the least of these my brothers, you did it to me." (Matthew 25:40) So, Dorcas clothed Jesus, exchanged his rags for fine clothing lovingly made, by doing so for the church's widows.

Living faith also experiences a growing concern for the rightness of things. When people are treated unfairly, just because of circumstances or social position or race or gender or any other unjust reason, it rubs us the wrong way. Not that it makes us angry and want to fight, so much as it makes us unhappy and intent to do something to make it right. We realize that God's character is not reflected in our societies—that's what it means that the world is fallen and not what it should be. But we long to see God's character reflected as much as possible, so we do things consistent with his character and try to make situations better. So, Dorcas cared for people that society did not care about, reflecting a sense of compassionate justice in what can be a cruel world.

And most of all, living faith motivates loving care for everyone because it senses that God is remaking humanity into something wonderful.

> Christ has been raised from the dead, the firstfruits of those who have fallen asleep. For as by a man came death, by a man has come also the resurrection of the dead. For as in Adam all die, so also in Christ shall all be made alive. But each in his own order: Christ the firstfruits, then at his coming those who belong to Christ. (1 Corinthians 15:20-23)

Dorcas believed that when Jesus rose from the dead, he became the firstfruits of a new humanity, one open to all races, both genders and every age—everyone, regardless of how valuable or worthless society saw them.

When Dorcas looked at the widows who flocked to the church, she didn't see women who had been abandoned by God. She didn't see cast offs who were only fit to beg in the streets for a crust of bread. She saw women who had become citizens of God's kingdom and who were being renewed right now, in his image. She saw women who already wore the royal robes of Christ's righteousness in the sight of God, women who were so highly esteemed that Jesus Christ died for them. Just as Jesus rose to newness of life, new life was already rising within them. They were beginning to taste his godliness pulsing in their heart. And one day, they would rise from their graves, rise in glory just like Jesus. On that day, everyone will see those who were abandoned by the world, but who belong to God—those who were considered cast offs, but who are actually his beloved.

The living faith that enabled Dorcas to see Christ resurrected enabled her to see these women raised with him. By faith, she could see the worth, the value bestowed on these Christian sisters by God. Society couldn't see it, but she could—with the same faith that saw her Savior alive. So, for Dorcas, everyone in the church was important, because they were being renewed in the image of God. Everyone outside the church, too. I doubt that Dorcas turned anyone away, even if they came for help without faith. Every person bears God's image and may yet find that image renewed through faith in the gospel.

Peter sensed how sorely the community missed Dorcas' ability to look at everyone in the light of Jesus' resurrection. As he walked onto the scene, perhaps he thought of Lazarus, Jesus' friend. Jesus had wanted to perform a sign that would underscore that, "I am the resurrection and the life. Whoever believes in me, though he die, yet shall he live, and everyone who lives and believes in me shall never die." (John 11:25-26)

So, Jesus had raised Lazarus from his tomb. Lazarus' resurrection was only a temporary sign, of course. He would die again, but his resurrection was a miracle that confirmed the truth of the gospel message. Perhaps the dear believers in Joppa were hoping for just such a sign.

Peter hadn't done this before, so he decided to simply imitate his master. He thought of the time when Jesus raised a twelve year old girl, the daughter of a local leader named Jairus. Jesus went into the room where the girl's body lay, sent the crowd out, took the girl by the hand and said in Aramaic, "Talitha, qumi", or "little girl, arise." That little girl came back to life! So, the simple fisherman asked them all to leave; he got down on his knees and prayed. Perhaps it was then that he realized that the Aramaic for Dorcas, gazelle, was Tabitha, just slightly different from talitha (little girl). So, he imitated his Master as best he could and said,

"Tabitha, qumi," or "Dorcas, arise." And she did; she came back to life!

When the church and the widows she had helped came back into the room, they saw a living testament that everything Dorcas believed was true. Everything she had preached to them with her hands was true. They were important to God; everyone is important, because Jesus really is raising a new humanity to life.

Only a relatively few people were ever healed or brought back from the dead in apostolic times. Miracles were never effective in encouraging faith because of their shock value. What apostolic miracles accomplished was to vindicate the gospel message as true. It is Christ who makes all the difference.

What shook Joppa and brought many to Christ in those days was not that one person temporarily came back from the dead. It was what Dorcas' resurrection illustrated, what it proved. It proved that her ministry was a genuine and true reflection of God's salvation. In Christ, those who are nobodies become somebodies. Those who have found heartache and pain and death in a world that has turned its back on the Creator, find that God has not turned his back on them. We can come to Christ with our morally filthy rags and tattered hopes and receive fine garments, ours without cost. The cost was borne by one who loves us and is willing to work with his hands (on the cross) to clothe us with God's grace.

What touched people's lives most was not Tabitha's extraordinary physical resurrection; it was how Tabitha herself was extraordinary. Her very life was a vision of what new life in Christ is all about. She could see the potential of Christ's life in everyone she served, and she treated them that way. She treated every widow as a daughter of the King, or a potential daughter if she would but open her heart to him. Each one left her knowing a little better how it feels to wear the dignity of God's own image.

No one comes to Christ without understanding and embracing the gospel message. But the beauty and power of the church lies not in its sermons, but in its Tabithas. Joyful widows who open their hearts and homes to others who feel alone. Young adults who come alongside widows and single moms to change oil, repair roofs and rake leaves. Women who lovingly prepare extra meals for brothers and sisters going through a crisis. Christians who give their voice to speak up on behalf of the infirm or appeal to the hearts of fearful mothers contemplating the abortion of their children. Folks who work hard to organize a flea market of donated items to make them available to needy families, completely free of charge. Others who prepare lunches or sleeping bags or other necessities for individuals who are homeless in the city. Christian men and women who band together to overcome their own substance abuse and welcome any who wish to share their support. Church groups and individuals who travel to less developed parts of the world to build encouraging and helpful relationships, and also provide clothing, a vehicle, or surgery that would otherwise be impossible. Christians who band together to go anywhere there is disaster and tragedy, whether it be Florida or Sri Lanka, just to help—no charge.

Why do they do these things? Because everyone is important. Every human being is important. True, sin cost us the identity and dignity God designed for us to have, but Jesus rose from the dead to restore those things. In Christ, we are being renewed in the image of our Creator and are beginning to appreciate that image in others. Underneath their brokenness and idolatry. we can see that image in every human being. And if they can see his image being renewed in us, in the way we treat each other and in the way we treat them, then perhaps they will seek him for themselves.

Living faith looks like Dorcas sewing clothes. Such dear ones may not be called to preach, but they illustrate the gospel eloquently with their deeds. In them, we see Christ raising a new humanity in which everyone is important.

All My Problems Are Solved

> Peter began to say to him, "See, we have left everything and followed you."
>
> Jesus said, "Truly, I say to you, there is no one who has left house or brothers or sisters or mother or father or children or lands, for my sake and for the gospel, who will not receive a hundredfold now in this time, houses and brothers and sisters and mothers and children and lands, with persecutions, and in the age to come eternal life.
>
> But many who are first will be last, and the last first." (Mark 10:28-31)

Jesus had just finished speaking to a man we call "the rich young ruler." He had come to Jesus asking what he needed to do in order to inherit eternal life. It's clear that the young man came with a rather shallow view of God's Law, since he somewhat glibly claimed to have obeyed all of God's laws since childhood. How do you reach a person with the message of grace, when he doesn't believe he needs grace?

"And Jesus, looking at him, loved him, and said to him, 'You lack one thing: go, sell all that you have and give to the poor, and you will have treasure in heaven; and come, follow me.'" (Mark 10:21) This command exposed the young man's idolatry, for he simply could not do what Jesus asked. He left, unsaved.

Jesus' disciples had listened to all this. This wasn't the first time they had heard Jesus speak of "treasure in heaven." The rich young ruler went away sad, but the disciples had chosen differently. What was this treasure Jesus spoke of? What could they expect for their sacrifices? That question was behind Peter's statement, "See, we have left everything and followed you."

The Bible says over and over that real faith leads to substantial sacrifices for Christ. Peter had made sacrifices. In fact, every believer is called to make sacrifices. Jesus said,

> Whoever loves father or mother more than me is not worthy of me, and whoever loves son or daughter more than me is not worthy of me. And whoever does not take his cross and follow me is not worthy of me.
>
> Whoever finds his life will lose it, and whoever loses his life for my sake will find it. (Matthew 10:37-39)

In the text concerning the rich young ruler, Jesus even mentioned the possibility of persecutions.

Jesus taught a way of life filled with self sacrifice.

> I say to you, Do not resist the one who is evil. But if anyone slaps you on the right cheek, turn to him the other also. And if anyone would sue you and take your tunic, let him have your cloak as well. And if anyone forces you to go one mile, go with him two miles. (Matthew 5:39-41)

He commanded his disciples to love, and in a fallen world love costs time, money, patience and forgiveness. The Christian faith is a lifestyle of sacrifice, believing from the heart that, "It is more blessed to give than to receive." (Acts 20:35)

As Peter watched that young man walk away, unwilling to embrace sacrifice, he must have thought, "In order to follow Christ as the Messiah, I've already given up my career and my family. And now Jesus is talking about being handed over, tortured and killed, so things could get a lot worse. What reward will I have?" In three verses, Christ answered that question by sketching a future hope that also gives encouragement for each present day. In doing so, he taught that in him, all our personal problems are solved.

Jesus' remarks can only be understood within a biblical view of history. In verse 30, he spoke of the "present time" and "the age to come." Instead of infinitely repeating cycles, the Bible understands our experience in three linear segments: a past, present and future. These time segments enable us to understand reality and our place in it.

The first segment goes back to the initial creation, an age of innocence when everything was "very good." We don't know exactly how long that was. (How long would it take for Adam to become familiar with and name all the animals?) Comparatively, that first segment wasn't very long, and ended abruptly when our first parents chose to incorporate sin into their very nature. They chose to assume authority over their own lives, as if no one had created them.

At that moment, history changed and we moved into what Jesus calls the "present time," or present age, which is virtually everything we've known up to now. Christians understand the present age as a time of conflict and suffering. The goodness of God's design and his image in us is constantly compromised, sabotaged and frustrated by our own sin. The human race is in continual conflict with God as we break his laws, in conflict amongst each other as we envy and fight, and in conflict within ourselves as we struggle with violated consciences. However, the present age is also a time of redemption. God provides a way to overcome sin through Christ, and he works to apply that redemption to millions of people over many generations. In the present age, we can be reconciled to God and begin to find healing in our relationships and in our personal identity.

The age to come is our future eternal state. It's a state Adam and Eve were meant to attain, a state in which everything remains "very good" forever. It is the age that begins when God's awesome final judgment wipes the earth clean, and the redeemed find that their old sin is gone. With renewed bodies and minds, we will begin to live as God intended.

Understanding the rewards of Christian faith requires that we grasp our blessing both in this age and the age yet to come. Ultimately, Jesus sets our hope on the future. Christ told Peter that he would receive "in the age to come, eternal life." In the Bible, "eternal life" is more than everlasting life. It is that, of course, but biblically, eternal life refers to life with the eternal one, or life with God. "This is eternal life, that they know you, the only true God, and Jesus Christ whom you have sent." (John 17:3)

Eternal life begins as faith invades the present age, but we will experience it in fullness only in the age to come when all the sin that hides God from us is completely done away. "For now we see in a mirror dimly, but then face to face. Now I know in part; then I shall know fully, even as I have been fully known." (1 Corinthians 13:12) In the age to come, "The earth shall be full of the knowledge of the LORD as the waters cover the sea." (Isaiah 11:9)

Peter would later say, "According to his promise we are waiting for new heavens and a new earth in which righteousness dwells." (2 Peter 3:13) In the age to come, loyalty and faithfulness will be all we know. The bravest, most tender and deepest love we ever approach in this age will be commonplace. There will be no war, no offense, no misunderstanding, no jealousy, no anger, nothing that will ever need forgiveness again.

Since disease and accident and are the by-products of sin, our Lord promises complete healing and wholeness in the future. "He has borne our griefs and carried our sorrows." (Isaiah 53:4)

Therefore, my eyes will be perfect, my back strong, my diabetes gone and I will have a full head of hair. Failure and frustration are bitter fruits of sin that also shall be no more. None of us will ever be lonely again or feel crushed by defeat. We will have much work to do, but work then will feel more like play feels now, since we will work with people we love in a world that no longer resists our efforts. And because we will work so well, we will be productive beyond our dreams. Such is our hope for the age to come.

Even so, Jesus also gave Peter encouragement for this age. "Truly, I say to you, there is no one who has left house or brothers or sisters or mother or father or children or lands, for my sake and for the gospel, who will not receive a hundredfold now in this time, houses and brothers and sisters and mothers and children and lands." This is because eternal life has invaded the present age. Faith in Christ enables us to taste eternal life with God now. And what a taste it is! We receive today a hundred fold more than we are called to sacrifice.

What does this mean? Some would use this comment to develop what is called a "health and wealth gospel," teaching that strong faith is marked in this life by terrific prosperity. Proponents and preachers of such views tend to drive expensive cars and live in expensive homes in order to exemplify what real faith looks like. They say that if believers have enough faith, then in this age they can live like kings and be healed of every ailment.

However, there are at least four indications just in this passage warning us that this would be an improper application of Jesus' words. First, it isn't just possessions that Jesus says will be multiplied to the faithful, but mothers as well (I never hear these preachers promising one hundred mothers-in-law), so perhaps Jesus was speaking figuratively. Second, Jesus reminds us in the same verse that we will experience this age's blessing along with persecutions. It seems that believers will not live in a protective bubble, after all. Third, in verse 31, Jesus follows this teaching with a reminder that those who are last in this life shall be first in the life to come. So whatever our blessings entail, Jesus says that those with strong faith will be "last" today. Fourth, Peter asked his question because he was not rich. He wore no fancy clothes and drove no expensive chariot. He never would. Faith leads to a life of sacrifice, not opulence. No, Jesus did not teach a health and wealth gospel. What then, did Jesus mean by this promise of a hundredfold return in this life?

It seems obvious to me that Jesus was talking about the delightful potential of Christian fellowship. Christians have the ability, if they choose to exercise it, of functioning as one huge spiritual commonwealth. In terms of homes and possessions, the New Testament records,

> All who believed were together and had all things in common. And they were selling their possessions and belongings and distributing the proceeds to all, as any had need ... breaking bread in their homes, they received their food with glad and generous hearts. (Acts 2:44-46)

> Now the full number of those who believed were of one heart and soul, and no one said that any of the things that belonged to him was his own, but they had everything in common ... . There was not a needy person among them, for as many as were owners of lands or houses sold them and brought the proceeds of what was sold and laid it at the apostles' feet, and it was distributed to each as any had need. (Acts 4:32-35)

In terms of relationships, Christians enter into a huge spiritual family. We don't all know each other that well yet, but when one born again Christian meets another, they often share an uncanny sense that they are going to live together for eternity. (Fortunately, we'll be perfect by then!) From the cross, our Lord taught that his disciples are family.

> When Jesus saw his mother and the disciple whom he loved standing nearby, he said to his mother, 'Woman, behold, your son!' Then he said to the disciple, 'Behold, your mother!' And from that hour the disciple took her to ahis own home. (John 19:26-27)

The Apostle Paul taught Christians to regard one another as family. "Do not rebuke an older man but encourage him as you would a father, younger men as brothers, older women as mothers, younger women as sisters, in all purity." (1 Tim 5:1-2)

In Christ, the age to come invades the present age through Christian fellowship. Homes? I am welcome in dozens and dozens of homes in my own congregation, thousands in America, and hundreds of thousands the world over, simply because I belong to Christ. Brothers, sisters, parents, children? I've got millions of them! Fields, possessions? When I have suffered a crisis, I've been supported with food for weeks, with money available from the church to see me through. To follow Jesus means that your life and your stuff is dedicated to him. His fellowship is one in which all the others feel the same way. So each one of us gains a hundred fold over anything we give.

Peter said, "See, I have left everything and followed you. What will I get?" Jesus replied, "Why Peter, didn't you know? You get everything! You will receive it all completely in the age to come, and you are already tasting it right now in our fellowship.

Peter, already we are welcome in dozens of towns, hundreds of homes. Already, your family is larger than you can count and we're just beginning. And just wait till you see what is yours when we're done."

Christian, do you understand that all of your problems are solved? That is such an outrageous thing to say, isn't it! Try saying it out loud, "All my problems are solved." I'm certain it sounded outrageous to Peter, considering all he had given up and the poverty of their little band. Yet when he thought about it, Peter would have to agree, "Someday in my future, there won't be mortgages and lean fishing seasons. There won't be war and crime. There won't be sickness and aching muscles. There won't be miscarriages and graves. Someday, I will never feel lonely or misunderstood or angry or frustrated with my career. Someday, I won't be frustrated with myself. Because of my Master, all my problems are solved. Temporarily, we are now the last of all people, dedicated to working with God for his glory and mankind's good. But I suppose I can really afford to do that, given that one day, I am destined to be first. Because I'm guaranteed so much to come, I can afford to keep less now. That's how Jesus seems to think. He knows he's going to be first forever, so he has no problem being last for a little while, for our sake. It's as if he can taste the glory to come … And you know something? So can I."

Peter might go on the think, "Looking at the other disciples I journey with, what a motley crew we are, and yet, we are family. I'm actually closer to these people than I am with most of my own extended kin. And I have to admit, we never starve; we are welcome in hundreds of homes. And we get to travel with Jesus together, side by side. That's not too shabby!"

While we still endure problems, believers know that ultimately those problems are already solved, and we can begin to taste the blessing of our future today. We can't name a problem that will follow us into eternity. No ache or pain that troubles our body. No unresolved conflict that burdens our soul. No debt, no guilt. And we can taste that future glory now by embracing a fellowship of faith that treats each other as children of God, precious ones for whom Christ died, a forever family.

There's a great line in the movie, Forest Gump. Forest has left all his finances in the hands of his friend and partner who invested heavily in a new company called Apple Computer. Overnight, they are millionaires. Money will never be an issue again. Forest's simple response: "Well, that's one less thing to worry about."

Imagine running through the mail tomorrow and discovering that long lost uncle Henry just left you $100,000,000. For you, money is now one less thing to worry about. It will take two months of legal processing before you get your check. Imagine what it would feel like to live those two months in the in-between, a millionaire with no money, already but not yet rich. In those two months, you would feel rich; you would feel like all your financial problems were solved. Moreover, you could afford to be generous with what little you have, knowing that immense wealth is on the way.

Now, imagine an inheritance that is more than mere money—an inheritance of land and sea and sky. An inheritance not of money, but of all the things money could ever buy. An inheritance, in fact, of the whole creation. An inheritance of a new family, a new reputation, a new career, a new life. An inheritance of a new body, strong and healthy, along with a new mind ready to use that body to do wonderful things. An inheritance which literally solves all of your problems. An inheritance that is already yours, guaranteed—you just have to wait a short while for it to be processed.

This is your inheritance, Christian, and you can already taste it in the church, if you want to. I'm not just talking about a sanctuary, preaching and music. I'm talking about Christ's people —people who celebrate the same inheritance you have, rejoice in the earth which shall belong to us, rejoice in each other, eager to share the small down payment of joy and blessing we each have received. We have a kingdom and a family that already make each of us richer than anyone else on this planet.

"All my problems are solved." Can you get your mind around that? Can you get your heart around it? Even as I struggle with challenges that are over my head, I know that, for me, they are already overcome, already solved, already neutralized in my future. This person I love will not always be disabled, or confused, or depressed. I will not always hurt or find it hard to control my behavior. In the age to come, I will have eternal life, as fresh and clear as God's crystal sea. And in the Christian fellowship of this present age, I have a one hundred fold return on everything I have dedicated to my Lord.

You ask, "Lord Jesus, see how I've dedicated my whole life to you. What do I get?"

He replies, "Didn't you understand, my friend? You get everything!"

How light and supple would your spirit be if every evening, as you lay down the burdens that weigh upon your soul, you could say, "Good night, Lord. Oh, I almost forgot...all my problems are solved, aren't they?" What self-sacrifice would you be capable of, if every morning you awoke to pray, "Good morning Lord... Oh, I just remembered, all my problems are solved! I can afford to serve you in any opportunity that comes my way today."

Christian, rejoice in being last in this world, putting God's glory and the needs of others before your own. After all, you can afford it. We can afford to be last because in the age to come, forever and for all time, all of our problems are solved.

What does such living faith look like? …

Paul

> For to me to live is Christ, and to die is gain. If I am to live in the flesh, that means fruitful labor for me. Yet which I shall choose I cannot tell. I am hard pressed between the two. My desire is to depart and be with Christ, for that is far better. But to remain in the flesh is more necessary on your account.
>
> Convinced of this, I know that I will remain and continue with you all, for your progress and joy in the faith. (Philippians 1:21-25)

For the Apostle Paul, the days and nights were long and difficult. Just before this passage, he described himself as "in chains for Christ." Given his comment that execution was a real possibility, we assume that he wrote during his imprisonment in Rome. Months earlier, Paul had been arrested in Jerusalem for preaching Christ, and as a Roman citizen he had claimed the right to appeal his case to Caesar. After a long trip, he was now under house arrest in the Roman capital.

Paul probably understood his situation as the fulfillment of prophecy. At his conversion, God said, "He is a chosen instrument of mine to carry my name before the Gentiles and kings." (Acts 9:15) It seemed that the way Paul would appear before Caesar and explain the gospel would be to appeal his case. At that time he might be set free, punished, or executed, but in any case, he would have fulfilled his mission.

As long as Paul could afford to rent a house, he was spared the dungeon, but being chained and house-bound for months and months was no fun. From his house, Paul could watch the world go by … without him. He learned of preachers who cared more about their reputation than the gospel. He heard how the church grappled with sin, argued over the truth and in general struggled to grow up—and there wasn't a whole lot he could do to help.

Sometimes, the hardest thing to do is simply to be faithful. To stay the course, and do what God has given you to do, even when you feel tired, in constant discomfort or physically restricted. Even when you feel forgotten, a bit unappreciated and useless. It's hard to remain faithful when you go to bed with such feelings only to wake up to find them still there week after week, month after month.

The book of Philippians is a letter from Paul to one of the churches he founded earlier in his ministry. They heard of his predicament and sent money to help pay for his rented rooms. Philippians is a thank you letter in which Paul touches on some truly profound issues regarding our faith and our mission. It is also a letter in which the apostle opens up his own heart and soul.

In the section quoted above, Paul ponders his attitude toward the future. He writes that his only goal is to honor his Lord, however his trial goes. "It is my eager expectation and hope that I will not be at all ashamed, but that with full courage now as always Christ will be honored in my body, whether by life or by death." (Philippians 1:20)

Paul finds himself frankly evaluating which option he would prefer: life or death. Of course, it wasn't his choice to make; it was God's, through the decision of Caesar. But in his mind, Paul considers the possibilities. On the one hand. "to me, to live is Christ and to die is gain." On the other hand, "If I am to live in the flesh, that means fruitful labor for me."

Paul hypothetically contemplates what he wishes would happen when he finally gets a chance to appear before Caesar and finish his mission. "Yet which I shall choose I cannot tell. I am hard pressed between the two. My desire is to depart and be with Christ, for that is far better. But to remain in the flesh is more necessary on your account." Finally, he makes his decision, "Convinced of this, I know that I will remain and continue with you all, for your progress and joy in the faith, so that in me you may have ample cause to glory in Christ Jesus."

This little window on Paul's motives and convictions demonstrates the power of a much neglected aspect of faith: hope. Hope fuels faithfulness when things get difficult. When Paul was converted, he devoted his life to the one who gave his life for him. Paul served his Lord for years, loving the people Christ loved even though that love was costly. In one letter, he remembered how costly.

> Five times I received at the hands of the Jews the forty lashes less one. Three times I was beaten with rods. Once I was stoned. Three times I was shipwrecked; a night and a day I was adrift at sea; on frequent journeys, in danger from rivers, danger from robbers, danger from my own people, danger from Gentiles, danger in the city, danger in the wilderness, danger at sea, danger from false brothers; in toil and hardship, through many a sleepless night, in hunger and thirst, often without food, in cold and exposure. And, apart from other things, there is the daily pressure on me of my anxiety for all the churches. (2 Corinthians 11:24-28)

How could Paul afford to love like that? How could he keep giving consistently? We see in Philippians an aged and tired Paul indeed wondering if he can afford another day. The strength to go on loving came from hope in his own future. "For to me to live is

Christ, and to die is gain … My desire is to depart and be with Christ, for that is far better. "

These were not idle words; Paul received visions of heaven. He knew more about the age to come than we do. He wrote, "The sufferings of this present time are not worth comparing with the glory that is to be revealed to us." (Romans 8:18) The future, his own future in particular, is something Paul must have thought about a lot. Paul regularly pondered how, in Christ, all of his problems were solved, ultimately and eternally. Paul saw his earthly death as a doorway to something wonderful for him.

Now, in his mind, Paul walks toward that door with outstretched hand to turn the knob. On the other side of that door is everything he longs for. But he hesitates; he looks back because the door is one-way. He considers a few more things he could yet do before he leaves for Paradise. And because there is so much waiting for him on the other side of the door, he can afford to let go of the knob and come back to give just a little bit more. As he put it, "But to remain in the flesh is more necessary on your account."

Mind you, what Paul can accomplish at this point seems rather limited. He's under house arrest. He can pray, he can share the gospel with his guards, and he can write letters. That's about it. But it's enough to focus his self-giving for one more day. He knows that all his problems are solved, so he can afford to spend one more day doing whatever he can.

A full-bodied, robust hope is the secret ingredient of a life that can afford to keep giving and loving. The word "hope" has two related biblical meanings. It can refer to an inner sense of confidence and anticipation of good things to come. It can also refer to the facts on which such confidence and anticipation is based. When these two wings of hope are welded onto either side of your life, they enable the human soul to soar.

Of course, you have to have both wings in order to fly. How many people there are in this world who are optimists, with a positive outlook on the future which has no basis in fact. They have little reason to believe that the world is truly becoming a better place, or that the ancient frailties and faults of the human race are being eradicated. They have absolutely no objective reason to hope for anything when life in this world is over. Their philosophies are castles in the clouds, mere pretense. Eventually, such pretending collapses under the strain of reality and they come crashing to the ground, either in this life as former-optimists-turned-cynics, or in the life to come as all hope wilts under the wrath of an offended Creator.

On the other hand, how many Christians have every objective reason to hope for help today and great things when Christ returns, yet never develop those facts into a positive and powerful outlook on the future? They allow the pessimistic state of our world to sabotage their souls from ever taking flight.

Paul once wrote, "So now faith, hope, and love abide, these three." (1 Corinthians 13:13) The greatest of them is love, but the most neglected, I think, is hope. When the facts of Christian hope are matched with a sense of assurance and excited expectancy, our lives can take flight. When we are truly convinced with good cause that all our personal problems are solved, then we can afford anything.

Yet, how many believers spend significant energy cultivating the kind of hope that bears fruit in a lifetime of faithfulness? How much energy we lavish on the upcoming weekend, our next career goal, our plan for retirement. Certainly, we should make plans for this life, but compare the significance of the next few years with the immensity of life in the world to come. Do we even talk about it with our families and friends?

Do you think such anticipation would be wasted time, drawing you away from the needs of today? That's the surprise of this text. Apparently, hope in the future does not draw us away from the needs of today. Instead, it propels us into today's needs with a renewed sense of freedom and freshness we can get in no other way.

Christian, all our problems have been solved! They have been solved in the sense that they are guaranteed a solution by God within a relatively short span of time. My needs have all been addressed, and I will reap those benefits very shortly. The more I understand that, the more I realize that this world, this age, has nothing I ultimately need. I don't need to get anything back when I love others. I can give whether or not I receive, because everything I need is already mine, waiting for me on the other side of the door. That perspective on the future powerfully changes how I use my opportunities today.

Think about our careers. Some of us have great jobs, but for many others, our career in this age may be far from the exciting adventure we thought it would be. After ten years or more, challenge can turn to drudgery. Few people feel properly appreciated for their labor or their loyalty. Our accomplishments may not rack up as high as we hoped. In fact, our careers may have exposed our limitations in ways that feel discouraging or even humiliating. We can end up feeling more like indentured servants than the movers and shakers we hoped to become.

But consider our future careers, the ones we will pursue throughout eternity! Did you think eternity would be one unending worship service? Eternity will involve unending worship, yes, but it will be the worship of minds and bodies creatively inventing and shaping everything according to God's desires. We'll have careers shaped by the talents God gave us, by the stewardship we demonstrated in this life, and by the infinite possibilities inherent in subduing a whole planet for God. Imagine your future career, always learning, and improving, working with great people whose spirits are as redeemed as yours, brothers and sisters all, who love you and appreciate you as you do them. Imagine the projects, the accomplishments, the satisfaction. I hope to get back to physics, and then move on to music, and then start to learn the ways of every animal God thought up.

I remember how, in college and later in seminary, I had a whole host of summer jobs I was less than crazy about. I was a soda jerk, a paper stacker in a printing house, the janitor's janitor in a maternity hospital, a security guard, a house painter and a computer operator. None of these jobs was really satisfying for me. But because I knew I was bound for something more permanent, I could do them with a smile, conscious that I could contribute something and touch people with Christ's love in the short time I was there.

Now I have learned that my "permanent" work in this life is just a summer job compared to my eternal career. Knowing something great is waiting for me later, I am compelled to pick up the burden one more day because I know that I will never again get to serve such a needy world. This may be the only chance I'll have to bless the folks I work with. I want to help them recognize their own God-given worth and the significance of their choices. I want them to know something of the love of Christ. Knowing that my career will only take off in the centuries to come, helps me go to work with a good word, ready to work hard and do my best.

Think about our relationships. Relationships are so hard to get right. It's so easy to offend and be offended, so hard to forgive and be forgiven. How many of your relationships are what you wish them to be—or more importantly, are what God wishes them to be? Some of us are so desperate to have healthy relationships that we are willing to abandon ones that are hard, hoping to find others that might be more successful.

But consider our relationships throughout eternity! If by God's grace, I and another gain Paradise together, what can I assume about our relationship? Even if we struggle and stumble with each other today, in the age to come our relationship will be perfect. We'll be free from our self-centered fears, we'll both be healed from our deepest hurts, and we'll both be open to listen and understand and care. Our souls knit with God's, we'll be able to go fishing or hiking, or do woodworking, or cook, or play music together and just soak up our mutual fellowship. Having that hope changes the way I view things now. No matter how difficult it is for me to relate to another believer, I know that in just a few years, we are going to be closer to each other than I presently am to anyone in the world. Our relationship, our reconciliation is assured. It's going to happen. Such confidence encourages me to taste that reconciliation now. Why wait to at least try to make it work, since our mutual love is inevitable?

Or think about our material well-being. The fact is, Christian, that you have no idea how wealthy I am. I am an heir of the whole world! And Christian, so are you! Having that kind of hope changes the way we view things. Sure, my resources are quite limited now. But I don't have to worry about what I might miss because I choose to help somebody else. I will miss nothing. I can afford to help.

The point I'm trying to make is that the more we are excited about our eternal future, the more that sense of well-being will thrust us back into this world, able to afford loving others. If all we think of our future in Christ is that it's going to be nice or will simply deliver us from pain, then we will approach dying, at best, as an escape. "O Lord, please take me home." "Well, at least she is at peace; no more pain." We may even find ourselves wanting out of this life, banging on the door of death: "Lord, let me in, I can't stand it here anymore."

But if our future hope is bigger than that; if it is as big as the promises of God, if we realize that all of our problems are solved —solved in such a way that I am going to be happy, fulfilled and useful for all eternity … then everyday, I will mentally walk up to that door of death and put my hand on the knob, since "my desire is to depart and be with Christ, for that is far better" …

And I'm going to hesitate. I'm going to look back, knowing that the door is one-way. I'm going to see the needs of this hurting world. I'm especially going to see those few needs that I can do something about. O my Lord, I've got so much. All my problems are solved. All my relationships are going to work. I'm rich beyond my ability to imagine. I've got a stupendous job waiting for me. But, "If I am to live in the flesh, that means fruitful labor for me … to remain in the flesh is more necessary on [their] account."

Hey, I can afford one more day, one more year, whatever God has for me here. What can I do to help? Even under house arrest. I can pray, I can share the gospel with the guards, and I can write a few lines of encouragement. Where's my pen?

I realize that this message may not strike some of us as entirely relevant just now. Maybe things are going so well that your eternal future seems irrelevant. Maybe you have so many immediate hopes and dreams that you have no time for eternity at present. Maybe a life of giving and loving is not really on your list of things to do at the moment. There's so much to get out of life, so much you want to experience for yourself, or for your kids, that you're working overtime to have it all.

As we grow in the Christian life, though, we learn that the best part of life is in giving. It really is more blessed to give than to receive, and giving to those who can't give back is like soaring high and free in the wind, with a view that stretches far beyond ourselves and our children.

But that kind of giving is costly; that kind of soaring takes energy. Sometimes you get to a point where you wonder if you can afford any more. Your flight of faith may lose altitude and you find yourself scraping the treetops. The wing of facts is as sound as ever, but the other wing of excited anticipation is unstable and starting to buckle. That's when you need to ponder the hope that is yours, Christian—what the world will be like, and what your place in it will be when Christ returns—what is waiting for you on the other side of that door we must all go through.

Can you and I honestly say, today, that to depart and be with Christ would be far better than staying here? I'm not talking about, "O, I guess I'll be OK when I die." I'm talking about a solid, genuine preference, in terms of what we actually want for ourselves, a preference to be with Christ. That's real Christian hope.

The great surprise is that when you and I develop that kind of hope, it will not lead us to embrace death. Instead, the anticipation of glory will cause us to hesitate at the door and look back. Once I leave, I'm headed for every good and holy desire I've ever had, for all my problems are solved. I am profoundly OK, or at least will be on the other side. But once I leave, I can't come back. Is there anything left for me to do before I go? After all, I can afford to stay another day. It's not like my eternity is going anywhere.

It's kind of like leaving your old house when moving to a new, grander one. I can't wait to move into my new home. But before I shut the door on the old one for the last time, is there anything I can do for the ones coming after me here, to make their lives a little easier? "Hold on a minute, I want to leave a note about the heater, and jot down where we left the batteries. Oh, and I want to sweep the floor; let's leave the place nice for them." There is something especially sweet about such a profoundly unselfish and uncluttered consideration of others, liberated from the need to receive anything in return. You have all you want, or soon will. As soon as you shut the door and move on, you don't really need anything you've left behind. So you're free to leave just a little extra. You want to pass a little more blessing on before you go on to something better.

One's entire life can be like that. The love that overflows out of happy hope can be the sweetest, most selfless fruit of faith. Paul wrote, "My desire is to depart and be with Christ, for that is far better. But to remain in the flesh is more necessary on your account." This kind of love is the least heroic and the most joyous, the beautiful fruit of hope.

Sitting under house arrest, what acts of simple love could Paul afford to offer as he rejoiced in his future hope? Well, he could afford to pray with a happy heart.

> I thank my God in all my remembrance of you, always in every prayer of mine for you all making my prayer with joy … it is my prayer that your love may abound more and more, with knowledge and all discernment, so that you may approve what is excellent, and so be pure and blameless for the day of Christ, filled with the fruit of righteousness that comes through Jesus Christ, to the glory and praise of God. (Philippians 1:3-11)

The Lord was pleased to use such loving prayers, inspired by hope in Christ, to hold the early church together through difficult days so it could grow and prosper.

And Paul could afford to share the gospel with the few people he did come in contact with.

> I want you to know, brothers, that what has happened to me has really served to advance the gospel, so that it has become known throughout the whole imperial guard and to all the rest that my imprisonment is for Christ. (Philippians 1:12-13)

I don't know if Paul fully understood the implications of what he wrote. The imperial, or praetorian, guard was a hand picked division of Roman troops. One of their ceremonial duties was to guard those awaiting appeal to Caesar. These highly respected men, who would over the course of time serve the Emperor in every province, saw Christianity close up, unobscured by propaganda. They saw Paul's faith in the context of his chains. They heard about his Savior. History records that in the years to come, they would carry that message all over the Empire. Paul's humble sharing, born of hope, reached more people than if Paul had been free to preach on the Roman street corner every day.

And filled with hope, Paul could also afford to write a few lines of encouragement. Friends, if you want to see God's stamp of approval on love that is sustained by a future hope, hope that inspires a life of giving just like Jesus', then just consider how God took those "few lines of encouragement" and placed them in the New Testament. The Lord has used this Letter to the Philippians to encourage not only the Philippian church, but also millions and even billions of believers. God the Father is thrilled to watch our souls soar on wings of hope in his Son!

Living faith connects your feelings to the facts of your future. Christian, revel in what is yours because of Jesus, and see what God does with the love you can then afford because you know that all your problems are solved.

I Have The Greatest Job In The World

The LORD called to Moses out of the mountain, saying, "Thus you shall say to the house of Jacob, and tell the people of Israel: 'You yourselves have seen what I did to the Egyptians, and how I bore you on eagles' wings and brought you to myself.

Now therefore, if you will indeed obey my voice and keep my covenant, you shall be my treasured possession among all peoples, for all the earth is mine; and you shall be to me a kingdom of priests and a holy nation." (Exodus 19:3-6)

Moses administered the Lord's covenant during a time when God's power was seen in the affairs of men in the most tangible and extraordinary ways in all of history. The work of our Lord Jesus was far more significant, but not on such a culturally grand scale. In the time of Moses, God reached into the mightiest superpower of the era, and against the will of its king, brought out an extended family of slaves. The Lord God molded human history with his own hands in order to make a model of what we call "salvation," a model of how he ultimately intended to call a multitude of people from every nation. He will call us out of the slavery of self-worship that has led to all the sorrow and death we know so well. He will call us to become, in a very unique and wonderful way, his people. We become a people who know and trust him, and therefore give ourselves willingly to his design. We become a people he can bless with glorious life eternally.

And all this good news was revealed, not on paper or in a dream, but by God carving the message into human history. Before he accomplished this plan in Christ, the Lord spent thousands of years modeling it in the nation of Israel so that we could understand it when Christ came.

At Sinai, the saving relationship, or covenant, that began with Adam and Eve moved into a new phase. For some time, it had been modeled in terms of a family, the family of Abraham. Now, that family had grown numerically and Abraham's offspring were about to become a nation. The model of God's salvation would now be fleshed out in terms of national laws and institutions. This chapter's introductory text outlines, in broad strokes, the nature of this covenant model.

It was on the third new moon after the people of Israel had gone out of the land of Egypt. They came into the wilderness of Mount Sinai. While Israel camped at the foot of the mountain, Moses went up to God. "The LORD called to him out of the mountain, saying ... 'You yourselves have seen what I did to the Egyptians, and how I bore you on eagles' wings and brought you to myself.'"

The most important point of God's saving covenant is that it is based upon sovereign grace. Israel did absolutely nothing to earn their deliverance out of Egypt. They were chosen in order to model his salvation and record the insights he gave them, so that one day the completed message could be sent out to all the world. They did nothing to deserve this calling; it was simply given to them.

This is how salvation works. God calls people; he reaches out and carries us to himself as on eagles' wings. "Now therefore, if you will indeed obey my voice and keep my covenant, you shall be my treasured possession." This covenant saves us from the worst slavery of all: the slavery of sin under which we all suffer. Sin is a festering insanity in the human soul that goads us to live as if God were not, or as if God were different than he is. Sin tries to bend all reality around the irrational dogma that mankind exists for itself and is the measure of all things. In order to do that, sin must reject the conscience God gave us, and ultimately reject his design for us to lovingly care for this planet. Sin turns the beauty of human life into a miserable madness in which we are all enslaved. God's covenant brings us back under his exclusive Lordship, the Lordship of the One who made all things good. Under that Lordship, we can live happily as God's treasured possession.

"For all the earth is mine; and you shall be to me a kingdom of priests and a holy nation." This is the original, pristine Israelite model of salvation: The Lord God living with his people, every one of whom is a priest to him, every one of them holy.

This pristine vision was soon carefully adapted into an inspiring 3D model of a house. In the wilderness, that first model was a tent called the Tabernacle. Israel realized that the Tabernacle and the later stone Temple were only symbolic dwellings, that God's presence could never be limited to a physical structure. But the symbolism of God living in the midst of his people was very precious.

A symbolic house needed a symbolic priesthood—one which represented all the people. One tribe of the twelve (Levi) was chosen to represent all the others. And within that tribe, one family represented the tribe as a formal priesthood while the rest became the priest's helpers. This was called the Levitical priesthood. This tribe was the only one that inherited no land when they reached Canaan. Instead, they lived off the tithes that the other eleven tribes brought to honor the Lord.

The Levitical priesthood is what we think of when we think of biblical priests, but we must remember that they represented what God considered to be an entire holy nation of priests. Just as the Tabernacle and Temple reduced the whole kingdom down to one structure, the Levitical priesthood reduced the holy calling of all the people down to one representative group who served at this Temple. Both were reduced models and symbols of God's larger vision: that God would live with all his people, and all of them would serve him as holy priests.

Thus, when Israel came to the Tabernacle on holy days and watched the priests, they were looking at models of themselves. In the priest's duties and ceremonies, they saw a symbolic enactment of their own calling to live with Almighty God. They would look and see people dressed in splendor.

> You shall speak to all the skillful, whom I have filled with a spirit of skill, that they make Aaron's garments to consecrate him for my priesthood. These are the garments that they shall make: a breastpiece, an ephod, a robe, a coat of checker work, a turban, and a sash. (Exodus 28:3-4)

In such a simple society, these uniforms were breathtaking. They represented glory and great honor. They communicated both a blameless character and a sublime calling. To underscore both, God told Moses, "You shall make a plate of pure gold and engrave on it, like the engraving of a signet, "Holy to the LORD." And you shall fasten it on the turban by a cord of blue." (Exodus 28:36-37) The word holy means set apart as special. It communicates the sentiment that "out of all nations you will be my treasured possession."

The important thing to notice is that this holiness, this special relationship of belonging to God, was true for the entire nation. "'You shall be to me a kingdom of priests and a holy nation.' These are the words you are to speak to the Israelites.'"—that is to say, to *all* the Israelites. When an Israelite looked into the Tabernacle and saw these amazing people, dressed in unimaginable splendor, the high priest wearing a plate marked, "holy to the Lord," he or she looked at a walking model of their own relationship to God.

Priests live with God. God's Law is at the heart of the Tabernacle, and over it God sits on a throne of mercy surrounded by angels. The whole interior is lit by a supernatural glow called "glory." Walls keep out everyone else in the world, but God's priests are allowed into a special holy communion. They eat with the Lord, enjoy the light of his truth and offer prayers like sweet incense. That's what it means to be a priest: to dwell in the intimate fellowship of the Lord God Almighty, glorifying and enjoying him forever!

God's priests depend on sacrifices provided by God for their forgiveness, to cover their sin so they may live with him safely. Of course, the Old Testament priests could not actually offer such a sacrifice; they could only model such offerings. That's why they had to keep making sacrifices all the time, every day, every year. Only when Christ functioned as the perfect priest was a sacrifice offered that properly satisfied God's Law and covered our sins. But in the Old Covenant, the people saw this great sacrifice modeled by their priests, and by faith they counted on it. At least three times a year, all Israelites traveled to the Temple to remember the covenant, see God's house and remember that all the people of Israel were God's home. They came to see the priests and remember who they, themselves, were.

Jesus came to turn the Old Testament model into reality. Peter declared to all Christians,

> As you come to him, a living stone rejected by men but in the sight of God chosen and precious, you yourselves like living stones are being built up as a spiritual house, to be a holy priesthood, to offer spiritual sacrifices acceptable to God through Jesus Christ ... you are a chosen race, a royal priesthood, a holy nation, a people for his own possession, that you may proclaim the excellencies of him who

called you out of darkness into his marvelous light.
(1 Peter 2:4-9)

Jesus originally said that his body was God's Temple, where God dwelled on this earth. But after his resurrection and ascension, Christ's spirit began to build a new Temple out of everyone who knows him by faith. God exists everywhere, but his address on Planet Earth is his church, his people. That's where he lives; that's the place of his fellowship. God's people are his Temple.

The New Testament reveals Jesus as the great High Priest over the house of God. His perfect life as a man earned Jesus the right to live in God's presence and blessing. And through the sacrifice of his perfect human self, Jesus also earned the right to share that privilege with every believer. In Christ, we who trust him are all God's priests. We are not welcome to enter God's house and presence because we merit such an honor. Rather, "you yourselves have seen what I did … and how I bore you on eagles' wings and brought you to myself." While we aspire to live lives worthy of our Lord, our priesthood is an honor given us by grace alone.

Christian, do you understand that you have been called by God to be his priest? This is true for both male and female believers. It has absolutely nothing to do with holding a church office or achieving some level of practical holiness. It is part of a calling every believer shares.

The idea that all believers are priests has been unfortunately encumbered by Roman Catholic and Eastern Christianity. I humbly suggest that the decision made centuries ago to mimic the Old Testament priesthood with a special clerical class was a serious mistake. At the very least, it encourages a profound misunderstanding of how the covenant works. The Old Testament priesthood was a real, but symbolic, office. We have no more need for it today than we need a literal Temple or animal sacrifices. The New Testament eldership is not a ceremonial office in the Old Testament sense. An elder is a functioning governor and shepherd in the church. A pastor is an elder with a special, often professional, emphasis on teaching. Thus, the pastorate is not a priestly office in the Old Testament sense. I have been a pastor for over 40 years, but I am not a priest because I am a pastor. I am a priest because I am a Christian.

And Christian, so are you. You are a priest because when God looks at you, he sees someone he personally carried on eagle's wings out of slavery to become his treasured possession. He looks at you and sees a golden plate proclaiming your holy calling to live in his personal fellowship.

Of course, our priesthood means nothing in the world at large. The world does not treat seriously things we do not get paid for. And it is certainly not our calling to "baptize" our careers and our society in an attempt to drag non-Christians into God's presence. This priesthood is exercised within Christ's church, the people of God, for we are "a holy priesthood, to offer spiritual sacrifices acceptable to God through Jesus Christ."

Many who engage in worship do not see it as a calling, but rather as an experience pursued for what it contributes to their welfare. The fact is, however, that Christians are called to worship God as his priests in this world. Of course, we benefit tremendously from exercising our relationship with God. But we do not worship only for ourselves, or even mostly for ourselves We worship because without our praise, the only worship this world would offer would be to idols, and the Living God deserves better. Humanity has turned away from the Lord; our sin has muffled the praise of the planet itself. It is the calling of God's priests to glorify him with the worship he deserves. Even though the world does not give us a paycheck for it, it is our job as redeemed human beings.

"Do not neglect to do good and to share what you have, for such sacrifices are pleasing to God." (Hebrews 13:16) In the Old Testament economy, the priests shared their meals in God's presence. Moreover, they administered freewill offerings and officiated at special Sabbath celebrations in which the whole community shared its abundance with one another, and especially with widows and orphans.

The first Christians took this priestly function seriously. "They had all things in common. And they were selling their possessions and belongings and distributing the proceeds to all, as any had need." (Acts 2:44-45) It is quite telling that it was after the first deacons were appointed to minister to the needs of Christian widows that a number of the Temple priests came to faith (Acts 6:7). They apparently saw the Christian community exercising this aspect of the priestly role better than the Temple bureaucracy. Caring for others, and particularly for members of our spiritual family, is not an optional convenience. It is our glorious calling, our job as God's priests.

Priesthood has to do with our place in the church, even though it is tempting to think of it in other terms. Sometimes, "the priesthood of all believers" is used to express our calling to serve God in every area of life—as farmers, blacksmiths, soldiers, homemakers, etc. That we can and must serve God in every capacity is most certainly true. We saw earlier that this is the Cultural Mandate is all about—our purpose as human beings from before sin entered the world and into life everlasting.

But while we do indeed share with Jesus a Cultural Mandate regarding all of human civilization, that is not what the New Testament talks about when using the language of priesthood. Rather, priesthood has to do with life in God's fellowship and within the fellowship of his people. It has to do with worship, the mutual commitment of Christians, and our welcome into God's kingdom of those newly born again.

Christian priesthood expresses how every Christian has a job, a personal calling from God, to build Christ's church. For most, this is not a professional position; it does not come with any pay. It is, however, just as much a job as our occupational careers. And since we can pursue this career in open fellowship with Christ and with fellow Christians, it is the greatest job in the world!

When a child looks ahead, he or she asks, "What shall I be when I grow up?" The world works hard to narrow the answer to that question down to a list of possible occupations. Depending on your social status, opportunities, and sometimes on your race or gender, the world lays out a list of things you can do or be: a butcher, a baker a candlestick maker, wearing a blue or white collar in business, the family or the professions. For the world, the question of, "What shall I be when I grow up?" is answered entirely by some economic place in society.

Occupations are important, of course. Along with other roles, they are a context in which we can make our fallen world a better place. But in addition to an occupation, every Christian also has a calling to serve God as his priest—not an ancient object lesson wearing archaic robes and a turban—but a real live, present-day priest of the Lord High God, whom we know in Jesus Christ.

That means that I have a career in the church, among God's people, that is just as real as the one in the world that I get paid for. The absence of a salary may tempt me to view my role in God's church as a mere hobby. But if my God is not a myth then my calling to be God's priest is a real spiritual career.

This profoundly exciting truth is lost on so many, because our understanding of church involvement is constrained by the idea of being a "volunteer." A volunteer is someone who is not paid for work in the church, and who therefore gets to serve at their convenience. But for Christians, the word "volunteer" misses the big picture. What we volunteered to do was to follow Jesus. He called us to follow, and we decided that we would. As we have seen, that calling involved becoming a priest to the Living God. We volunteered for that. But having volunteered for that role, it now belongs to us as a spiritual career in which we serve at his convenience.

Balancing two jobs is a challenge, to be sure, but I must approach each as a holy calling. Related to creation, I am called by to the Cultural Mandate to build the best society I can for this planet. Related to redemption, I am called by the Great Commission to build Christ's church as one of his priests.

If priesthood is a real part of every Christian's calling, then it is something we must carefully teach our children. When we help our children think about what they will be when they grow up, we talk about college or other career training, but that only deals with their occupation. We must also teach them their priestly calling in God's church, and help them prepare for it. We must teach them, by example, the privilege and responsibility of worshiping the Living God in a world full of idolatry. We must show them the importance of caring for other Christians as family, whether or not they happen to be our friends. We must demonstrate how every personality, talent and resource can be used in some way to bring the gospel to a broken world. We must help them see the glorious picture Israel's children saw when they looked, wide-eyed, into the Tabernacle courtyard, so that when they prepare to confess their own faith, they will realize that the Lord God is ordaining them as priests in his church.

Christian, as Christ's priest, you have the greatest job in the world! You are called to serve God in his earthly house. His holiness is written all over you, and it is your privilege to show others what it means to know and serve the Living God.

What does such living faith look like, when every Christian takes their career as a priest seriously? ...

Co-workers In Rome

I commend to you our sister Phoebe, a servant of the church at Cenchreae, that you may welcome her in the Lord in a way worthy of the saints, and help her in whatever she may need from you, for she has been a patron of many and of myself as well.

Greet Prisca and Aquila, my fellow workers in Christ Jesus, who risked their necks for my life, to whom not only I give thanks but all the churches of the Gentiles give thanks as well. Greet also the church in their house. Greet my beloved Epaenetus, who was the first convert to Christ in Asia. Greet Mary, who has worked hard for you. Greet Andronicus and Junia, my kinsmen and my fellow prisoners. They are well known to the apostles, and they were in Christ before me. Greet Ampliatus, my beloved in the Lord. Greet Urbanus, our fellow worker in Christ, and my beloved Stachys. Greet Apelles, who is approved in Christ. Greet those who belong to the family of Aristobulus. Greet my kinsman Herodion. Greet those in the Lord who belong to the family of Narcissus. Greet those workers in the Lord, Tryphaena and Tryphosa. Greet the beloved Persis, who has worked hard in the Lord. Greet Rufus, chosen in the Lord; also his mother, who has been a mother to me as well. Greet

Asyncritus, Phlegon, Hermes, Patrobas, Hermas, and the brothers who are with them. Greet Philologus, Julia, Nereus and his sister, and Olympas, and all the saints who are with them. Greet one another with a holy kiss. All the churches of Christ greet you.

I appeal to you, brothers, to watch out for those who cause divisions and create obstacles contrary to the doctrine that you have been taught; avoid them. For such persons do not serve our Lord Christ, but their own appetites, and by smooth talk and flattery they deceive the hearts of the naive. For your obedience is known to all, so that I rejoice over you, but I want you to be wise as to what is good and innocent as to what is evil. The God of peace will soon crush Satan under your feet. The grace of our Lord Jesus Christ be with you.

Timothy, my fellow worker, greets you; so do Lucius and Jason and Sosipater, my kinsmen. I Tertius, who wrote this letter, greet you in the Lord.

Gaius, who is host to me and to the whole church, greets you. Erastus, the city treasurer, and our brother Quartus, greet you.

Now to him who is able to strengthen you according to my gospel and the preaching of Jesus Christ, according to the revelation of the mystery that was kept secret for long ages but has now been disclosed and through the prophetic writings has been made known to all nations, according to the command of the eternal God, to bring about the obedience of faith—to the only wise God be glory forevermore through Jesus Christ! Amen. (Romans 16:1-27)

Paul may have written these lines in Corinth, just before setting off for Jerusalem. Paul knew that danger, opposition and possible imprisonment awaited him there. If not, he hoped to travel on to Spain and continue the spread of the gospel. Rome would then become a base of operations for that western mission. Therefore, Paul wrote a letter to the Roman church to enlist their prayers and support. Paul wished the letter to be as pastoral as possible, so he reviewed the gospel in such a way as to encompass both the Gentile and Jewish segments of the larger congregation, and he greeted by name every member of the Roman church he either knew or had heard of. This list gives us an intriguing window into the early church.

The first thing immediately noticeable is the large role of women in the church. Phoebe is the first person mentioned, probably because she was the courier who would take the letter from Corinth to Rome. Paul began by asking the Roman church to receive her as a representative of the Corinthian church. As we go on, nine of twenty-six people Paul mentioned are women. They include Phoebe, two wives, someone else Paul says had been a mother to him, perhaps recalling her generous hospitality, and two hard workers who likely were sisters.

We also see how the church in a given city was more like what we would today call a presbytery, a united collection of local churches. There were no church buildings until after Constantine. Before then, churches met in homes, the largest of which could host no more than 50 people. The "Church in Rome" was a collection of such house churches. Paul mentions five that he knows of, each associated with various households. Among these house churches, some apparently had Jewish roots, while others seem to be led by Gentiles.

We see names common to slaves and names common to freedman. We know that some were trades people and others served in the royal court. One person mentioned was the director of public works.

Some of these are names of people who are familiar to us from other parts of the Bible. We know Priscilla and Aquila from the Book of Acts. We didn't previously know Andronicus and Junias by name, but since Paul says they knew Christ before him, they are almost certainly included among the groups of people mentioned in Acts. There is good reason to believe that Rufus is mentioned in the Gospel of Mark as the son of Simon of Cyrene, the man who carried the cross of Jesus.

But most of these folks are new to us. Paul greets them because they were all known to be hard workers, hosts and servants in a variety of capacities. Some of them are no doubt leaders and may have held a church office, but it isn't certain that any of them are religious professionals. In other words, few, if any, of these people got paid for what they did in the church.

Today, we would probably call such people "volunteers," but I don't think they thought of themselves as volunteers, the way we use that term today. For us, volunteering is something we do at our pleasure. Theirs was a holy calling to serve within Christ's church, at his pleasure. In general, one did not work in the early church for money. A Christian had one career as a livelihood, and another career in the church; one for money and another for love. No, these are not religious professionals. They are just Christians, like you or me, whose names God saw fit to record in his Word because of their faithful service.

The Apostle Paul was not a religious professional either. If I were applying to refinance a mortgage or open a bank account, I would be asked about my job or career. They would need to know that I'm gainfully employed. Depending on my choices, I would say "pastor" or "clergy." I count myself very blessed to be a religious professional. But imagine Paul opening a bank account in Rome, and asked to fill in his career. What do you think he would write? "Apostle?" No. For one thing, the bank would have no idea what "apostle" meant. But more importantly, Paul did not make his living as an apostle.

This is a surprise to most people. The apostles were the first Christian missionaries, and today Western missionaries are typically supported by sending churches who issue official calls stipulating salary and benefits. But such a system did not exist at the beginning. It is true that Paul taught that those who preach and teach the gospel ought to be financially supported by their church, much as the priests and Levites of the Old Testament were supported. But Paul himself resisted asking for support like that. Elsewhere, Paul wrote,

> If others share this rightful claim on you, do not we even more? Nevertheless, we have not made use of this right, but we endure anything rather than put an obstacle in the way of the gospel of Christ.
>
> Do you not know that those who are employed in the temple service get their food from the temple, and those who serve at the altar share in the sacrificial offerings? In the same way, the Lord commanded that those who proclaim the gospel should get their living by the gospel.
>
> But I have made no use of any of these rights, nor am I writing these things to secure any such provision. (1 Corinthians 9:12-15)

Occasionally, Paul did handle financial contributions from churches, but Paul rarely, if ever, asked for money for himself. He did not support himself through the church. He felt it was crucial,

271

as the first Christian preacher many would ever see, that there be no possible suspicion that he was in it for the money.

So how did Paul support himself? Was he independently wealthy? Apparently not, since friends on occasion helped him financially, whether he asked for it or not. As a young man, he had left home to be trained as a rabbi or scribe, but as we have seen, he did not make a living from his teaching and preaching skills.

However, it was an ancient practice for Jewish boys to learn a trade, usually his father's trade, before leaving home. Apparently, Paul was raised by a father who made tents for a living. When Paul first visited Corinth, "He found a Jew named Aquila ... and because he was of the same trade he stayed with them and worked, for they were tentmakers by trade." (Acts 18:2-3)

Not only does this tell us how Paul made his living, but we also see how he got to know the Aquila and Priscilla mentioned in Romans (who must have later returned to Rome after Emperor Claudius died). Aquila operated a tent making business with his wife. They had become Christians before they met Paul, and after becoming acquainted in Corinth, Paul worked in their business to earn a living. They became an economic and spiritual team. In fact, they apparently moved the whole business to Ephesus in order to work together in planting the church there. I imagine Paul was looking forward to the same partnership in Rome.

So, the great apostle Paul, who worked as hard, or harder, than anyone to build the church of Christ, had a regular job like anyone else. When opening a bank account, he would have filled in "tentmaker." His employer: a business called something like "Tents with a Mission" operated by Aquila and Priscilla. I'm sure that, given their common sense of mission, Paul's hours were extremely flexible. But Paul still had to show up for work, complete his projects, get paid and do taxes just like everyone else. Paul had a job in the world for money—making the world a better place by making good tents, and he had another job in the church for love—preaching the gospel and planting churches.

And the same was true for all these folks mentioned in Romans 16. See how Paul called them "coworkers." They all had other careers, too. The homemakers built families, the servants tended the estates of others, the city planner served the larger community in many ways. What they all had in common was how they used those jobs not only to build their society, but also to enable them to pursue the job they loved most: building the Church of Jesus Christ.

A Christian's calling or career has two parts. One stems from the Cultural Mandate, that overarching calling to have dominion over the earth. We pursue that calling through our many roles in our society at large, including the jobs we get paid for. These jobs in the world have a spiritual dimension giving them eternal significance, as we make the world a better place.

But we can only do so much to make this fallen world a better place. The great joy of Christians is that we get to have another job, another aspect of our calling, one that stems from the Great Commission. Christ's call to work alongside his Spirit to build his church extends to all his followers. If we are Christians, then the Great Commission is our commission. It is a divine call to a permanent, part-time job making disciples. Christ calls us to walk alongside him and be his voice, his mouth, his hands to bless. We are called to be his body sharing and modeling the gospel, bringing into this age, a taste of the age to come. It is the work of priests. That's why it is our work.

So, in addition to our career in the world, we also get to have a career in the church, too—a genuine career, though one without pay. Phoebe, Epenetus, Aquila, Priscilla—none of them got paid. None of the people who hosted the 30 to 50 people called a "church" got paid. None of the men and women whom Paul said were his coworkers got paid. But they had a career in Christ's church, just as surely as Paul did. After all, he didn't get paid for his church career, either.

These people did not think of themselves as "volunteers" at their convenience. They were called to unpaid careers in the church, just as surely as they were called to paid careers in the world. As disciples of Jesus, they were a priesthood. None of the Old Testament trappings of robes and incense, but a genuine, royal priesthood just the same.

We don't think of ourselves as volunteers for our employers. We are committed to doing what we are trained and hired to do. We feel responsible to do our jobs and do them well. In fact, Paul exhorted us to work for our secular employers as if we were working for Christ.

Well, doesn't that logic work at least as well if we turn it around? Should we not work for Christ in his church at least as well as we work for a secular employer, with at least the same sense of responsibility? Of course, in this age our paying job frames our available time and resources. But notice that some of the "coworkers" named in Romans 16 were servants or slaves in the royal court. If servants who had no control over their schedule could find time to build the church, I imagine anyone can.

What are the goals and responsibilities of someone who sees the church as an unpaid career? In Romans 16, Paul mentions those goals in summary fashion: "For your obedience is known to all, so that I rejoice over you, but I want you to be wise as to what is good and innocent as to what is evil. The God of peace will soon crush Satan under your feet. The grace of our Lord Jesus Christ be with you." These are our goals, no matter what our roles and gifts, no matter what program we happen to be involved with at present.

The one who sees church as a second career has goals that go beyond any program. If you work in the military, whether you are a front line soldier, or an analyst, or help with logistical support, your goal, always, is to protect your country. If you work in a hospital, whether as a physician or nurse or administrator or technician, your goal, always, is to heal people. If you work in the church, if you develop an unpaid career in the church of Jesus Christ, then whatever program you may be involved with at the moment, whatever office or relationships or projects, Paul says that your goal is to build a community that obeys our Lord Jesus, is full of joy, wise about what is good, and innocent about what is evil. Your goal is to build a community united and at peace with God, so that Satan's work among us is crushed and we radiate the grace of Christ in this world.

That is your job, Christian. Not just somebody else's job in the church. It is your job. Whether you are a business owner or employee or homemaker in pursuit of the Cultural Mandate, Christ has called you to an unpaid career pursuing the Great Commission. The one you do for money, whether you love it or hate it, the other you do for love only.

Our Cultural Mandate responsibilities are tremendously important. The Great Commission, however, is not only important; it is by far the more urgent. We will exercise dominion over a renewed earth forever in God's renewed kingdom. But bringing a taste of sanity, hope, purpose and salvation into this needy world is something we can only do in the small window of our lifespan in this age.

The church is made strong through those who pursue unpaid careers building it up. We have never needed such people more. To those hard workers in Rome, Paul wrote, "The God of peace will soon crush Satan under your feet." Look around, Christian; look at the world, at this country. Look at our own families. Who is crushing whom today? Are we crushing Satan or is he crushing us? In a world that is severed from God, severed from its Head, and running around like a dying chicken—in that kind of a world, the church is called to reflect the future glory of an amazing kingdom. The church is the world's only taste of the kingdom of God, a kingdom of disciplined truth and realistic hope and demonstrable love, a kingdom that halts the advance of Satan and actually walks over him as it grows.

Do you think Satan will ever be crushed through what we do in pursuit of the Cultural Mandate alone? What we do to make the world a better place will bless many, but is that what Paul says will crush the work of Satan?

What pushes back Satan, whether in society or in our own homes, is a strong church that keeps the message and model of the gospel crystal clear. What defeats Satan is a community born of Christ's Spirit living amidst the larger community that lives in darkness. Besides the church, who else in our society is going to exalt, honor and fear God? Who else is going to lift up what is good and expose what is evil? Who else is going to win the hearts and minds of a culture like ours that is politically free to do as much evil as it wants? For that matter, who else is going to win the hearts and minds of our own children? Who else?

The church is not a business, but the church needs committed career workers as much as any business does—as much as any army or any hospital. Sure, you can use occasional volunteers in a hospital or an army or even a business, but you need a host of career people to make them work. In Rome it was the Aquilas and Phoebes, the Tryphenas and Tryphosas, who made the church work.

If Satan is going to be crushed in our day, then a lot of us must take up unpaid careers in the church, making the health and growth of the church our second job. That job may find us hosting small groups or teaching children or streaming music, worship and teaching, or taking teens camping or serving as officers. Our job may find us bringing Christ into high schools and colleges, or into jails or to the homeless, or applying God's Word directly to social issues. It might find us giving special care to the elderly or infirm.

There are lots of jobs in the Great Commission. Each one is an opportunity to work alongside Christ and see him work. Throughout history, each has been held by Christians who understood faith as a priestly career. If Paul were to write a letter to my own congregation, I know some of the blessed names he would include in his list of greetings.

Unfortunately, in this day and age, some of us are slow in developing our church careers. Maybe we've accepted the enslaving notion that our secular jobs have an exclusive right to our best efforts. Maybe we've thought that moving around so much makes a church career impossible (though it doesn't seem to make a secular career impossible). Maybe we've thought of the church more as a consumer commodity than a career. Whatever the reason, it's not too late to get started.

Paul's career in the church developed over time. After coming to faith, he worked at least fourteen years teaching in a local church and helping the poor. He spent years retooling his mind, understanding the Old Testament in terms of Jesus. Eventually, he was set apart as a missionary. God used him in a variety of ways, as you would any committed worker.

As a new Christian, I remember plotting my own dual career path. My livelihood goal was either to teach physics or work on fusion generators for a living. My church goal was to someday work as an elder, for love. I had many jobs in my church career before I became an elder. My first job was watering grass at the church facility, then I led Bible studies, then joined a summer-long evangelism project, and then I helped administer a campus Christian group. No pay, but all part of my career in Christ's church. Eventually, I left the dream of fusion generators and got a job as a church janitor while studying at seminary. Since then, I've been a professional pastor. If I stop getting paid as a pastor tomorrow, I expect the Lord would still have something for me to do.

The fact is that Christians are called to the most exciting career a person can have. Where else can you build a community alive with God's power? In what business could you produce the ultimate answer to human brokenness? In what army or government agency could you fight the deepest conspiracy of all? In what hospital could you give your patients eternal life? You can make this world a better place in a thousand different ways, but where else can you become wise in what is good and become innocent again in what is evil? Where else can you open heaven and bring down a taste of future Paradise, lifting souls and uniting people who would otherwise remain divided? Where else can you shield yourself and your children from lies that target us as deadly arrows? Where else can you find acceptance in spite of your faults, and find what it takes to accept others in spite of their faults? Where else can you reshape the spiritual landscape of the most barren places on earth by sending out brothers and sisters with the seeds of life?

If the church languishes in America, it is not because of insufficient volunteers. It's because so few of us see the service of God in the church as an unpaid career, something we do with the determination of a professional, but for love alone.

Paul made tents for a living, but that did not make him a church "volunteer." He had a career in Christ's church. The bank wouldn't understand that. To them, he was a tentmaker. But to God, he was a priest.

A career in the church is part of your calling too, Christian, every bit as much as it was for Philologus and Julia, Apelles and Rufus, Ubanus and Mary, Timothy or Teritus. Take hold of your priestly calling, for you have the greatest job in the world!

Discussion

God is who he says he is

- What is the significance of the meaning of God's name, "I Am Who I Am"?
- What was it about God's character that motivated Jonah to flee?
- Are there aspects of God's revealed character that you must work at accepting?

God is in control

- Do you know, from the Bible, what God's agenda is?
- How could Mordecai be so certain of God's protection? (What part did Israel have in God's agenda?)
- Assuming that God has placed you where you are right now in order to advance his agenda, what choices lie before you?

This world is not what it should be

- What difference does it make whether or not the world is supposed to be different than it is, according to a divine design?
- Why did Nehemiah care so much about Jerusalem?
- If you could take off from your job for three years to pursue God's design, what would you work on?

God will make all things right

- Describe as best you can what you expect the world will be like after Jesus returns.
- Why did Jeremiah buy his kinsman's field in Anathoth?
- What are some decisions you might make today, which would only make sense if Jesus were coming back?

Jesus makes all the difference

- If there is a Savior who could reconcile God and mankind, why would it have to be Jesus?
- What did Nicodemus' faith initially lack? How does such faith come about?
- Are you willing to follow Jesus openly, in ways that are plain to everyone?

I am a disciple of Jesus

- How does the Holy Spirit contribute to Jesus' ministry?
- What were John's disciples at Ephesus missing, in terms of the Christian faith?
- What does it mean for you to be a disciple of the risen Jesus himself, rather than just a follower of ancient teachings?

Spiritual growth: from the inside out

- Contrast a relationship with God based on his Law with one based on faith in Christ, using elements of a marriage for illustration.
- From your experience of life, do the best you can to speculate on the nature of Mary's "seven demons."
- Where to you need Jesus to bring you freedom from something that still binds your soul?

All I have to do is fear God

- Describe the biblical concept of fearing God.
- List some implications of keeping one's faith in a religious box, separated and unrelated from other areas?
- How would being able to see God as the greatest factor affect the way you approach decisions, challenges and opportunities?

God is always right

- Discuss the usefulness of intuition and revelation when it comes to divine guidance.
- How did Joseph know what to do, in order to find God's greatest blessing?
- What do you know God wants you to do, right now, so that he might bless you? How do you know that?

Christ is worth it

- Why is Jesus the only one uniquely qualified to deal with the tragedy of our human condition?
- Which is more impressive to you: how Stephen gave his life for Christ all at once, or how he gave it little by little, day by day?
- When it comes to giving your life, how much is Christ worth?

I can make this world a better place

- How does "waking up" to the reality of Christ turn a person's entire life into a calling?
- How did his spiritual awakening affect Zacchaeus' business?
- How might your ongoing spiritual awakening affect your career? your social responsibilities?

Everyone is important

- How did Jesus turn around the question, "Who is my neighbor?"
- Why was Dorcas, or Tabitha, so precious to those who knew her?
- Whom do you know who particularly needs to treated as the image of God, right now?

All my problems are solved

- How is our hope for the future tied to our understanding of the ages of history?
- How did Paul's future expectations affect his enthusiasm for today's opportunities?
- What determines how much you can afford to invest of yourself in service to Christ?

I have the greatest job in the world

- Describe how every Christian is a priest.
- What is the difference between being a volunteer and pursuing an unpaid career in Christ's church?
- There are many roles involved in the Great Commission. What do you do?

About the Author

Dr. Glenn Parkinson has been learning and preaching the Bible for over 40 years. Converted while completing his undergraduate degree in physics, Glenn's goal is to discover the natural themes and patterns that weave God's Word into a coordinated and meaningful whole. And as a Reformed Pastor with a doctorate from Westminster Theological Seminary, he believes that every truth should be used as an engine for living in ways that please the Lord.

Glenn lives with his wife and best friend, Micki, and also cat Lilly, who valiantly battles the computer for lap time.

Also by Glenn Parkinson

Like the Stars
a Christian alternative to culture war

Share Your Master's Joy
a partnership that lasts forever

Living Faith
convictions that bring faith to life

Tapestry
The Book of Revelation

Made in the USA
Middletown, DE
21 October 2020